PEER COUNSELING

In-Depth Look At Training Peer Helpers

Third Edition

A Companion Book
to

PEER POWER: Becoming an Effective Peer Helper
Book 1, Introductory Program, 2nd Edition
(Developing 8 Peer Helper Skills)

Book 2, Applying Peer Helper Skills, 2nd Edition

Resource Audio Tape Available: PROBLEM SOLVING

Judith A. Tindall, Ph.D.
Psychologist & Consultant
Rohen & Associates
Psychological Center
St. Charles Missouri

 ACCELERATED DEVELOPMENT INC.
Publishers
Muncie   Indiana

PEER COUNSELING

An In-Depth Look At Training Peer Helpers

Library of Congress Catalog Card Number: 88-82677

International Standard Book Number: 0-915202-85-9

© Copyright 1989 by Accelerated Development
First Edition copyright 1978
Second Edition copyright 1985
Modification and reprint September, 1989

1 2 3 4 5 6 7 8 9 10

Technical Development: Tanya Dalton
                       Delores Kellogg
                       Marguerite Mader
                       Sheila Sheward

Cover Design: Donna Johnson

Printed in the United States of America

ACCELERATED DEVELOPMENT Inc., PUBLISHERS
3400 Kilgore Avenue, Muncie, Indiana 47304-4896
(317) 284-7511

DEDICATION

Peer Counseling: An In-Depth Look At Training Peer Helpers is dedicated to my husband Boone and son Jarrett. They have given feedback on the material and offered support as the material was developed. They have participated in the development of support tapes and other materials. The hope is that the materials will give trainers and others designing, developing and delivering peer helping programs assistance as they move ahead in their Peer Helping Activities.

Judith A. Tindall

PREFACE

Peer Counseling: In-Depth Look at Training Peer Helpers and the accompanying exercises entitled Peer Power: Becoming an Effective Peer Helper, Book 1, Introductory Program (Developing 8 Peer Helper Skills), and *Book 2, Applying Peer Helper Skills,* grew out of my interest in helping non-professionals to learn to help others with personal problems. When I looked for ways to teach lay counselors, I found very few ideas or models that would do the job of training well. As a result, I was faced with the dilemma of wanting to teach counseling skills to non-professionals and not having any model or program that I felt would be effective for this task.

In the research that I have completed, I found that group counseling alone was not sufficient to teach effectively helping skills. Other studies supported my conclusions that group counseling did not do what I wanted it to do. Therefore, I decided to investigate other ways of imparting counseling skills to the lay person.

I discovered through our research, which used highly structured step-by-step training procedures, that I was able to teach counseling (communication) skills to nonprofessionals to a degree of effectiveness that was statistically significant. As a result of my findings I decided to refine the training program of the research design so that a professional social worker, teacher, counselor, or minister could use the program to train peer counselors, lay helpers, peer facilitators, or tutors.

In 1973, I presented the first mimeographed copy of our training program to a national convention. Since that time I have presented my model at local training centers, professional meetings, and state and national conventions. We estimate that approximately 10,000 individuals have indicated an interest in training peer counselors by attending these various meetings. In addition, many have corresponded with me to request help in training peer counselors and to share their successes and failures in these ventures.

As a result of my experiences in these workshops and meetings, I decided that I had an obligation to other professionals to put my ideas and training procedures into a form that they can use effectively. In my training procedures I have used the ideas and concepts developed by Dreikurs, Carkhuff, and Sprinthall. As a result, a step-by-step model for training peer counselors forms the basis of this trainer's manual, *Peer Counseling*, and the accompanying exercises for trainees, organized into two books for effective skill building, *Peer Power: Book 1, Introductory Program* (Developing 8 Peer Helper Skills), and *Peer Power: Book 2, Applying Peer Helper Skills.*

In the trainer's manual I also wanted to include some of the rationale behind peer counseling, some of the research data and some sample programs to give a more complete understanding of non-professional human relations training. The purpose of these three books—*Peer Counseling: In-Depth Look at Training Peer Helpers* and *Peer Power: Becoming an Effective Peer Helper, Book 1, Introductory Program,* and *Book 2, Applying Peer Helper Skills* fill the gap caused by the lack of written materials on peer counseling for professionals who feel the need to train others but have no format to follow.

The *Peer Counseling* manual is intended for those interested professionals such as teachers, counselors, ministers, religious educators, social workers, and others in the helping professions. The *Peer Power* exercises are intended for those interested in learning human relations skills (communication, crises reduction, peer helping and peer counseling). The manual for trainers and the exercise books for trainees are not panaceas for trainers nor a replacement for effective existing programs, but they can serve to open wider the exciting developments in human relations training and will identify an effective procedure for the implementation of a peer counseling training program.

Dr. Gray and myself would like to thank all the teachers, administrators, counselors, and supervisors in the Pattonville School District, Rockwood School District, and Southern Illinois University that helped to form a basis for our first edition.

I personally want to thank H. Dean Gray for his expertise and clear thinking and hard work that put together the first edition. Since the first edition the following people, John Canale, M.D.; Norm Creange, Ed.D.; Jan O'Neill, B.S.; Shirley White, Ph.D.; Karen Johnson, M.A.; Hazel Sprandel, Ph.D.; and Elizabeth Foster, Ed.D.; have taken the time to read the material and give us feedback.

Judith A. Tindall

CONTENTS

MODULES FOR BOOK 1
INTRODUCTORY PROGRAM

X. EVALUATION OF THE PROGRAM 329

APPENDICES **379**

REFERENCES **395**

ADDITIONAL READING **401**

INDEX **407**

ABOUT THE AUTHOR **417**

LIST OF FIGURES

Chapter I

AN OPEN LETTER TO THE TRAINER

Dear Trainer:

The goal of this book is to provide a program designed to teach professionals a method of training peer counselors or helpers. Peer counseling training is the major delivery system of affective education or deliberate psychological education. Strategies in this program are to give away counseling skills and attitudes, or more specifically, to teach helping skills to lay persons. This program will enable the trainer to teach facilitative interpersonal communication skills and techniques. The training will enable lay helpers to work with others, either formally or informally, in a variety of helping roles.

The philosophy of a counselor "giving away" skills and "training" to others in peer counseling requires a strong commitment of energy, self-awareness, time, and probably additional training. This book and accompanying student books entitled *Peer Power, Book 1* and *Book 2*, will help you become aware of the scope and tasks of a successful peer training program. The program design has been developed and field tested by us for several years.

Several personal attributes are essential before a trainer can complete a peer training program successfully. The success of training lay helpers depends upon four attributes:

1. a belief in the validity and integrity of teaching others helping skills;

2. a possession of energy necessary to initiate, develop, and complete a training program;

3. the ability to modify model training procedures to fit the system in which the training takes place; and

4. the willingness to trust those trainees that have been trained to carry forth the work.

A trainer first must be both dedicated to the concept and understanding of the value of training lay leaders in affective interpersonal communications skills. Also, one must be competent in using and teaching such skills. A trainer, who is functioning at high levels of effective communications skills, enhances the chance of trainees functioning at effective skills levels. Even though the trainer may have had experience in counseling, this experience does not assure effectiveness in peer counseling teaching. Research by Carkhuff (1969) warrants the conclusion that often times a counselor has lower peer helping skills as a result of that counseling experience. One can very easily develop habits and behaviors which are destructive and ineffective for peer training and not be aware of it. Therefore, trainers for peer training programs need to improve continuously and add to competencies in their personal helping skills before and throughout the process of training others.

The first requirement for being effective in training peer counselors is *possessing a high level of awareness of one's own values, feelings, goals, and aspirations.* A trainer must have a strong and accurately developing awareness of self and others in order to carry out an effective training program. Without this ability to know one's self accurately, a high probability exists that the trainer will exhibit behaviors that can detract and damage an otherwise effective program. The leader of any program of this nature exerts a tremendous influence, either negative or positive, on trainees learning the basic communication skills. Unless trainers are cognizant of personal feelings and emotions and how these feelings are communicated to others, their impact on trainees will be haphazard, sometimes destructive, sometimes effective, but never will the impact be consistently helpful in the growth of the individual trainee.

A second attribute is *an awareness on the part of the trainer of the significant amount of time and effort*

required to organize people in an educational system, church system, or community system that is not geared nor oriented to include peer counseling training. As is true with the other requirements of peer training, if the time and effort is not given willingly, or, if the trainer is not able to give the time to organize a program adequately, the probability of success will be reduced.

The time commitment to develop and complete a program requires high levels of physical and emotional energy. A peer training program requires energy levels which enable concentration for relatively long periods of time. For example, a key training procedure, which relates directly to this energy need, is found in the feedback process of the program. The feedback procedure requires that the trainer both identify the effectiveness of a trainee's communications skills and feed that appraisal back to the trainee. To do this consistently and well requires a high enough level of energy to concentrate for significant periods of time. High expenditures of energy require that one be in good physical condition. Otherwise, difficulty will occur in maintaining energy levels sufficient to be an effective rater or trainer.

Third, the **willingness to take creative risks is important.** The *Peer Counseling: An In-Depth Look at Training Peer Helpers* book provides only a skeletal format and program, but for a specific program to be effective, each person must use personal creativity to develop needed modifications. Although it is important not to change the skill building pattern, the program design needs to be adapted to the unique conditions existing in the system being served. Because each system operates somewhat differently, adaptations require creative thinking and planning to fit the program design into the structure of the setting in which the training takes place. For example, an open school could have peer counseling located in many parts of the building, whereas a traditional school may have to fit a training program into an often rigid physical and curricular structure.

Fourth, the **competency and integrity of the trainees must be trusted.** An element of risk always exists when one is training helpers because possibly they will go beyond skill limitations in helping other people. Experience shows, however, trainees become acutely aware of their limits as the result of training. Considerable time and effort in the training program are spent in clearly identifying the responsibilities of the helper when dealing with material that may be confidential or beyond the helper's capacity. The final requirement, then, is to trust trainees after giving them a thorough training to have the integrity which will support that trust.

When using the training procedures described in this book, the experience has been that no inappropriate helping behaviors of any consequence have occurred. Apparently, the training helps to establish the qualities of competence and integrity needed to be able to trust trainees. To date, this trust has been supported by hundreds of peer helpers.

One caution to you, the trainer, is not to use this book as a "cookbook" process. The program design demands a high degree of structure for success. Hopefully, the program design will represent a disciplined structure rather than a recipe for training. A trainer is urged to blend personal creativity into implementing the program to specific needs without destroying the integrity of the process and the program design.

To you, a potential trainer, an invitation is issued to participate in a highly exciting program for increasing competencies in the helping skills. This *Peer Counseling: In-Depth Look at Training Peer Helpers* has been developed to help people interested in an action program for training peer counselors. The accompanying two books entitled *Peer Power: Becoming an Effective Peer Helper, Book 1, Introductory Program,* and *Peer Power: Book 2, Applying Peer Helper Skills,* contains content and activities to assist trainees in gaining and applying the essential skills under your supervision.

Sincerely,

Judith A. Tindall, Ph.D.

H. Dean Gray, Ph.D.

PEER COUNSELING AND ITS COMPONENTS

Interest among counselors and other persons in the helping professions has been growing significantly over the last few years; interest in teaching non-professionals skills, attitudes, and concerns of effective human interrelationships has also expanded. Training programs are relatively new and terminology is in the formulative stage. By reading this chapter, you will be exposed to the frequently used terminology in peer counseling and the meanings commonly associated with these terms.

PEER COUNSELING

The most important term is the concept of *peer counseling.* For the purpose of the program, peer counseling is defined as a *variety of interpersonal helping behaviors assumed by nonprofessionals who undertake a helping role with others.* Peer counseling includes one-to-one helping relationships, group leadership, discussion leadership, advisement, tutoring, and all activities of an interpersonal human helping or assisting nature.

AFFECTIVE EDUCATION

Because the trainee's experience is one of learning how to teach, the trainer must be aware of the concept of *affective education* or *deliberate pyschological education.* The terms "affective education" and "deliberate psychological education" (DPE) essentially are interchangeable, and both refer to educational concerns that deal with feelings. References to DPE strategies relate to procedures or programs that teach or train people in the concepts and skills involved in improving interpersonal affective psychological behaviors and attitudes. Feelings become the central focus of DPE programs, and peer counseling training becomes a core concept of these programs. Teaching people to become more facilitative and effective in interpersonal relationships is the goal of DPE programs, and peer counseling training is one of the major delivery systems to that goal. In other words, DPE strategies attempt to aid in developing counseling skills and attitudes or, more specifically, to teach helping skills to lay persons.

Affective education includes all educational experiences in which the major emphases are related to understanding feelings, emotions, and interpersonal relationships. Teaching interpersonal skills is directly related to affective education parameters.

DEFINITIONS

Learning peer counseling requires a training program. This *Peer Counseling: In-Depth Look at Training Peer Helpers* and accompanying exercises provide a training book. The program requires trainers, trainees, support from staff and administration, and a training format and procedures. Certain terms may be new to you. So you and others can communicate easily, terms used in your training program will be used as explained in this section. Terms and meanings frequently associated with the training aspect are the following ones listed.

Trainer. The trainer—a professionally educated counselor, psychologist, teacher, nurse, clergy, social worker, human relations specialist—is any person in the field who assumes the responsibility for basic and advanced training. This process includes organizing, developing, implementing, and following through with procedures for a complete peer counseling program. A more complete description of the trainer's responsibilities will be found in Chapters VIII and IX of this book. The profile and development pattern of a trainer are provided in Chapter V.

Peer Facilitator/Supervisor. This person serves in the following roles: trainer, supervisor, grant writer, administrator, facilitator; or any role that involves being in charge of peer helpers and their projects.

Trainee. The trainee is a person who is involved in a peer counseling training program. This person is learning to function as a peer counselor.

Participants and Group Members. These collective terms are used to refer to trainees. Each term is used as appropriate in the context of this book and the trainee book *Peer Power: Becoming an Effective Peer Helper.*

Program Design (Model). A specifically designed program to prepare peer counselors.

Role Playing. Role playing refers to a training procedure in which a trainer or a trainee assumes the role of helper, helpee, or rater or any additional role which enables a training technique to be demonstrated.

Feedback. Feedback is the process by which listeners communicate to others the reaction that they have to the quality of communication of the speaker. The format of this program requires that trainers and trainees act as raters to give feedback to trainees who are practicing various skills.

Helpee. The helpee is any trainee who is functioning as the individual with a personal concern.

Helper. The helper refers to any trainee who is functioning as an individual assisting the person with a personal concern.

Rater. The rater is any person whose function is to give constructive feedback as to the quality, accuracy, and effectiveness of the helper's helping responses.

The terms "helper," "helpee," and "rater" will be used to describe the roles that trainees will be assuming during the training period.

Peer Counselor. The term "peer counselor" refers to a person who assumes, either by choice or conscription, the role of a person helping contemporaries. This definition excludes professional counselors but can include all paraprofessionals when they function as interpersonal peer helpers. The term "peer" denotes a person who shares related experiences, values, and lifestyle.

The terms "helper," "lay helper," "peer helper," "peer facilitator," "peer counselor," and "paraprofessional" are often used interchangeably in the literature. Peer counselors are nonprofessional counselors who provide counseling skills to aid peers. Peer counselors may either assist or work independently of professional counselors.

Paraprofessionals. Persons who have completed satisfactorily a peer counseling program are referred to as paraprofessionals. They are considered an important member of the team when peer counselors work with professional counselors. Peer counselors are often able to help do things that professionals alone either could not do as quickly or could not do at all.

Helping. Helping has many ramifications. In the peer counseling literature helping refers to giving assistance to a person who is in need of personal psychological assistance. The helper is the peer counselor who provides the assistance; the helpee is the one who receives the help. On completion of a basic skill training, a trainee assumes the role of helper (peer counselor).

The helper (peer counselor) has the skills and the psychological strength to provide the helpee with the assistance needed. Thus, helpers must in some manner communicate concerns, feelings, problems, or other human needs for which the helpee wants assistance. The helping process could occur in a group setting as well as on an individual basis. Helpers, therefore, offer interpersonal human assistance to helpees.

Communication. As used in the trainer book and the trainee book, communication refers to verbal and nonverbal (body language) messages between two or more individuals. Specifically, the communication is between the helpee and helper. The purpose of the communication is to facilitate self-exploration and/or understanding. Because helpees must communicate concerns, feelings, problems, or other human needs, helpers (peer counselors) must possess skills necessary to enable an understanding of what is being communicated.

Helping Process. The helping process is the composite of all activities associated with the helper's helping the helpee. The helping process may be diagrammatically summarized as shown in Figure 2.1.

Responding. Responding is the process by which the helpers provide constructive information concerning the helpees' communicated behavior. Feedback enables helpees to know that they have been understood and that the helper is able and willing to assist them.

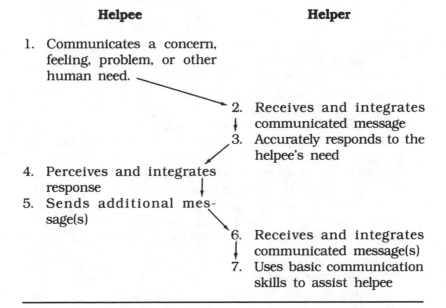

Helpee	**Helper**

1. Communicates a concern, feeling, problem, or other human need.

      2. Receives and integrates communicated message
      3. Accurately responds to the helpee's need

4. Perceives and integrates response
5. Sends additional message(s)

      6. Receives and integrates communicated message(s)
      7. Uses basic communication skills to assist helpee

Figure 2.1 Diagrammatic summarization of the helping process.

BASIC COMMUNICATION SKILLS TO BE TAUGHT

The format for training will follow patterns that were introduced by Carkhuff (1969), Ivey (1973), Gordon (1970), Jakubowski-Spector (1973a, 1973b), and others and are modified to teach interpersonal helping skills to nonprofessionals. The program design will teach basic interpersonal skills presented in Figure 2.2, that is communications skills that have been identified by eight areas: attending, empathizing, summarizing, questioning, genuineness, assertiveness, confrontation, and problem solving. These eight as are used frequently in the *Peer Counseling* book and the two *Peer Power* books are defined for future reference as follows:

Attending behavior relates most directly to the concept of respect, which is demonstrated when a helper gives the helpee undivided attention and which by means of verbal and nonverbal behavior expresses a commitment of focus completely on the helpee. The term connotes an active behavior on the part of the listener and is a prerequisite to effective helping. Learning about verbal and nonverbal communications and their effects is essential for peer helping.

Empathy or "empathizing," as used here, is equivalent to Carkhuff's (1969) "minimally facilitative level of empathic response." Empathizing responses must communicate an accurate awareness of the feeling and meaning of the helpees' statements and of the conditions that generated those feelings and statements. Empathic responses do not go beyond the helpees' demonstrated level of understanding. In other words, the helpers respond with an accurate identification of what the helpees have communicated and do so in such a way that the helpees may easily perceive the helpers' understanding. To utilize empathy skill the peer helper needs to be able to discriminate among messages from the helpee and to paraphrase the meaningful ones.

> **Discrimination** is a part of empathy. It is the ability to separate effective and facilitative interpersonal communication from ineffective and destructive behaviors. Discrimination of effective behaviors precedes any other communication skill.

Paraphrasing, the feeling and meaning of what the helpee communicates, is also a part of empathy.

Summarizing is any helpee behavior that organizes several helpee statements into one concise statement. Initiative responding is listening so as to be able to respond in a manner that sheds new light on and adds new dimensions of awareness to the solution of a problem.

Questioning is the process of inquiring so as to prompt a reply. Questioning pertains to a subject under discussion and oftentimes an area of concern to the individuals present. Effective questioning from the helpers prompts the trainees to consider their concerns in greater depth, to identify, to clearly understand a problem, and to consider alternatives.

Genuineness is communicating honest feelings in such a way that the relationship between two or more individuals is maintained or enhanced. Helpers must be genuine in all behaviors.

Assertiveness involves the ability to express thoughts and feelings in an honest, straightforward fashion that shows respect for the other person.

Confrontation is communication that identifies discrepancies in another person's behavior.

Problem Solving is the process of moving a person through phases of exploring a concern, understanding the reason for that concern, and evaluating behavior that affects solving the concern.

The basic skills that are being taught in the program are fundamental communication helping skills. A summary outline of the communication helping skills is provided in Figure 2.2.

BASIC COMMUNICATION SKILLS

Figure 2.2 Basic communication skills.

APPLYING PEER HELPER SKILLS

After learning the eight basic peer helper skills as outlined in *Peer Power: Book 1*, participants are provided with an opportunity to utilize those skills and learn additional ones in *Peer Power: Book 2, Applying Peer Helper Skills*. In *Book 2* are several modules for applying the peer helper skills in areas where peer helpers are frequently utilized. Any or all of these areas may be appropriate for your situation and your peer counselor training program. Information for the trainer to offer both introductory and advance programs are contained in this *Peer Counseling* book. As for the trainees two separate books are provided so that you may select the book most appropriate for trainees with whom you are working at the time.

Drugs and Alcohol Abuse Intervention and Prevention

Chemical abuse is one of the leading problems in America today. Most of us are not aware of the types of chemicals available, the kinds of problems that these chemicals create, the extent of these problems, or how to treat individuals who have chemical abuse problems. This training will increase helper's awareness of these issues.

Wellness/Stress Management

Wellness implies leading a healthy life—having the body, mind, and emotions in balance with each other and with the human environment. When these components are out of balance, a condition of stress ensues. Stress management techniques enable peer counselors to help individuals find and change or control their own stressors.

Enhancing Self Esteem

Helpers learn to focus on the group members' strengths to help them gain or regain self-confidence and to emphasize the positive rather than the negative side of personality.

Leadership Training

Group and organization leadership training involves determining and balancing task-type and people-type styles of leadership, communication skills, mediation and judgment skills, and leadership expertise.

Facilitating Small Discussion Groups

At times peer counselors are asked to lead small discussion groups with peers. Some of the groups are open ended groups and others are problem solving. The module will give the participants practice in leading small discussion groups.

Leading Classroom Groups

Peer leaders (helpers) for classroom groups are often needed to assist in distributing information to large groups because information given by a peer is often better accepted than when provided by professionals. Topics include health issues, getting along with friends, value clarification, and others.

Peer Helping Through Tutoring

Peer Counselors are often called on to assist others in learning a new skill, assisting in formal teaching or working with students that have difficulty learning. This module will assist Peer Helpers as they work in their role of tutoring.

Recognizing Eating Disorder Problems

Eating Disorders has become an increasing concern with emphasis on thinness and achievement. Anorexia, Bulimia, and Compulsive Overeating are a problem with all ages. Peers are often the first to notice odd eating behavior. This module will assist Peer Helpers to assess their own eating habits and recognize eating problems in others.

Suicide Prevention

Peers are often the first to know of someone considering suicide. This module will assist the trainees in recognizing the symptoms and some action steps to take. Activities to assist those left behind are also presented.

Coping with Loss

All people cope with loss, some losses have more impact than others. Coping with loss is part of the life cycle. This module will assist the trainees to understand reactions to loss but also help them cope with their own loss and assist others who are coping with loss.

**Ethical Considerations
In Peer Counseling**

This is still one of the most important modules in Peer Counseling. This might be addressed prior to starting any training and addressed throughout each activity and later as the Peer Counselor is delivering their activities.

CHANGING COUNSELOR ROLES

Counseling or training of people to be capable of assisting others who suffer social and psychological problems is entering an expanding and important stage of development. No longer can professional counselors feel comfortable about their competence when their counseling activities are restricted to individual sessions or small group processes. Both philosophic and economic conditions negate the number of individual sessions and small group processes as the measure of counselor effectiveness. The philosophy which assumes that counseling skills are, in reality, human skills and need to be taught to as large a number of nonprofessionals as possible is the relevant philosophic condition. The relatively small number of people whom counselors can help each day identifies the economic condition pertinent to the decline of these traditional counseling activities as accurate measures of counselor effectiveness. The emergence of peer training, psychological education, and confluent education in public and private community systems further indicates that the traditional roles and functions of the counseling profession are faced with new and interesting challenges.

Brown (1974) suggested that the emergence of nonprofessionals is the direct result of both an increasing demand for counseling services and the inability of professionally trained personnel to provide all of these services. Sensitive professional counselors, therefore, are feeling pressure from their critically perceptive colleagues to examine closely roles, functions, and philosophy of counseling as it relates to the major foci of educational, religious, governmental, and community agencies.

Administrative functions often impinge upon counselors' opportunities to help greater numbers of people. The vast majority of professionals in the counseling area have felt restricted by an ever-increasing demand to perform administrative and quasi-administrative tasks at the sacrifice of directly helping people. Many administrative tasks are necessary to improve the roles that counselors perform. Although administrative tasks are sometimes important and needed, they still detract from those functions that relate directly to helping others. Therefore, to devise effective means to assist more people in a limited time becomes important.

Economically, the condition is the same. In a time of high taxes, inflation, and increasing demands on limited funds, one-to-one counseling becomes expensive and difficult to justify. Public and private support of counseling will continue to increase demands that counseling skills become available to larger groups of people.

Dr. Frank Riessman discussed at the 1987 *National Peer Helper Conference* in St. Charles, Missouri, the rationale of "The New Peer Wave: Why Now?" He cited such factors as what is occurring in the redesign of teaching from being teachers to classroom managers, facilitators of learning and planners. He also discussed the adolescent crises. The public has become dismayed by all of the problems of adolescents. In light of the limited resources available for school counseling staffs, it would be better for counselors to plan, facilitate, and monitor peer counseling rather than provide all the counseling themselves; and this is not just for economic reasons but also because peers reach peers more effectively.

Peer approaches have been utilized for the last 20 years. Excellent research data are available to support peer helpers' effectiveness in such helping forms as peer tutoring, peer coaching, and peer editing. For example, in the business community, peers have been active in reaching out to troubled employees. One such program is the "Volunteers Group of McDonald Douglas Corporation" in St. Louis, Missouri. A new wave of peer movements is occurring in churches called "peer ministry" or "youth ministry." This is the result of trying to provide services to the community.

Recently, with the forming of the *National Peer Helpers Association* (1987), a new spirit has swept the country as more than 350 attended the first conference in St. Charles, Missouri, and with more than 550 attending in Ft. Collins, Colorado, in 1988 from all the states and many foreign countries. The organization has published articles in popular magazines and has had overwhelming response to the idea from both teens and adults.

Clearly the "crystal ball" focuses upon the need to reexamine, reeducate, and retrain counselors for new and expanding roles in community systems. People in schools, churches, and other public and private agencies have pigeon-holed counselors into roles that these agencies can no longer afford nor tolerate. The counselor's responsibilities include the need to identify, develop, and sell new counseling concepts to these agencies. The counselor, better than anyone else, is able to fulfill those responsibilities.

SCHOOL COUNSELING

In education, school guidance programs consist tradi-tionally of informational and administrative guidance activities plus a varying amount of individual or group counseling. Although each of these activities is an important function of a good counseling program and should be maintained, the pressure to develop a more efficient and effective use of the counselor's time and skills demands that these activities cannot continue to be the major concerns of the counselor. As Ivey and Alschuler (1973) stated:

> . . . individual treatment, group counseling, advising, behavior therapy, values clarification, and so forth, are not valid per se; they simply are less effective than a systematic combination of several different procedures used to reach a single goal. (p. 594)

Certainly the activities and training of the counselor must change in order to maintain congruence with the changes occurring in the world to which counselors legitimately relate.

The concepts of peer training, deliberate psychological education (DPE), and other affective education concepts are relatively new to the field of education and, generally, have not been emphasized in counselor education until very recently. The assumption can be made, in light of recent emergence of DPE, that its concepts currently do not lie in the mainstream of counselor education.

The multiple administrative functions assumed by counselors partially explain why counselors have been slow in meeting the changes affecting them professionally. School administrators, generally not aware of effective counseling roles, frequently assign administrative tasks on a regular basis to counselors. Counselors who accept these activities either prefer the more clearly defined tasks of administrative detail to the risks of developing effective counseling relationships, or they are unable to define a counseling role and function realistically in relation to their administrators.

In addition, counselors in the field and in training are burdened with the lack of training facilities in affective awareness. The recent emergence of affective education created a lag between the need for experienced teachers and the ability of teaching institutions to meet that need. However, the demand for nonprofessionals in counseling, as identified by Gartner and Riessman (1974), is forcing counselor educators to face the problem of training trainers of laymen. As yet, only a few effective procedures or educators are available to meet the need to train trainers of peer counselors.

Finally, appropriate research results are very limited which can aid the professional who is looking for ways to train nonprofessional helpers. The writing that has been completed either has a very poorly designed delivery system or does not relate specifically to the concern of how to train trainers.

Consequently, all indications appear to support the statement that counselors on the job have little training and/or skill in affective education strategies. Frequent letters containing requests for information and good attendance at workshops on peer counseling lead to the conclusion that counselors are becoming aware of the need to change.

Graduate programs, however, tend to emphasize traditional counselor training. Testing, theories, program administration, and academic constructs still predominate in undergraduate and graduate counselor training institutions. Conversely, indications of changes are occurring as identified by the competency programs being implemented by Michigan State, Oregon, Texas, and others. Also, the training programs and ideas of Carkhuff, Ivey, Eagan, Gazda, and others are being incorporated into institutions of higher education. These facts are evidence that some changes are being made. Practicing counselors not only have difficulty in being aware of developments in peer counseling training and deliberate psychological education but also have difficulty in receiving adequate training in these strategies if and when the training is desired.

As a result, counselors often are involved in schedule changing, report writing, and various other clerical tasks that only remotely relate to the counseling function. The prevailing climate and conditions often prevent or make extremely difficult for professions, who wish to change their roles, to do so. They must overcome the handicaps of administrative duties, a lack of initial training, and the difficulty in becoming retrained adequately.

Aspy (1972), however, contended that the counseling profession in education is moving and must continue to move in directions that will increase the counseling professions service to the major focus of education, that of merging the affective and cognitive dimensions of learning into one integrated experiential learning process in the educational mainstream.

Elementary school counselors and teachers are finding that peer helpers can be effective as tutors, discussion leaders, one-on-one helpers, and in a variety of other roles. Robert Bouman, Ph.D., and Robert Myrick have developed programs on the elementary level for peer helping. Elizabeth Foster of the Pare County Schools of Wake County Schools in Manteo, North Carolina, has established a strong peer tutoring program.

The number and kinds of problems at all ages are endless. For example, loneliness, low self-esteem, health issues, violence in the schools, different cultures trying to communicate, and declining academic skills, all can be helped through a peer helping program. These issues cannot be addressed only by professionals; the professionals must have help—through training others.

Some answers to the school counselor's dilemma are to be found in the ideas generated by the emerging concepts of psychological education and the activities related to it, such as training peer counselors, consultation, and the teaching of human relations skills and attitudes. Marguerite Carroll (1973) stated that she is not only a believer in psychological education but also feels that psychological education has a high priority in training and commitment. Carroll stated in an article in the School Counselor that psychological education is

> . . . a regeneration of our profession by reordering our affiliations, engaging in a profound degree of retraining and committing ourselves to a deep involvement in the concept of learning. Progress has never been a bargain; we have to pay for it. (p. 395)

RELIGIOUS COUNSELING

The religious community today must relate to internal problems. Declining church attendance, the advancing age of existing members, and an increasing challenge in keeping members involved and interested in church programs are causing some clergy to look for new ways of approaching people (Olsen, 1974). Religious leadership faces three challenges in attempts to keep churches viable in the community:

1. meeting the pressure of maintaining traditional responsibilities;

2. meeting the increased demand for counseling services; and

3. meeting the increased need for a significant number of people who are competent in human relationships, communication, and other interpersonal concerns (Olsen, 1974, p. 27).

Traditional religious responsibilities of the clergy have remained constant or have increased, and additional new demands for counseling help often have been added. This additional work load has forced clergy to find new ways to meet the responsibility of this role. In recent years, religious education has trained religious leaders in counseling techniques, increasing their interest in and capacity to assume counseling responsibilities. Even with training, however, priests, pastors, or rabbis cannot hope to meet all the needs of their members.

Another challenge facing religious leaders is the increasing demand by members of the congregation for help in improving their interpersonal relations skills. To meet this challenge, the base church concept is evolving. A major goal of the base church is to establish a system by which people relate more effectively with others and to learn better interpersonal relationship skills and attitudes.

Since the base church concept consists of small groups of people in open, face-to-face contact characterized by warmth and intimacy, new skills and leadership training are needed. In order for the implementation of the base church concept to be successful, the leadership must have interpersonal relations skills developed to a high level of facilitation and be able to teach these same skills to the members of the base church. Without effective people with these interpersonal relations skills, the base church concept will not satisfy people's needs any better than the traditional religious groups.

Olsen (1974) felt that the base church concept of small group interaction will bring to the surface the same individual "hang-ups," insecurities, frustrations, guilts, and idiosyncrasies exposed by the traditional church struggles, but it will expose them more quickly and more effectively. The combination of a small group format with a desire to know and relate to others on more than a superficial basis creates experiences within the base church which require many people to possess highly developed interpersonal skills. The small group church concept is validly related to religious concerns since when church members in base church programs are given the opportunity to experience affective human interaction produced by effective leaders, they often report their experiences as highly meaningful in a religious sense.

Olsen (1974) maintained that human potential experiences can be effective only if they foster growth in all participants in the experiences. He espouses the extended use of encounter groups, Gestalt concepts, psychodrama, sensory awareness, and all of the strategies employed in teaching for improved affective education. In order to meet the expanded needs of church members to develop better interpersonal relationships, religious leaders would be wise to teach others their own counseling and interpersonal skills.

Also, by establishing training programs for nonprofessionals within the church, the church leaders can make better use of lay leaders in religious education, internal leadership and outreach crisis intervention, tutorial and other community responsibility programs with a degree of effectiveness not previously possible. Lay leaders often have the desire to improve the basic communication skills and look to their minister, priest, or rabbi for help. If the training is not provided, the members can be alienated by the professionals in churches or synagogues often feel left out and retaliate by leaving the church or reducing their involvement in its activities (Olsen, 1974, p. 36).

A strong movement can be found in all faiths in reference to "peer ministry" and "youth helper" programs. Les Stohl of the Lutheran Church reported that more that 15,000 youths attended conferences centered around these issues. Barbara Varenhorst has done a considerable amount of work using her training model in Peer Ministry.

BUSINESS AND INDUSTRY

With the new fear of drug testing on the job and the loss of productivity as a result of stress and personal problems, business and industry are looking at a variety of methods for dealing with problems relating to such issues as drug and alcohol issues, stress, attendance, family problems, and midlife transitions.

Many companies have established employee assistance programs, (EAP). These programs sometimes provide all of the counseling for the employees, or the counselor may see the employees once and then refer them to other professionals in the community. In some companies, the EAP counselors are highly trained professionals; in other companies, they are peers who have completed some helping training. Still other companies also have peer helpers to help troubled employees and bring them to the attention of the EAP counselors.

American industry is very competitive, and one way of being competitive is to keep the employees emotionally healthy. This, of course, cannot be done only by professional counselors; companies and corporations must rely as well on paraprofessionals for help.

OTHER COMMUNITY AGENCIES

The paraprofessional concept has received acceptance and provided impetus in community agencies that are concerned with people in trouble. Illustrations of such agencies are crisis centers, drop-in centers, and teen centers. Gartner and Riessman (1974, pp. 253-254) identified five major reasons for the development of nonprofessional helpers:

1. the consumer previously was not served adequately by people who could understand his or her problem;

2. the poor were locked out of achieving professional skills by the usual paths;

3. nonprofessionals filled a gap between professionals and the complaining public;

4. jobs were needed that government agencies could provide, and

5. delivery of services, especially to the poor, was lacking.

As a result of these needs and conditions in the community, a rush to provide nonprofessional services in many counseling roles began. As the need to fill the void created by an insufficient number of professionally trained counselors became apparent, attempts were made to train nonprofessional or paraprofessional staff. Traditional counselor training institutions were unable to provide adequate help. Emphasis in training has been, and still is, directed mainly toward training professionals. To date, the facilities and procedures for teaching nonprofessionals has been inadequate. Programs to train nonprofessional counselors have focused typically on academic and theoretical understanding rather than on the skills needed to facilitate client change (Brown, 1974). Because the demand for helping agencies is so great and the technology to train lay helpers so meager, the results often are frustrating, damaging, and ineffective.

The gap between the great demand for help and the deficient quality of training procedures emphasizes the need for methods and processes that can be given to staff members for training nonprofessionals in workable helping communication skills and attitudes. When training methods are available and staff members are trained adequately, the result can be a vital program of peer helpers.

Bridgeton, Missouri, provides an example of a teen center that struggled for two to three years until staffed by a person who had received adequate training in helping skills and additional trainer skills. The staff member proceeded to develop a program in which peers were trained on a continuing basis, and the center has functioned as a social teen center—a center where peers can help other contemporaries with problems and concerns. Programs such as this can serve as models for adolescent centers in which both social needs and interpersonal needs are met. Other community service groups such as Boy Scouts, Girl Scouts, and Big Brother/Big Sister organizations would be able to expand their effectiveness if individuals within these organizations were to have the necessary peer counseling training and experience to meet the needs of those who seek help.

One of the problems facing the leadership in community social action groups is faced similarly by school counselors, that is, an incapacity to keep abreast of the changing human service scene. The result of this failing is that the scope of their creativity is limited to the traditionally described counselor role. The face of the country is changing, and helpers of others must either adapt to that change or see their impact severely diminished.

In looking for research to support the upgrading and dissemination of peer counseling skills, it is important to look at research that offers a variety of techniques such as pre-help and post-help testing, comparison groups, objective and self-report, subjective evaluation. Currently in the literature are some research articles that consider the effectiveness of peer counseling. According to Scott and Warner (1974), however, most of the available articles are subjective. In the following review of peer counseling programs we have attempted to present programs that are both objective and subjective in nature.

If you are in need of a more complete bibliography, you may want to write to Dr. Rey Carr, Director of the Peer Counseling Project, University of Victoria, Victoria, British Columbia, VBW 2Y2. He has compiled a bibliography entitled *Peer Counseling: An Annotated and Indexed Bibliography, 1978-1986.*

An effective way to accomplish these changes is to accept the premise that counseling skills should not be kept secret but rather should be given away. Counselors are in a most advantageous position to distribute these skills.

Peer counseling therefore becomes an important concomitant to the educational goals not only of schools but also of other helping community agencies. The training of peers in basic communication skills can contribute greatly to improving the impact of interpersonal relationships on the entire community.

Chapter IV

BRINGING YOU
UP-TO-DATE

This chapter has been included in the *Peer Counseling* book only after much debate. The final decision to include a chapter on research finding in a "how-to-do-it" *Peer Counseling* book was predicated on the possibility that research support may be needed when the idea of peer counseling program development is presented to administrators and decision makers regarding program offerings. Often administrators and co-workers will give support to and become involved in an idea only when it has been successful in some other place or system. Because that attitude frequently prevails, the following representative samples of the research and of recently attempted programs in peer counseling (many successful, some with problems) hopefully will foster support for ideas in your setting.

RESEARCH TECHNIQUES USED

Pretest-Posttest Method

Rapp, Dworkin, and Moss (1978) reported the effects on peer helpers of a middle school peer program. The researchers' findings indicated there was no decline in the academic performance of peer helpers, nor was there any increase in their self-concept or positive attitudes toward school. Bowman and Myrick (1980) described a peer program with students in grades 3 through 6 who were trained to be "junior counselors." All peer helpers showed positive gains in self-concept when pre- and post-evaluations were analyzed.

Comparison Group Method

In a study using the comparison group method to evaluate a peer program, Emmert (1977) found that a group of students who had received peer-helper training had statistically different and higher empathy scores than did a group of students who did not receive the training. In another study, Bell (1977) used this method to investigate the effects of participation in a structured peer counseling program on junior high peer counselors' self-concepts and academic achievements. He found that, although trained peer counselors did not display increases in self-concept, they did demonstrate higher academic achievement than did trained peer counselors who did not work with other students.

Bowman (1982) examined the effects of helping projects on fifth grade student helpers in nine elementary schools. No significant differences (.05) were found in the peer helpers in terms of self-concept or attitudes toward others. Significant differences (.05), however, were found in the problem-behavior students for improved classroom behavior and school attitudes.

Tindall (1978) attempted to assess the effect of training versus nontraining on high school students' ability to function as peer facilitators in an individual setting. The control group consisted of five students at a high school working in an office; the experimental group consisted of eight students serving in a peer counseling role at a high school. Two expert judges rated the experimental (trained) students significantly higher as individual helpers than the control (untrained) students on both the 15-minute taped interview (p < .007) and the written "Index of Communication" (CI) (Carkhuff, 1969) (p < .002). Interrater reliability among the expert judges was found to be .76 for the taped interview and .80 for the written index.

Cooker and Cherchia (1976) conducted a study to ascertain the effects of training versus nontraining of peer leaders in a high school setting. They looked at the effect of training on the peers' ability to function as facilitators in a group setting with fellow students as participants. They also looked at the effect of communication skills training on the subject's level of facilitative communication. They selected the control and experimental groups from 60 students (28 male, 32 female) attending an Oxford, Mississippi, high school. The participants were chosen by a faculty-student committee to be trained as group facilitators. Selection was made with the intent to represent a cross-section of the student body. The committee selected students for their leadership ability among fellow students; their ability to recognize and to influence others was seen as important in terms of leadership. The group was composed of 19 sophomores, 24 juniors, and 17 seniors. Of the group, 42% were nonwhite and 50% were white. Upon completion of training, each facilitator was expected to lead discussion groups of 10 to 12 fellow students, randomly assigned from the remainder of the student body of 625 pupils. This was initiated to make peer groups an integrated part of local drug education programs. The intent was to give students an opportunity to participate in small group discussions in which students held the responsibility for content and direction. A 40-20 split was used so that a substantial number of trained facilitators would be available for the next school year. Those selected for the experimental treatment were randomly assigned to 1 of 5 training groups of 8 students each. Each group met with a trainer for a total of 8 hours, 1 hour a week over an 8-week period.

The CI was used, as was a 15-minute taped interview with a coached client who presented a standard situation. Both the written and taped responses were rated by two counselors familiar with the scales.

Cooker and Cherchia (1976) found a significant difference in the means of the posttests on the CI and interviews. The CI scores yielded a significant difference between groups, $F(1,59) = 41.42$, $p < .05$; and on the taped interviews, a significance at $F(1,59) = 36.54$, $p < .05$. The researchers also found that in both the CI scores and the interviews the trained students in the role of group facilitator were rated significantly higher than untrained students. The expert judges' ratings were $F(1,59) = 36.54$, $p < .05$; and peer ratings were $F(1,59) = 6.71$, $p < .05$. This indicates that trained students functioned at higher levels in facilitating small groups than did untrained students. The real significance of this study is revealed in the finding that training peer helpers is more desirable and productive than not training them. The assumption that existing leadership skills or qualities are sufficient for adequate peer helping may thus be invalid. It appears that professional helpers need to spend some of their time disseminating their skills by training others.

Other studies using comparison groups researched different counseling methods: with disruptive youths (Creange, 1982); changes in behavior (Lobitz, 1970; Samuels, & Samuels, 1975; Vriend, 1969); and different training methods (Allbee, 1976; Gray & Tindall, 1974).

Self Report.

Gumaer (1976) used the Likert-type scale in his self-report study. His findings suggested that both the peer helpers and the students they worked with had positive attitudes toward the peer helper experience and believed it should be a part of every school.

Tindall (1979) reported results using the *Youth Listener Evaluation Survey*, which was given to a random sample of students, grades 10 through 12, as part of the Guidance Evaluation Survey. The researcher wanted to know the following:

A. Have you ever heard of this
   program?   Yes 84%   No 16%

B. Do you think that there is
   a need for this program?   Yes 83%   No 17%

C. Have you ever talked with
   a Youth Listener about a
   personal concern of yours?   Yes 13%   No 87%

(IF YOU CHECKED YES,
PLEASE ANSWER THE QUESTIONS BELOW)

1. How did you feel after talking to the Youth Listener?	1	2	3	4	5
	Worse		Somewhat Better		Much Better
	6%	4%	11%	43%	36%

2. Rate how well the Youth Listener listened.

1	2	3	4	5
Did Not Listen		Listened Halfway		Listened Well
5%	2%	6%	23%	65%

3. Rate the amount of concern shown by the Youth Listener.

1	2	3	4	5
Not Concerned		Somewhat Concerned		Very Concerned
7%	—	9%	33%	15%

4. How would you rate the outcome of your problem after talking with the Youth Listener.

1	2	3	4	5
Things Got Worse		Nothing Changed		Things Got Better
3%	—	16%	40%	41%

5. Would you feel comfortable talking to a Youth Listener again?

Yes	No	Unsure
88%	9%	3%

Barbara Varenhorst (1987) reported on a study done by Ailsa Edge in which Edge randomly chose 133 students in grades 7 through 11 to respond to a questionnaire. Of this group, 80% said that they would consider friends as being likely individuals to help them with problems, while 36% indicated that they were unsure about the adequacy of the Fulton Peer Counseling Program in training students to assist others, and 47% were unsure of the methods by which they could contact a peer counselor. However, 14% indicated that they talked over a problem with a person who they knew was a peer counselor.

Additional studies include Hamburg and Varenhorst (1972) and Hensley and Mickelson (1978).

Summary

Obviously other highly controlled research is still needed, but sufficient subjective and objective studies are available to indicate the success of peer counseling. Many authors have written about peer counseling. Sobey (1970) wrote about lay helpers; Eisdorfer and Golann (1969) referred to the concept as the "New Professional"; Gray and Tindall, in 1978, developed the book, *Peer Counseling, first edition,* for training peer counselors. The American School Counselor Association (see Chapter 12) has developed a position statement on peer counseling. The California Personnel and Guidance Association has developed "Guidelines for the Paraprofessional in Human Services" (see Chapter 12). Samuels and Samuels (1975), Myrick and Bowman (1981), and Foster (1982) have recently written books concerning peer training.

As the peer helper movement has gained momentum, more presentations on this topic have been appearing on programs at state and national guidance conferences each year. March 1983 saw creation of a periodical devoted entirely to peer helper programs—the *Peer Facilitator Quarterly.* Many states and areas have also started their own local information exchange. Peer counseling conferences are happening throughout the country at local levels. It appears that peer counseling has grown from a small beginning in the late 60s to what is now a recognized, viable way of helping.

TRAINING PEER COUNSELORS

Perhaps the most critical component in any peer helper program is training. The procedures chosen to train students can make a difference between a successful program and an unsuccessful one. Although a number of peer programs were launched in the 1970s, some that lacked planning and organization soon floundered. In others, however, the planners ensured success and support for their program by being more systematic in their approach, defining the training programs in detail, and carefully selecting the peer projects and tasks (Myrick & Bowman, 1981).

A growing body of research contains information to indicate that a more systematic approach to teaching helping skills will lead to more successful interventions (Allbee, 1976; Bowman & Myrick, 1980; Briskin & Anderson, 1973; Cooker & Cherchia, 1976; Kern & Kirby, 1971; Kum & Gal, 1976; McCann, 1975; Tindall, 1978). Gains in self-esteem, classroom behavior, and academic achievement are reported for peer helpers and their helpees in programs that have fully defined goals and objectives of training (Myrick & Bowman, 1981).

Allbee (1976), in his study of different types of structured training, compared three groups: (1) the Ivey "Microcounseling" training group, (2) the Carkhuff model trained group, and (3) an untrained group. He found significant differences in most dimensions between the trained and untrained groups. He found no significant difference between the peer counselors trained using the microcounseling model and those using the Carkhuff model. If time is a factor to the professional trainer, the approach presented by Carkhuff would seem to be more efficient.

Another training model has been presented by Zwibelman (1977), who used basically didactic and experiential aspects in a model consisting of three distinct elements: (1) a therapeutic contact with a high-functioning trainer, (2) a highly controlled program of techniques, and (3) a group experience in which the trainee is allowed to integrate personal values into the program.

A peer counseling program instituted by Hamburg and Varenhorst (1972) consisted of training through didactic instruction and practice through role playing. Although they found personal growth of the trained students, it was not related to the effectiveness of the training. Those studies that measured the changes in the skill levels of facilitative behaviors (Truax & Carkhuff, 1967; Gray & Tindall, 1974) support the hypothesis that individuals can change their behavior in interpersonal skills and, as a result, they do improve in growth-producing behaviors.

Apparently an important aspect of training peer counselors is to use a model structured in listening skills as opposed to nontraining and simply personal growth activities. If the goal is self-concept development and personal growth, perhaps it should be called "group counseling" rather than peer counseling training. This is not to say that personal growth does not take place with peer counseling, but the weight of evidence is not as clear as it is in communication skills training.

Looking at those outcomes subjectively, researchers have concluded that changes in behavior are taking place, and the probability is evident that the training of the peer counselors has influenced those changes. The subjective and objective results of the studies that have been completed to date influence the conclusion to which Scott and Warner (1974) agreed—that beneficial effects occur when peer counseling is used in schools.

In this book, studies are cited that describe how peer counselors are being used in a variety of settings and systems. Problems, as well as successes of programs, are presented to provide the most inclusive understanding of the peer counseling concept and program possibilities.

SETTINGS AND PURPOSES

Peer counseling programs in the schools have been used essentially to augment the impact of the counselor or professional in the system. According to Scott and Warner (1974), peer counselors have been used as adjuncts to the counseling program, with specifically defined roles. In other cases they have been used in group settings as co-worker with the counselor. The authors found that these uses crossed the age dimensions from elementary schools through college levels.

College Level Programs

By far, the largest number of studies dealing with peer counseling have been conducted at the college level. Four of the studies (Froman, 1972; Luther, 1972; Murry, 1972; Upcraft, 1971) used peer group counselors to help students with academic problems. In each case, the peers were used in addition to the regular counseling program. All four researchers reported that peer programs were beneficial. The studies by Murry, Froman, and Luther were experimental in nature. Murry found student counselors to be effective in the academic area but not in the social area. Froman reported that peer counseling and individual reinforcement counseling significantly improved the chances of high-risk students' succeeding academically and remaining in school. In Luther's study the grade point average and self-esteem of marginal students were improved.

Colorado State University implemented a program designed to improve racial understanding at a predominantly Anglo university through the use of peer counselor-trained students of minority races as aides. This program was reported in an article by Thomas and Yates (1974), who were involved in the training and development of the program at Colorado State. Minority students were trained in counseling and informational techniques and were used to help other minority students to develop feelings of strength and power. A second and more widespread task of the peers was to explain the feelings, needs, and concerns of minority students to Anglo students and campus groups. The program developed both successes and frustrations among the Anglo students, who found difficulty in changing their deeply ingrained biases and beliefs. Thomas and Yates were encouraged by the program, although they received both positive and negative feedback. No statistical data are available to support or to reject the concept or the program.

Another program that used peer counselors at the college level was reported by Ware and Gold (1971). They trained students as peer counselors at Los Angeles College to help other students who were having academic difficulties during the first and second semesters of their freshman year. Data were gathered to determine whether or not students in academic trouble who were seen by peer counselors stayed in school longer than did those who did not see peer helpers. Ware and Gold (1971) identified the degree to which peer counselors were effective in preventing students from dropping school because of poor academic adjustment to college during the first semester of their college experience. They concluded that peer counselors affected significantly the staying power of marginal freshman students. Ample evidence, although not statistically significant, was collected to support as well the conclusion that peer influence positively affected students' academic performances throughout their college lives.

Junior High and High School Programs

Scott and Warner (1974) identified 7 studies on peer counseling at the junior high and high school level but maintained that the evidence found in these studies was conflicting. Engle and Szyperski (1965) and Margro (1973) found little difference in anxiety and self-concept between students functioning as peer counselors and their "clients." In contrast to these findings, Hamburg and Varenhorst (1972), Koch (1973), Lobitz (1970), and Vriend (1969) all reported significant changes in academic, social, and personal areas of student concerns. Gray and Tindall (1974) claimed that there were highly significant changes in levels of helping skills when participants in new programs were compared with those in control groups. In addition, Gray and Tindall found that there were significant changes in the academic behaviors of their "clients." Teachers reported improved grades for the peer counselors as well as increased effectiveness and maturity in class. Leadership roles increased markedly, although the increase was not tested statistically.

Shorey (1981) conducted a study with 90 thirteen-year-old middle school students in which she compared peer group counseling with achievement motivation counseling. The results showed that there were no significant differences in achievement or acting out behavior but that there were significant increases in attendance for both groups.

Terrell, McWilliams, and Cowen (1972) trained 24 students to lead 36 counseling groups in the schools. Although the evaluation was subjective in nature, the results were positive. Kelley (1980), however, in his study with secondary students in an alternative high school, found that peer group facilitation does not foster positive changes in self-concept. Kern and Kirby (1971) used seventh and eighth graders, and their evaluations showed significant positive changes in behavior in students with whom paraprofessionals were working.

Murphy (1975) studied the effects of peer group counseling with chronically absent sophomores on the variables of attendance, achievement, and behavior. Specifically the intent of the study was to see if peer group counseling would decrease significantly the number of absences among chronically absent sophomores between the second and third marking periods. These absences were compared with those among a like number of control students. The testing of the hypothesis and the analysis of the data revealed the following finding: students with chronic attendance problems who received the treatment had significantly fewer absences than did the noncounseled at the .01 level. It was not possible, on the basis of the study, to state that there was a significant decrease in the number of times a chronically absent student was sent to the office for discipline.

Research into and studies of disruptive behavior and its remediation have sought alternatives to punitive action; these alternatives have frequently been specific counseling approaches. Alternative approaches that offered individual or peer counseling have resulted in schools' being able to meet more effectively the discipline needs of students (Mizell, 1978). A Dade County, Florida, school system found that the implementation of peer group counseling programs resulted in a decrease in disruptive incidents and an increase in students' self-concept (Samuels & Samuels, 1975).

Creange (1982) compared the effects of individual and peer group counseling on a sample of disruptive high school students. The measuring instruments were attendance, grade point average, incidence of disruptive behavior, and self-concept as measured by the *Tennessee Self-Concept Scale* (TSCS). A sample of 24 disruptive students had been randomly selected at each of 4 high schools for a total of 96 students; each sample was then divided into 3 subgroups. One group received weekly individual counseling; a second group, peer group counseling; and the third group, which served as the control, the minimal counseling usually provided by the schools. Attendance, grade point average, incidence of disruptive behavior, and the TSCS scale were given both before and after the 10-week duration of the study.

The results of the study were that over a 10-week period individual counseling sessions by credentialed counselors with disruptive students yielded data that indicated this type of intervention had improved the attendance of female students. Peer group counseling, individual counseling, and routine counseling sessions with disruptive students over a 10-week period yielded data that indicated that all three of these types of intervention reduced the disruptive behavior of these students.

Neither individual counseling, nor peer group counseling, nor routine counseling sessions affected significantly school achievement as measured by grade point average with disruptive students. Neither individual counseling, nor peer group counseling sessions affected significantly self-concept as measured by the TSCA. In the area of attendance, high school girls appear to have been more receptive to particular counseling strategies than did high school boys.

Hensley and Mickelson (1978) described a high school peer counseling group as one trained to deal with students described as "high risk." The high-risk students had poor attendance, poor academic standing, limited peer interaction, limited involvement in school activities, and limited classroom interaction. The peer counselors were trained in the individual areas of values clarification and trust building and in the group skill areas of group leadership, active listening, problem definition, and problem solving. They were trained to arrive at a competency in these skills through experiential exercises and role playing, with the use of audio tapes as skill levels advanced. The students spent more than 100 hours in training. They then were used as an outreach function of the counseling center to contact, to deal with, and/or to refer the high-risk students.

Evaluation of the program found that in 1977 their 18 peer counselors grew in number to 32 by the beginning of the second semester. These students reported having had 993 counseling contacts with students, parents, and teachers. During the first semester of 1978, 21 peer counselors reported just under 1,700 contacts. The various types of problems dealt with were little different from those handled by most school counselors. A closer look shows communication problems leading the list—those mostly between student and student, teacher and student, and parent and student; skipping classes and drug abuse follow; with the remainder ranging through runaway, pregnancy, death and dying, and requests for college and career information. Many of the problems were referred to professional counselors. A study done of the students who were counselors indicates that their clients viewed the program in a very positive way and felt that it was helpful to them.

Elementary School Programs

Studies with elementary school programs include both older students helping elementary age students and elementary students helping elementary students. These students have been used as special friends, tutors, discussion leaders, and peer helpers. Peer helpers can play a significant role in improving both the learning process and the learning environment. Through training and preparation, they learn how to assist both teachers and peers. They become an extended hand of teachers and counselors, enabling more students to participate actively in learning experiences so that the learning process becomes more personalized (Myrick & Bowman, 1983).

The concept of students helping students in elementary and middle schools is not new. In the past 10 years it has received increasing attention in the professional literature (Briskin & Anderson, 1973; Gumaer, 1976; Kern & Kirby, 1971; Mastroiani & Dinkmeyer, 1980; McCann, 1975).

Peer helpers as young as third graders have been trained successfully for a variety of projects, all of which can be carefully planned and structured for success (Bowman & Myrick, 1980). For example, McCann (1975) developed a training program to prepare sixth graders to work individually with other students in a school drop-in center. The counseling program consisted of eight one-hour sessions that focused on listening skills, nonverbal communication, self-disclosure, reflective listening, and developing alternative courses of action when faced with a problem. The center was open to fifth grade students twice a week during recess or lunch. Kum and Gal (1976) conducted a similar program. Briskin and Anderson (1973) developed a program to teach behavioral principles to peer helpers. Sixth grade peer helpers were assigned to work as contingency managers for two disruptive third graders.

PREVENTION PROGRAMS

Sciacca (1987) reported another way of using peer helpers. This has to do with training students as peer health education teachers. He defines "peer health education" as the teaching or sharing of health information values and behaviors by individuals of similar age or status group. Thus student peer health education is the teaching of health information and behavior by fellow students. Some topics are smoking, drugs and alcohol, and sexuality.

Telch, Kellen, and McAlister (1982) illustrated the effectiveness of a program that utilized high school peer educators to teach junior high students the skills to resist the pressure to smoke. The students not receiving the peer education program, after 33 months, reported smoking at a level three times that of the peer education group.

Luepker, Johnson, and Murray (1983) documented the results of a three-year study of cigarette smoking among 1,081 seventh graders in three different schools. School number 1 received no special smoking prevention curriculum; school number 2 received a smoking prevention curriculum taught by adult teachers; while school number 3 received the same smoking curriculum taught by student peers of the same age. The education program taught exclusively by adults was found to be effective during the first year; however, by the end of the second year, the smoking rates were as high as those in the school receiving no intervention. In school number 3, where peer educators were involved in the teaching, lower smoking rates prevailed over the entire three-year study.

In 1984, Botvin, Baker, Renick, Filazzola, and Botvin reported a 20-session program that focused on reducing adolescent smoking, alcohol, and marijuana use. Ten public schools were randomized to either a teacher-implemented curriculum or a "slightly older peer" implemented curriculum or no curriculum. Substantially lower smoking, alcohol, and marijuana use rates occurred following the intervention for the peer education group, as compared to both the teacher-led and the no-treatment group.

The results of these studies indicate that substantial evidence is available to show that peer health education programs can be effective in the schools.

Prevention programs have been highly funded with some evaluation. Tobler (1986) conducted a meta-analysis. She located more than 240 programs that were evaluated during the period from 1972 to 1984. Of these 98 studies, encompassing 143 different program modalities, met her criteria. The program modalities were collapsed into the following five categories:

1. **Knowledge only.** Presentation by teacher of legal, biological, and psychological effects of drug abuse-scare tactics.

2. **Affective only.** Self-esteem building, self-awareness, feelings, values clarification—experiential activities.

3. **Peer program.** Positive peer influence; peer teaching, peer counseling, helping, and facilitation; peer participation—subdivided into those focusing on refusal skills (saying "No") and those concentrating on interpersonal and intrapersonal life skills.

4. **Knowledge plus affective.** Combination of numbers 1 and 2.

5. **Alternatives.** Activities more appealing than drug use.

Tobler found that peer programs were dramatically more effective that all of the other programs. She concluded from the study that (1) the knowledge-only and effective-only programs for average adolescents should be discontinued; (2) the focus should be on peer programs that emphasize refusal skills as well as communication and decision-making skills; and (3) for the at-risk youths, the peer programs should be supplemented with alternatives (e.g., community activities, physical activities, mastery learning, job skill).

Feldman and Caplinger (1983) suggested that the power of the peer group as a socializing agent is in developing positive behaviors. The critical element in the success of the peer program approach may be the sense of connectedness (participation in meaningful activities) and involvement (assumption of responsibility) that the youths experience. Another word is "empowered."

Based upon available evidence, in the prevention field peers are effective in prevention.

Agency Programs

As have schools, community agencies have turned to nonprofessionals or paraprofessionals to meet some of the problems that face the counseling profession. Problems in agencies are different from those in the schools. First, nonprofessionals may or may not be peers with those with whom they are working. Second, nonprofessionals who work for agencies often are paid for their services. In fact, they become the "New Professionals," as they were called by Eisdorfer and Golann (1969). Nonprofessionals who are not hired by the agency are volunteers who come from the community and are not responsible to the agency other than through their desire to help. These two conditions create problems different from those faced by the schools, where the peer counselors are both a part of the system and served by the system.

In dealing with nonprofessionals who are employed by the agency, Gartner and Riessman (1974) identified five reasons why nonprofessionals have been added to the helping system:

1. Consumers, particularly the poor and minorities, were troubled by the inadequacies of traditional service delivery and by the reluctance of professionals to understand their needs, both physical and psychological.

2. A recognition was made that the poor were locked out of achieving professional status by traditional credentialing paths, which required long periods of education prior to job placement.

3. Professionals, who at first felt highly criticized by the poor and minorities, were reluctant initially to accept paraprofessionals, but soon accepted them gladly as a buffer. The paraprofessional was sometimes called a bridge to the poor. In a sense, the paraprofessional was the lesser of two evils, the other "evil" being the poor or minority consumers who were highly critical of teachers, social workers, and other human service professionals.

4. A need for jobs existed and the traditional private sector was not providing them. The idea that individuals who possessed a community understanding and background could begin working with very minimal training was consequently a positive aspect of the paraprofessional movement and was used to generate needed jobs.

5. In some cases, particularly in terms of service delivery in poor neighborhoods, a manpower shortage was present that could be filled by paraprofessionals. (pp. 253-254)

In agencies, motivation is more often to oil a squeaking wheel than to expand and improve the services of counselors who cannot meet the needs of their clients. By training paraprofessionals, agencies are enabled to meet the needs that are voiced by the poor and minorities. In this way agencies are not forced to deal with the problems brought about by clients' being denied services they desire. Training of nonprofessionals thus has become the most expedient way to solve the problems that many agencies face in their effort to meet the increasing counseling loads.

One main outcome of paraprofessional programs, according to Gartner and Riessman (1974) is that the training resulted in some important contributions to the field of counseling. One of those contributions is a new awareness that the minimally educated and/or peer can be trained to provide counseling services and in many cases perform as well as those trained professionals who have long years of education and experience. According to researchers, the evidence is increasing, and as a society, we are becoming aware that many persons can provide counseling services to those who need them, that these service providers need to have neither academic credentials nor advanced degrees to do a good job in the one area of interpersonal communication. The fact that almost a million individuals have been trained to some degree and are providing services on a paraprofessional level is cited as evidence that a serious need for counseling is present and that nonprofessionals are filling much of the void existing in counselor personnel. The authors even point out that when helper status is gained, values and goals change, and peer counselors tend to behave like professionals. The peer counselors' concerns become wages, personal education, and other typical worker issues rather than the concerns and issues of the clients whom they are supposed to be helping.

Nicoletti and Flater-Benz (1974) reported on the use of volunteers in community mental health agencies as a means to overcome the crunch resulting from efforts to increase helping outreach in the community with ever decreasing funds. The researchers feel that many agencies have a strong group of volunteers who could be trained and used as peer counselors. Nicoletti and Flater-Benz (1974) have been pleased with the results of their program, which has been in operation for two years. Benefits that they feel have accrued are ones that were mentioned also by Gartner and Riessman (1974). Volunteers provide a beneficial link between the professional and the client. This role of the volunteer provides the client with a role model who is from the community, but who also is knowledgeable in the area of mental health. However, these volunteers did discover a problem with this arrangement. With helpers and clients living in the same area, the clients often imposed on the volunteers at home or in other places, in addition to using the service offered by the agency.

Studies are needed in terms of effect on the helpee(s). Most studies are on the helper and training. Control and experimental studies need to be performed for the helpees, the community, and the systems in which they exist.

Summary

It appears that peer counselors have been used successfully in elementary, junior high school, high school, colleges, and agencies. They have been used successfully with disruptive students, high-risk students, drug and alcohol programs, health education, prevention programs, and race relations; they have been successful leading small discussion groups, serving as special friends to new students, and helping to change classroom behavior of problem students—gains in self-esteem, academic achievement, and improved attendance—through such functions as tutoring and drop-out prevention; lastly, they have provided help for agencies and assistance to teachers.

CAUTIONS RELATING TO TRAINING

The impact of peer counseling is becoming increasingly extensive, and interest in peer counseling programs continues to expand. However, several considerations must be taken into account before successful programs can be initiated. For example, a program may be planned, developed, and implemented without taking into consideration many aspects of the program that relate directly to the helpee in training or to others who are affected by the training. Peer counselors of various kinds and degrees of training are found in schools, juvenile detention centers, nursery schools, day care centers, support groups, crisis intervention centers, state hospitals, drug rehabilitation programs, and poverty agencies. Because the peer counselor may work in such a wide variety of settings, the professionals have the responsibility to give nonprofessionals good training, exposure to ethical standards, proper supervision, and support so that the trainee can contribute the best potential available.

Allen (1973) wrote succinctly regarding professional responsibilities to the nonprofessional helper. He deplored implications that individuals exposed to twenty-four-hour drug crisis training or one-weekend encounter group training are prepared adequately to do effective peer counseling of any type. He objected to the lack of interest in developing safeguards against unethical practices of the trainees. Such inadequacies often develop into hurried attempts to solve the dilemma of persons needing help because there are too few trained professionals available to meet those needs.

Allen (1973) not only criticized ineffective programs and unethical procedures but also offered some solid guidelines for the development of well-constructed training programs. He felt that any effective program needs to include as representatives in its development the persons who will be affected by the program. Trainers, trainees, consultants, and all supportive personnel need to be involved in planning, implementation, and evaluation of any program for it to be successful.

One of the difficulties with many programs is a lack of role definition for the peer counselors. Allen (1973) felt that the training of nonprofessionals cannot be justified on the basis that they will be used to fill in on responsibilities that the professionals do not want to meet or do not feel are important enough tasks. If the nonprofessional becomes merely an aide of a flunky, then the program cannot be justified. Another point that Allen stressed concerned the selection of trainees, for which he suggested a specific program. However, a difference of opinion as to the most effective selection procedures exists. Some trainers have conducted programs without selection of trainees and have felt that the peer counseling training was successful (Dellworth, Moore, Mullich, & Leone, 1974; Golin & Safferstone, 1971; Gray & Tindall, 1974; Varenhorst, 1973).

After selection of trainees has been completed (using a method that seems feasible to the trainer within the situation), the question arises as to how much training needs to be given. Allen (1973) cautioned against too much training, which can result in a serious change in the trainees' value systems. Such a change risks alienating the trainees, because their values may no longer be compatible with those of the group they are supposed to be helping.

Allen (1973) covered two points that are not made elsewhere in the literature on peer counseling. First, he indicated that one of the goals of training is to improve the professional or social position of the trainee as a result of the training and subsequent responsibilities. If this position is not changed, the person has no real need to be subjected to the training or the role function after the training. The second point relates to a legal concern. Law suits against schools are more prevalent than ever before, and the proper caution must be instituted to prevent trainees or their supporting systems from becoming involved in legal suits as the result of improper training or inappropriate behavior.

Brown (1974) supported the idea of using caution by stressing that a successful program must have three aspects adequately controlled:

1. the kinds of training,

2. effective interactions of peers and professionals, and

3. proper supervision and control.

Should you be involved in basic training, and if these trainees, after completing training, were asked to do certain projects or move to a practicum, then stringent criteria would need to be developed to select the qualified helpers for the project. Ongoing supervision and advanced training are essential for an effective program.

To have a group of paraprofessionals being helpers in a prevention program by giving classroom lessons without first experiencing quality basic training, as suggest in *Book 1* is hard to imagine.

When these criteria are properly followed, the results can be similar to those found by Carkhuff (1969), about which he stated:

> Using indices of behavioral improvement as criteria, the paraprofessional counselors were found to have achieved a level of therapeutic effectiveness only slightly below that of the experienced counselor and considerably above that of graduate school trainees. (p. 125)

In the ASCA Position Statement (see Chapter 12) is discussed training.

ESSENTIAL CONDITIONS
FOR PEER COUNSELING

Even though the number of studies that have been completed with peer counseling is limited, individuals in professional settings as well as lay persons are concluding that the concept is workable. Further development is needed and should be watched with interest. However, for the time being, training of peer counselors is worthy of counselor support and effort.

When several conditions are met satisfactorily, peer counseling can be an innovative and worthwhile dimension of the counseling profession. Based on experience and research reported in the literature, peer counseling is satisfactorily meeting certain needs. However, for it to be successful, peer counseling must be undertaken with specific developmental training, supervision, and evaluation procedures. In summary, the necessary conditions as reported in literature are as follows:

    1. Everyone involved in the program needs to be involved in the planning.

2. A specific planned training program is necessary. The program format may be in the form of classes, a series of workshops, training seminars, or whatever is needed, but it must have built in an effective training component.

3. Short encounter groups or one-time workshops of short duration are not adequate to train helpers effectively.

4. A lengthy training program is not necessary, but it must be well structured and long enough to enable trainees to integrate the training.

5. Individuals who have the qualities of sensitivity, warmth, and awareness of others make effective trainees.

6. Supervision of trainees is important. This includes an ongoing follow-up program while the trainee is functioning in a peer counseling role.

7. Evaluation and research must be a part of the training and peer counseling program to measure progress and isolate problems.

8. Persons involved in the program need to be interested in the concept and the application of peer counseling.

9. Anyone who plans to implement a peer counseling program in the schools will need effective responses to some of the following questions:

   a. How will teachers or staff react to this program? Will it be one more resented interruption?

   b. How will parents react? Will they give flack to the administration?

   c. Will peer counselors' clients take advantage of the program?

   d. What are the program's chances for success?

10. Do not use the peer training and subsequent employment of nonprofessionals as aides to do the flunky work with which professionals do not want to be bothered. The peer counselors must be an integrated part of the total program with responsibilities comparable to those of the professionals.

11. The ethical aspects of the training must be taught adequately and supervised fully.

12. Peer counselors should work with their peers rather than with groups that have far different value systems.

13. Peer counselors can work successfully with support groups (AA's, Weight Watchers, etc.) if properly trained.

14. The trainer needs to be able to be a trainer, coordinator, facilitator, organizer, and evaluator.

Chapter V

DEVELOPMENT OF THE TRAINER

In any peer training program, the trainer becomes the vital link in changing a trainee with poorly developed skills into one with highly effective facilitative skills (Carkhuff, 1969, 1972; Egan, 1975). The result of several research studies led Carkhuff (1969) to reiterate that the trainee is not able to function at higher levels of effective behavior than the trainer. In essence then, the trainer needs to be a constantly effective high level helper. Not only does the trainer have a responsibility to possess, at a highly integrated level, the skills that are taught, but he/she also must demonstrate to trainees the process of integration through frequent and consistent modeling behaviors. Since human growth is a continuing dynamic process and never completed except by death, a decision to delay training others until one's own skills are maximized may prevent the initiation of any training program. Therefore, training programs should be planned, organized, and initiated with the awareness that the success of any training program depends upon the trainer. The process of self-growth as a trainer supercedes the ability to organize, develop, and administer programs. The starting point in any effective training program becomes the trainer.

PROFILE OF A TRAINER

Any attempt to draw a picture of one composite person and maintain that it is representative of effective trainers is ridiculous since effectiveness and maturity are packaged in an endless variety of human packages. To be an effective trainer, a person must be an effective helper. What, then, are the characteristics of a good helper? Ideally, these characteristics are rather comprehensive and inclusive of what many social scientists call the effective person. It is what Ivey (1971) called the "intentional person," what Carkhuff (1969) and Carkhuff and Truax (1969) called an "effectively living" person, Maslow's (1968) "self actualized" person, or Jourard's (1971) "transparent person." The kind of maturity which is manifested in the desire for self-growth and development is, essentially, what these authors mean. Maturity that is committed to physical, emotional, intellectual, social, and even spiritual development needs to be the trainer's focus for self-development. The important point is for the trainer to exhibit and model internal strength and self-confidence along with a dedication to personal growth. Characteristics of effective trainers that can be identified are imperative. Some of these characteristics are intellectual curiosity, physical fitness, pragmatic outlook, optimism, problem-solving skills and deductions, and a good role model.

Intellectual Curiosity

Intellectual curiosity is a vital link in the trainer's development. The trainer needs to be interested in and have respect for intellectual activities that are infused within all research, creativity, innovative process, and strivings for better ways to do things. He/she must keep an accurate perspective on personal intellectual capacities, neither selling self short nor being overconfident. Along with the awareness and respect for personal intellectual curiosity, the trainer must accept and respond to effective intellectual capacities in others. This response includes the ability to distinguish between positive and effective intellectual curiosity and that quality of intelligence which is essentially nonproductive or destructive in others. Intellectual competency includes the interest and ability to act effectively.

Physical Fitness

The trainer needs to be aware of the importance of physical fitness. The process of helping and training peer counselors is hard work and demands large portions of physical and emotional energy.

A potent trainer maintains good physical condition through the use of a proper diet and adequate exercise. In our society, diet and exercise are often times neither adequate nor proper. The demands of high energy levels require that specific efforts are made to develop an exercise program that is taxing and consistent. The program should include exercises that are constant and strenuous enough to develop muscle tone and high energy levels.

Pragmatic Outlook

A trainer basically implements theories and concepts into action thus becoming, essentially, a pragmatic person. Because his/her responsibility will be to implement practical and specific action programs, the trainer must be able to translate theoretical psychological concepts into effective processes. Few psychological theories translate easily into everyday, on-the-spot behavior suggestions that can be used as a recipe for helper action. That translation is the trainer's responsibility. Not only is pragmatism required, but initiative is also needed to experiment and create new ways of teaching counseling concepts and skills. Because each situation is different, a training program will face some obstacles and problems that cannot be anticipated. Therefore, the burden of solving those difficulties lies on the trainer. Meeting and overcoming scheduling, administrative, logistic, and personnel problems is a responsibility that is almost impossible to unload or even share. Practicality and tenacity, then, become two tools of a successful peer training program.

Optimism

Another personal characteristic that is very helpful in a training program is the trainer's optimistic outlook with regard to his/her own ability to accomplish challenging tasks. Optimism and the next characteristic to be discussed, problem solving, relate closely with creativity and practicality in program implementation.

Optimism is important because in many incidents peer counseling and peer counseling training are classed with those "new fangled" frills that generate defensiveness and caution in many peers and/or administrators. It is not an idea that generates confidence among those who think competency comes only with a Master's Degree, experience, and a pay check. Peer counseling concepts frequently require selling the concepts to others who (1) have not thought about, (2) are threatened by, or (3) can't conceive of students, lay workers, or peers being effective in helping people. These behaviors, if successful, can be very threatening to co-workers who may think that helping trainees is their prerogative. Pessimism is not intended here, but the realities of experience are that peer counseling often requires that the trainer educate others and "sell" the construct to others in his/her field.

Many times resistance stems from people who are resisting without having thought about the possibility of training peer helpers. The concept acts as an irritation in their status quo existence, and the peer counseling ideas require new energies on their part to cope with the new concepts. The inertia obstructing an effort to establish a new thought pattern, idea, or concept is often the only obstacle to be overcome by the objectors. Active resistance can appear when dealing with co-workers who tend to be threatened by anything that causes them to rethink their well-ingrained educational constructs. The co-workers are not so much opposed or antagonistic as simply frightened or uneasy that some dire new consequences will result from these new behaviors. Introduction to innovative concepts ignites the fear in others that the ideas will create problems that cannot be dealt with easily. The newness or change from the prescribed way of doing things requires the trainer to have a degree of self-confidence as well as confidence in peer counseling objectives so that resistance is viewed as a challenge to be overcome and not as a wall blocking the path.

Problem-Solving Skills

Problem-solving skills and interest in overcoming obstacles are the characteristics that support optimism and become the vehicles through which the optimism becomes justified. The skill to solve problems can be learned and can be developed as thoroughly as any of the other skills taught in the program. One of the trainer's responsibilities is to develop the attitude conducive to learning problem-solving skills, and see that the process is internalized, not irrational. No manual can teach people how to have the desire to overcome problems effectively. Technology can assist in the process but not the desire. Fortunately, the quality of optimism toward challenges usually accompanies the interest in getting problems solved.

The two qualities, optimism and problem-solving skills, are vitally important for a successful program. Without these qualities the obstacles placed in the trainer's way in a traditional, often times very conservative system can generate an overwhelming sense of frustration and disappointment. When the qualities of optimism and problem solving are developed, some very exciting programs are available. In addition, the trainer gains the awareness that he/she is not only helping others in school, church, or a community system but also that some very important skills are being taught to a widely increasing circle of people.

Dedication

Many counselors are dedicated strongly to being helpful to others. A peer counseling program requires this kind of dedication. If counseling is just a job, then one is cautioned about starting a program. If, however, a counselor feels frustration at being the only person to meet many needs, then a peer program makes sense. A program of giving away helping skills or training others in these helping skills can become an effective way for the counselor to widen his/her ability to meet the needs of others.

The kind of person with all the characteristics just presented does not exist in one body, but the characteristics are ones that can be used as guides. A trainer does need to function at high levels in all of the qualities mentioned. Most of the qualities presented are found to some degree in effective, mature, and genuine people. A trainer for peer counselors has the responsibility of striving for high levels of these qualities if only to develop as a person. Effective personal qualities and competent trainer qualities generally are congruent.

Role Model

As a trainer, you need to be a good role model for the peer helpers. You must possess high-level helping skills. You also must represent ethical and legal behavior. For example, if you as a trainer were working with recovering alcoholics as peer helpers, it would be important to model for them the kind of behavior that you would expect of them. Another example might be the issue of confidentiality. When you expect the peer helpees to keep things confidential, you must also respect the ethics of the group. You must be a professional and personal role model.

TRAINING

Since the basic format used for training has been developed by R. R. Carkhuff (1969) and others who have followed his lead, understanding the basic training concepts is necessary. In this *Peer Counseling: In-Depth Look at Training Peer Helpers* the intention is not to restate the rationale and research which has preceded the model development. This information can be found in the following original sources: Carkhuff, 1969, 1971; Gazda, 1973; Egan, 1975. These sources identify the underlying theoretical concepts in the highly structured training format. A portion of the time to be spent in program development includes a thorough understanding of the training concepts which support the program in this *Peer Counseling: An In-Depth Look at Training Peer Helpers.* The research and model developed by Robert Carkhuff and associates should either be understood or studied either prior to or during the training period.

Highly structured training models, such as the Carkhuff model, often appear overly restrictive and highly regimented to someone who does not understand the reasons behind the procedures. As a result, the uninformed trainer tends improvise, modify, or otherwise structurally change the basic format without purpose or understanding. The outcomes, then, are less than satisfactory, and the original model is held responsible when, in fact, the trainer is causing the end result to be less than adequate.

Practicing Skills

Developing skills requires both discipline and focus which come with organized practice. Communication skills learned in this program are helpful if they are learned using the same methods that are used in any skill development, that is, by introducing small segments of new behavior based upon extensions of previously learned behaviors. These new behaviors then are practiced in the presence of others who can give direct feedback on the level of development and effectiveness of each skill segment. Included in this learning process is the need to maintain a training discipline which does not allow trainees to go beyond the concept taught until the total skill is presented and integrated. Without the discipline needed to maintain focus, people tend to revert to old and ineffective behaviors. The process is similar to the process involved in learning a skill in sports, music, or art. Trainees, who are allowed to move to new skills before they have incorporated effectively more basic concepts, eventually find themselves handicapped. Many trainees in a wide variety of skills are required by their trainers to go back to basic patterns and behaviors because of sloppy, undisciplined, previous practice or instruction.

Therefore, we emphasize strongly the need for basic skill development and discipline, which seems mechanical at first but later shows its effectiveness in meeting training goals.

Training as Therapy

One of the expectations of an effective training program is the development of therapeutic results for both the trainer and the trainee. Carkhuff (1969) and Aspy (1972) identified the positive effects of training as therapy. In the training program a high probability is that the trainer and the trainees will develop new behaviors and attitudes. These new behaviors will be directly related to the helping behaviors that are an integral part of the training. People involved in the training tend to integrate the basic communication skills as an integral part of their own lives, thereby developing behaviors and attitudes identified as desirable for a mature person.

In essence, the process established in this source book can become a delivery system, not only for training new skills but also for increasing the probability that the participants will become effective and fully functioning.

Additional Training Models

Any person, who is seriously interested in becoming an effective trainer in human relations skills, can profit from understanding training models. Gordon (1970), in his parent and teacher effectiveness training, utilizes many social awareness communication models for teaching nonprofessionals the awareness of a technology of interpersonal communications. In order to enable people outside of the profession to understand some of the basic principles of communication skills, he has developed a training process without depending upon much of the usual psychological jargon.

The Ivey (1971) model identified alternative training processes which can supplement and augment a training structure. Egan (1975) offered a variation in his approach to the Carkhuff model of human relations training. Egan approached the process with emphasis on the importance of a complete training package that spans the areas from exploration to action strategies. Gazda (1973) offered an alternative explanation of the scales and what the scales mean in addition to giving a graphic understanding of their interrelationship.

A trainer's familiarization with the variety of ways to approach a single training model can augment and supplement the training process to meet individual needs. In addition, further study into the concepts of Gestalt, namely into the use of fantasy, will enable the trainer to teach questioning and summarizing responses that easily expand helpee awareness. This source book sets up a basic structure, but the trainer would be wise to explore the variety of ways in which others have used the basic format with the express purpose of borrowing techniques and procedures.

Understanding Values

In addition to personality characteristics and supplementary training strategies, understanding the role of values and the process of valuing in helping is a necessity. Values are an integral part of all helping relationships. When helping another person, the helper is faced with several ways to respond to the helpee. The helpee's experiences and value systems are the conditions which underlie the helper's understanding of what the helpee may be relating. Therefore, the responses any helper makes need to be closely related to the helpee's values or value systems.

If a trainer and/or helper is unaware of the value systems that are functioning, the probability of his/her responding with implied or actual bias without being aware of that bias is increased. This lack of awareness can lead to control, manipulation, or seduction in a situation where the trainee does not understand what is happening. An awareness of personal values and the ability to identify them for others can reduce the tendency to influence others prejudicially.

Thus, learning and understanding personal values, value systems, and the process of valuing are recommended to the trainer. In this way training will incorporate human understanding of values and their significant role in the helping process. By understanding the relativity of the concept of values, the trainer can teach and practice tolerance for a wide variety of divergent value systems. In this way tolerance of divergent values becomes integrated in the trainer's teaching.

Several resources are available for using values clarification in the training. These resources will be explained later in the section on training procedure. Other sources which will aid in understanding of values and of the use of valuing within training are found in Raths, Harmon, and Simon (1966) and Simon, Howe, and Kirschenbaum (1972). For an understanding of values as a concept and the role they have in living, Kohlberg (1971) is suggested. Studying these resources will give background so that the training format can be understood in the larger context of improving human relations.

SELF DEVELOPMENT OF THE TRAINER

The long list of skills, attitudes, and experiences that are requisites to effective training of peer counselors may seem overwhelming. The requirements included are ones of a "paragon" peer counselor trainer. Thus most of the resources for growth have been included with information about how they fit into the blueprint of trainer growth. No one person can reach absolute levels of knowledge and experience in all of these areas, but gaining some expertise in each will assist in training efforts.

A key to effective training for anyone interested in becoming a trainer of others is continued self development. Today an individual can experience a great number of interpersonal situations designed to enhance self-awareness and growth. Many proponents of self development call for bizarre and radical experiences as the keys to that development, but also many legitimate programs are designed to help persons to experience positive self development. Assertive training, human potential experience, Gestalt workshops, group counseling, behavior modification, deliberate psychological education, and understanding self are some of the effective and legitimate models that can assist an individual in growth as a person and a leader.

Assertive Training

Assertive training uses many of the techniques of the Carkhuff model but works toward different goals. The focus of assertive training is to develop self-confidence, inner strength, potential, and worth. Helpers who cannot assert positively their personal worth and the worth of their contribution to others are not able to train others effectively to be strong helpers. Assertive training is a continuing process and to be effective, must be fully understood and adequately practiced. If assertive behavior is not understood or behaviorly practiced, alternative behaviors can become either destructively aggressive or impotently passive. Neither of these behaviors can result in trainer or trainee effectiveness as a helper.

For additional reading on assertiveness, the following are suggested:

Alberti, R. E., & Emmons, M. L. (1978). *Your perfect right: A guide to assertive behavior, 3rd edition.* San Luis Obispo, CA: Impact.

Alberti, R. E., & Emmons, M. L. (1975). *Stand up, speak out, talk back.* New York: Pocket Books.

Ellis, A., & Harper, R. A. (1961). *A guide to rational living.* Englewood Cliffs, NJ: Prentice Hall.

Jakubowski-Spector, P. (1973). *An introduction to assertive training procedures for women.* Washington, D.C.: American Personnel and Guidance Association Press.

Phelps, S., & Austin, N. (1975). *The assertive woman.* San Luis Obispo, CA: Impact.

Rathus, S. (1972). An experimental investigation of assertive training in a group setting. *Journal of Behavior Therapy and Experimental Psychiatry, 3,* 81-86.

Behavior Modification

The scope of this *Peer Counseling* book limits the discussion of the merits of behavior modification in relation to more humanistic concepts. The only point to be made is that learning theory has a central part in the training of peers to be caring, feeling, and communicating human beings. Since behavior modification is an integral part of the training process and since the goals and outcomes of the training will be in behavioral terms initially, the trainer is to do both of the following: (1) become knowledgeable of behavioral concepts and behaviors and (2) avoid setting up an artificial straw man to do battle between behaviorism and humanism. The trainer is to avoid the academic dialogue which often places humanists and behaviorists against each other and thus creates an artificial condition which detracts from the value of each.

The training format of this *Peer Counseling* book uses the behavior modification process to teach humanistic concepts effectively. The training model employs specific learning theory concepts to teach new skills. The better the concepts are understood, the more useful they can be in the training program development. Ample research by Carkhuff (1969), Carkhuff and Truax (1969), Ivey (1971), Gazda (1973), and others supports the procedure of employing behavior modification technology to teach some very humanistic behaviors.

For further understanding of the principles of learning theory as they apply to helping skills, the following sources are suggested:

Abt, L.E., & Stuart, I.R. (Eds.). (1982). *The newer therapies: A sourcebook.* New York: Van Nostrand Reinhold.

Bandura, A. (1969). *Principles of behavior modification.* New York: Holt, Reinhart and Winston.

Gossberg, J. M. (1964). Behavior therapy: A review. *Psychological Bulletin, 62,* 73-88.

Ivey, A. E. (1973). Microcounseling: The counselor as a trainer. *Personnel and Guidance Journal, 51,* 311-316.

Kanfer, F.H. (1980). Self-management methods. In F. H. Kanfer and A.P. Goldstein (Eds.), *Helping people change* (2nd ed.). New York: Pengamon Press.

Krumboltz, J. D. (1966). *Revolution in counseling.* Boston: Houghton Mifflin.

Krumboltz, J. D., & Thoresen, C. E. (Eds.) (1969). *Behavioral counseling: Cases and techniques.* New York: Holt, Reinhart and Winston.

Lazarus, A.A. (1981). *The practice of multimodal therapy.* New York: McGraw-Hill.

Nye, L. L. (1973). Obtaining results through modeling. *Personnel and Guidance Journal, 51,* 380-384.

Rose, S.D. (1983). Behavior therapy in groups. In Kaplan & B.J. Sadock (Eds.), *Comprehensive psychotherapy.* Baltimore, MD: Williams and Wilkins.

Sprinthall, N. (1971). *Guidance for human growth.* New York: Van Nostrand, Reinholt.

Ullman, L. P., & Krasner, L. (1965). *Research in behavior modification.* New York: Holt, Reinhart and Winston.

Deliberate Psychological Education (DPE)

The idea that affective education is of significant value in any teaching behavior is in direct support of the philosophy of peer counseling. Since peer counseling is one segment of the DPE concept, participating in a DPE program will enhance a trainer's potential for success as a peer counselor trainer. A trainer must be creative and imaginative so as to bring to human learning experiences both affective and cognitive learning. Affective education is not restricted to schools but is equally viable in religious and social agencies within the community. Consequently, a trainer must be aware and knowledgeable regarding what DPE is contributing to learning today. It is not the purpose of this manual to explain fully DPE concepts and strategies, but complete information can be found in the following articles and books:

Alberti, R.E., & Emmons, M.L. (1978). *Your perfect right: A guide to assertive behavior (3rd ed.).* San Luis Obispo, CA: Impact.

Aspy, D. N. (1974). *Toward a technology of humanizing education.* Springfield, IL: Merrill.

Gazda, G., Asbury, F., Balzer, F., Childress, W., & Walters, R. (1977). *Human relations development.* Boston, MA: Allyn & Bacon.

Gladding, S. (1986). Imagery and metaphor in counseling: A humanistic course. *Journal of Humanistic Education and Development,* Vol. 25, No. 1.

Hayes, R. (1987). Research in humanistic education. *Journal of Humanistic Education and Development,* Vol. 25, No. 3.

Ivey, A., & Alschuler, A. (Ed.) (1973). Psychological education: A prime function of the Counselor. *The Personnel and Guidance Journal, 51* (9), 586-682.

Mosher, R., & Sprinthall, N. (1971). Deliberate psychological education. *The Counseling Psychologist, 2*(4), 3-117.

Psychological education: A prime function of the counselor. *The Personnel and Guidance Journal, 51*(a), 586-722.

Sprinthall, N. A. (1971). *Guidance for human growth.* New York: Van Nostrand, Reinholt.

Sprinthall, N. A. (1973). Special feature: Psychological education. *The School Counselor, 20*(5), 332-361.

Weinstein, G., & Fontain, M. (1970). *Toward humanistic education.* New York: Praiger.

Gelstalt Workshops

The contribution of the Gestaltist is akin to the awareness taught by Otto. However, the focus of Gestalt methodology lies even more within the framework of creating awareness in self. Gestalt uses the concept of awareness and immediacy in combination to create an intensive focus upon immediate internal feelings and experience.

Several aspects are considered in the teaching and learning value of the Gestalt methodology in the training format.

1. A trainer's being in touch with his/her immediate feelings and experiences as a person sharpens his/her skill in developing more effective alternatives to his/her general behavior and reactions and to those peculiar to the training role.

2. An understanding of the concepts and techniques of Gestalt therapy will enable the trainer to provide the same growth-producing experiences with trainees.

As a trainer and trainees experience themselves more completely, they develop a greater variety of coping and facilitative behaviors which augment and integrate the training skills. Understanding the importance of being aware of self with regard to feelings will enable the trainer to transcend the mechanical aspects of training to an integrated understanding of human feelings and of how they affect his/her behavior.

For these reasons a familiarity with focus and strategies of Gestalt methodology is recommended to the trainer. Familiarity could be gained solely through reading, but attendance at Gestalt workshops where the trainer could tie reading and experience together is recommended as a better alternative.

Feder, B. (1980). Safety and danger in the Gestalt group. In B. Feder and R. Ronall (Eds.). *Beyond the hot seat: Gestalt approaches to group.* New York: Brunner/Mazel.

Passons, W.R. (1975). *Gestalt approaches in counseling.* New York: Holt, Rinehart and Winston.

Perles, F. (1973). *The Gestalt approach and eyewitness to therapy.* New York: Bantam.

Zinker, J., & Nevis, S. (1981). *The Gestalt theory of couple and family interactions.* Cleveland, OH: Gestalt Institute of Cleveland.

Understanding the Self

The need to understand yourself is very important as you approach working with individuals of different types and styles of learning. Based on the theory of C.G. Jung and developed and refined by a mother-daughter team, Isabel Myers and Katherine Briggs, who developed the *Myers-Briggs Type Indicator*, this instrument has helped individuals understand themselves as well as others. In understanding themselves, they begin to understand their work team, family setting, and intimates.

An excellent resource is *Please Understand Me*, by D. Keisley and M. Bates.

The *Myers-Briggs Type Indicator* can be ordered from the Center for Applications of Psychological Type, 2720 N.W. 6th Street, Gainesville, Florida 32609. The Bates and Kirsey book, *Please Understand Me*, can be ordered from Prometheus Nemesis Books, Post Office Box 2082, Del Mar, California 92014. Also, *Gifts Differing* by Isabel Briggs Myers and Peter Myers, 1980 Consulting Psychology, Palo Alto, California 94306.

Group Experiences

Much of the training of peer helpers is conducted in groups. For the trainer to be familiar with both theory and practice of group interaction will be helpful. Although the training structure is disciplined and highly focused, many instances occur whereby the understanding of group dynamics can be very helpful to the trainer. For example, group discussion of training experiences is an integral part of the training design and requires that the trainer have experience in group techniques and discussion techniques. The more skills and experiences the trainer gains, the more effective training procedures will become. Group experiences are helpful to the trainer in several ways. These ways include:

- Group experiences enable the trainer to learn experientially the dynamics which make up each group experience.

- Group experiences enable the trainer to gain awareness and understanding of himself/herself and of others. A significant part of most group experiences is feedback from others. This feedback often is lacking in everyday living. Learning from others how to communicate through the use of the feedback loop is a helpful part of the format used. Feedback as a teaching/learning technique and its use in groups can provide valuable experience that is of benefit to trainers when they employ the same process in training.

- Group experiences provide the trainer with an awareness of both good and poor human relations behavior. Within groups (because of their intensity) human behaviors that enhance or destroy growth quickly become apparent.

- Effective groups are able to create some degree of intimacy and allow risk-taking behaviors. The ability to take risks and become intimate are qualities of human relations that are necessary factors in effective helping behaviors. Groups can provide experiences that demonstrate the productive and destructive potential of risk taking and/or intimate behaviors. By intimate behaviors, we mean those behaviors which bring two or more individuals psychologically closer. As a result of intimate behaviors, self-disclosure, and trust become by-products of new relationships.

ADDITIONAL READING

Groups

Different group experiences are available today, ranging from Encounter and T-groups to discussion groups. One must decide what level of group will be helpful. Suggested reading that will expand knowledge about groups follows:

Association for Specialists in Group Work. (1980). *Professional standards for training of group counselors.* Alexandria, VA.

Corey, G. (1985). *Theory and practice of group counseling.* Monterey, CA: Brooks/Cole.

Corey, G., & Corey, M. (1982). *Groups: Process and practice.* Monterey, CA: Brooks/Cole Publishing.

Corey, G., & Corey, M. (1987). *Groups process and practice.* Monterey, CA: Brooks/Cole.

Corey, G., Corey, M., & Callanan, P. (1982). *A casebook of ethical guidelines for group leaders.* Monterey, CA: Brooks/Cole.

Corey, G., Corey, M., Callanan, P., & Russell, J. M. (1982). *Group techniques.* Monterey, CA: Brooks/Cole Publishing.

Eagan, G. (1982). *The skilled helper.* Monterey, CA: Brooks/Cole.

Gazda, G. M. (1975). *Basic approaches to group psychotherapy and group counseling (2nd ed.).* Springfield, IL: Charles C. Thomas.

Gazda, G.M. (Ed.). (1982). *Basic approaches to group psychotherapy and group counseling.* Springfield, IL: Charles C. Thomas.

Glanz, E., & Hayes, R. (1967). *Groups in guidance* (2nd ed.). Boston: Allyn and Bacon.

Gordon, T. (1951). *Group-centered leadership.* Boston: Houghton Mifflin.

Hoper, C., Kutzleb, U., Stobbe, A., Weber, B. (1975). *Awareness games.* New York: St. Martin's Press.

Muro, J., & Freeman, S. (1968). *Readings in group counseling.* Scranton, PA: International Textbook.

Olsan, M. (1970). *Group counseling.* New York: Holt Reinhart and Winston.

Otto, H. (1970). *Group method to actualize human potential.* Beverly Hills, CA: Holistic Press.

Pfeiffer, J. W., & Jones, J. (1972). *Structural experiences for human relations training.* Iowa City, IA: University Assoc. Press.

Schultz, W. *Here comes everybody.* New York: Harper and Row.

Sax, S., & Hollander, S. (1973). *Reality games.* New York: Popular Library.

Yalom, I.D. (1975). *The theory and practice of group psychotherapy.* New York: Basic Books.

Zimpfer, D. (1976). *Group work in the helping profession: A bibliography.* Washington, D.C.: American Personnel and Guidance Association Press.

Zimpfer, D. (1984). *Group work in the helping professions: A bibliography, 2nd ed.* Muncie, IN: Accelerated Development Inc.

Wellness/Stress Management

Wellness/stress management experience has been advocated by several authors. The whole concept involves striving toward becoming a healthy person. Knowledge of stress management and wellness concepts and activities may assist the trainer in becoming more effective.

The following are suggested books:

Anderson, R. A. (1971). *Stress power? How to turn tension into energy.* New York: Human Science Press.

Ardell, D. (1986). *High level wellness.* Berkeley, CA: Ten Speed Press.

Benson, H. (1975). *The relaxation response.* New York: Avon Publishers.

Cataldo, M. & Coates, T. (1986). *Health and industry.* New York: John Wiley and Sons.

Cooper, J. (1977). *Aerobics.* New York: Bantam Books.

Eshman, E. R. (1980). *The relaxation and stress reduction workbook.* Richmond, CA: New Harbinger Publisher.

Gherman, E. M. (1981). *Stress and the bottom line.* New York: AMACOM.

Girdano, D., & Everly, G. (1979). *Controlling stress and tension: A holistic approach.* Englewood Cliffs, NJ: Prentice-Hall.

Greenwood, J. W., & Greenwood, J. W. (1979). *Managing executive stress: A systems approach.* New York: John Wiley & Sons.

Hendricks, G., & Roberts, T. (1977) *The second centering book.* Englewood Cliffs, NJ: Prentice-Hall.

Jacobson, E. (1978). *Progressive relaxation.* Chicago: University of Chicago Press.

O'Donnell, M.P. & Ainsworth, T. (Ed.). (1984). *Health promotion in the workplace.* New York: A Wiley Medical Publication.

Ornstein, R., & Sobel, D. (1987). *The healing brain.* New York: Simon and Schuster.

Pelletier, K. (1977). *Mind as healer, mind as slayer: A holistic approach to preventing stress disorders.* New York: Dell Publishers.

Ryan, R.S., Travis, J.W. (1981). *Wellness workbook.* Berkeley, CA: Ten Speed Press.

Sehnert, K. W. (1981). *Stress/unstress.* Minneapolis: Augsburg Publishing House.

Syele, H. (1975). *The stress of life (Rev. ed.).* New York: Mc-Graw-Hill Books.

Truch, S. (1980). *Teacher burnout and what to do about it.* Novato, CA: Academic Therapy Publications.

Drugs and Alcohol

Much literature exists on chemical abuse. Groups such as AA and Alanon are excellent references. You also may wish to contact hospitals specializing in treating chemical abusers and receive some of their materials. Following is a list of references:

Bratter, T., & Forrest, G. (1985). *Alcoholism and substance abuse.* New York: The Free Press.

Deluca (Ed.) (1982). *Fourth special report to the U.S. Congress on alcohol and health from the Secretary of Health and Human Service.* Rockville, MD: National Institute on Alcohol Abuse and Alcoholism.

Heinemman, M. E., & Estes, N. J. (1977). *Alcoholism development consequences and intervention.* St. Louis: C. V. Mosby Co.

King, J. (1983). *Alcohol/drugs and kids: A handbook for parents. St. Louis:* St. Louis Area National Council on Alcholism.

Other Resources

Hazelden Books, Hazelden Educational Materials, Box 176, Center City, Minnesota 55012.

Johnson Institute, 100700 Olson Highway, Minneapolis, Minnesota 55441-6199

National Council on Alcoholism, located in most major cities.

Human Potential Experience

Human potential experience as espoused by Otto (1970) and his associates will assist the trainer in developing ways to help trainees understand the dynamics of their own behaviors and feelings. The Otto source provides ways to supplement training strategies in situations where the understanding of a specific human interpersonal experience will clarify the underlying rationale for a particular training strategy or technique. Knowledge of group experiences explored by Otto can help the trainer to work effectively with training problems caused by affective road blocks to learning occurring within the trainees. Using the appropriate affective human potential experience increases the trainer's chance to break through the "hang-ups" that trainees may have at a particular point in the training.

Reemphasis

The single most important attitude for the trainer is to really want to be involved in a program and then to be willing to take the risks that such involvement entails. The growth gained by trainers in their efforts to prepare for and initiate a program are worth almost any outcome. Once the trainer begins to explore skills, attitudes, and experiences of peer counseling training, the potential for learning and development of personal skills is great.

SETTING UP A PEER COUNSELING PROGRAM

The development, organization, and implementation of any new program involve an extended amount of time, energy, and commitment. If counselors decide to change their approach or technique in counseling, risks involved and time expended are minimal, but if the counselor decides to implement a peer counseling program, much planning time is needed and a realignment of priorities is necessary.

Any successful peer counseling program must be planned, developed, and implemented in an organized sequence. The four major steps are as follows:

- The **first step** in program planning is to **assess the needs** of the group to be served in order to develop the strategy for bringing about the change that is needed.

- The **second step** is a **commitment to become informed** about the concepts of peer counseling, what it is, its philosophy, and how to propose a program.

- The **third step,** that of **gaining support** from administration, staff, and community, also is necessary to the success of the program. The procedure towards gaining this support is to inform the people being served as completely as possible.

- The *fourth step* is to *develop evaluative procedures* to determine the effectiveness of the program.

The first three steps will be discussed in this chapter. Chapter 9 contains information regarding total program evaluation, the fourth step.

ASSESSING NEEDS

Professional counselors, psychologists, social workers, teachers, and religious leaders, who are responsible for the mental health of the community they serve, can improve their effectiveness by being actively involved in a systematic assessment of the psychological and helping needs of the population they serve. Assessment of needs can vary from a simple thinking about community needs to a comprehensive assessment which involves testing, interviewing, and other psychological evaluation methods. Many school systems are using standardized testing to help identify student, parent, teacher, and administrative needs. One such assessment reference points out that high school students who have a problem talk first with students their own age; they speak with relatives second, then school counselors, and finally with teachers. This kind of need assessment, which indicates the tendency of students to consult their peers, would support the development of a peer counseling program which could be helpful to students.

Another assessment strategy is interviewing students in order to determine the practicality of a peer counseling program in a specific system. "Focus" groups are another form of doing needs assessments in schools, religious institutions, agencies, business, and industry. Teachers and administrators also have a responsibility to respond to an assessment of the needs for a peer counseling program. Plans to develop a peer counseling program in a teen-age drop-in center require that the community needs be surveyed concerning the feasibility of such a program. If a group of peer counselors is to be employed to work with "child abuse" families, the families could be interviewed concerning their feelings about having a peer counseling program that would affect them.

Finally, the counselors in a system could decide on a program that would be helpful in developing a more open place to attend the training sessions. The idea to emphasize is that the consumers of counseling and psychological services should be involved in determining needs. When the needs are identified, then ways of meeting those needs can be devised.

LEARNING ABOUT PEER COUNSELING

Before writing a proposal for a peer counseling program, the literature in the field of peer counseling must be examined. The person responsible for development of the program must be able to answer as many of the questions as possible that will be asked concerning peer counseling. Professional literature needs to be examined in a deliberate manner. For example, ERIC (*Educational Resource Information Center*) is an important source to be contacted in a search for peer counseling sources. A second resource is correspondence with people using peer counseling in their programs.

A third resource, which was just formed in 1987, is the *National Peer Helpers Association.* The address is 1950 Mission Street, Room 7, San Francisco, California 94103. The purpose of the organization is to provide networking opportunities and support for peer helping programs. The association has four journals that are printed yearly. They describe programs and research throughout the country. They also hold a national conference each year. The first conference, which 350 individuals attended, was held in St. Charles, Missouri. The second conference, which 550 attended, was held in Ft. Collins, Colorado. In addition, the organization has developed *Standards and Ethics,* a materials resource list, and provides a variety of other help.

The association is made up of trainers and some peer helpers. It is one of the fastest growing associations in this country. The organization has international membership.

Counselor visitations to other places that have peer counseling programs is a recommended procedure. The interested counselor should try to spend a full day at a location to get a feel of the total responsibilities of the counselors in charge of the program. Observation of the training procedures, administration of the program, and innovative ideas will help to identify concepts and practices that would transfer effectively to another program.

Ira Scott Sachnoff reported in his *High School Peer Resource Program: A Director's Perspective*, the result of a survey he conducted with directors of successful programs. These directors ranked in order of importance the different ingredients in the program. As you start your program or refine it, you might refer to this list:*

Rank of Importance	Program Category
1	Strong program coordinator
2	Good training
3	Clear goals
4	Student commitment and ownership
5	Support from faculty
6	Supervision
7	Project director's contact with students
8	Having a mixture of students
9	Confidentiality
10	Recruiting
11	Students' having decision-making power
12	Value explanation and reflection ،
13	Good community resources
14	Rewards and incentives

*Reprinted with permission from Ira Scott Sachnoff, *High School Peer Resource Progress: A Director's Perspective.*

The programs of professional meetings and workshops are sometimes devoted to peer counseling. Attending these workshops helps in gathering more information, gaining additional skills in operating a peer counseling program, and/or meeting other people who are involved in peer counseling programs.

A person's job setting need not limit his/her learning about peer counseling. An important point is to learn as much as possible about a wide variety of peer counseling models in a variety of settings. For example, a crisis center counselor can learn much about training and advertising from school peer counseling programs. From observations, reading, and interviewing, a proposal can be developed that will fit individual work settings more creatively.

PEER COUNSELING PHILOSOPHY

Reading and observations will compel an examination of personal feelings about a peer counseling program. Investigation of peer counseling will indicate that the prospective trainer needs to believe in the concepts of developmental and pragmatic counseling as opposed to "crisis" counseling. In other words, he/she must be sold on and be able to sell the idea of developmental counseling and affective education to fellow counselors as well as to the rest of the staff. An understanding of the philosophy underlying peer counseling models enables the trainer to realign priorities in a guidance and counseling office. This realignment of priorities includes an understanding of oneself as a "trainer" and an increased concern for the mental health and communication skills of large numbers of people. The prospective trainer recognizes the necessity of being willing to give away his/her skills to lay people or paraprofessionals.

PEER COUNSELING PROPOSAL

The extent of a proposal depends on the scope of a program and the amount of financing required to operate it. The proposal could be a few pages written to a supervisor describing a small scale program operated by one person, or it could be a comprehensive grant proposal requesting state or federal funding.

The smallest proposal can be a conversation with an administrative superior. Even with regard to a concept of small scope, one must be well organized. The organizational process must include for an effective proposal an extensive understanding of the concept of peer counseling. Its assets and liabilities also should be included. The proposal needs to include a feasible plan and procedure for implementing the ideas of peer counseling within a specific system. A general idea of the costs, both in time and money, is vital to selling a program. In addition, as much support as possible needs to be gained from individuals who will be benefited by the program.

Two additional concepts can be helpful. *First,* one's ideas need to be organized on paper, either in outline form or in simple prose. These documents then are available whenever they are needed to promote a proposed program. *Second,* one needs to keep the contacted supervisor deluged with information, assuring that the administrator is informed during all stages of program development. Comprehensive information will increase the probability of the administrator's support for the program.

Often a program can be developed within the building itself, such as in school, but many times it cannot. Additional community, agency, or other outside support is sometimes needed. Outside support usually is of a financial nature, and when finances are involved, a program enters the competition with all the other financial obligations of the supporting group. When a program goes outside of the school, church, or local group for aid, an extensive proposal often is needed and always is helpful.

In developing an extended proposal, specific guidelines are worth following. Each funding source, whether local, private, state, or federal, follows specific guidelines in choosing the programs it will endorse. Guidelines are usually published by the funding agency. The *first step* to take, therefore, *is to identify the agency or agencies that might lend support.* This knowledge can be achieved in one of several ways. Contact the person in the local area whose responsibility it is to secure grants and funding. Also, the local library can provide information regarding both governmental and private funding agencies. Other sources are state and federal governments which have offices where information regarding funding for specific groups can be obtained. A letter or telephone call requesting this information can direct an applicant to the right source.

The **second step,** after determining which agencies are supporting projects of this nature, is for the prospective trainer **to complete the proposal according to the agencies' guidelines.** In addition, he/she should request assistance from the funding agency in offering constructive criticism for the proposal. When writing an agency to request guidelines, no obscurity should occur in the trainer's statements about the program he/she would like to develop. Many granting agencies will help in the writing of the proposal if they feel that the applicant has a sound, viable idea. The idea should include a clear-cut need, a rationale, and a plan for meeting that need, all described in general terms when the funding agency is contacted.

Finally, the **third step,** before submitting a proposal, is **to work with people who have had experience developing and funding a project.** If a person has contacts with people responsible for funding, get their feedback on a proposal before final submission.

Clearly identifying goals, behavioral objectives, and outcomes is essential. The more specific objectives, goals, and outcomes are, the stronger the proposal will appear to the funding agency. By being as specific as possible, a proposal puts the funding agency in the best position to evaluate the objectives of the proposal which are relative to their interests. A source to consult in writing behavior objectives is R. Mager, *Preparing Behavioral Objectives* (Belmont, CA: Fearon Publishers/Lear Siegler, Inc., 1962). Write objectives of a program in terms of training outcomes. For example, the behavioral objective, "Students in training will increase their mean score on the communication exercise by 1.0," indicates goals of a program which can be measured objectively.

BUDGET

In developing a budget, include specific categories and costs both to the funding organization and to the supporting agency (school, church, or agency). Hidden costs must be identified carefully and included in the proposal. These hidden costs include heat, transportation, telephone, physical setting, equipment, and a variety of support personnel. Listed are two examples of budget possibilities. The first (Figure 6.1) would support a small project located within the agency. The second (Figure 6.2) is typical of the budget of a large funded project.

Duration of Project—September 1988 through January 1989

I. Activities

1. To select peer counselors.

2. To conduct basic training for peer counselors every Tuesday and Wednesday for 1 hour for 10 weeks.

3. To assign peer counselors to their counseling responsibilities.

4. To provide advanced and follow-up for 10 weeks once a week.

II. Staff

One counselor 2 hrs/wk for 20 wks 2 x 20 x $28.00/hr	$1,120.00
One secretary 2 hrs/wk for 20 wks 2 x 20 x $7.00/hr	280.00

TOTAL SALARIES $1,400.00

III. Materials

Video/Audio equipment, 2 hrs/wk

1 *Peer Counseling* book	1 x $12.45 ea	$ 12.45
10 *Peer Power, Book 1*	10 x $11.95 ea	119.50
10 *Peer Power, Book*	10 x $8.95 ea	89.50
4 video tapes	4 x $50.00 ea	200.00
10 audio tapes	10 x $3.00 ea	30.00
10 audio *Problem Solving* tapes	10 x $9.95	99.50

SUBTOTAL   550.95

TOTAL COST $1,950.95

Figure 6.1. Sample budget for a small project located within an agency.

Four examples of large locally supported peer counseling programs are found in Dade County, Florida; Palo Alto, California; Spark program in New York City; and St. Louis, Missouri. The Dade County program is supported by 1.2 million dollars annually in local funds recommended by an administration and appropriated by a school board that recognized a need and, with community support, reacted to that need. Palo Alto has developed an extensive school-wide peer counseling program. Youth Emergency Service is a crisis center for runaways in St. Louis, Missouri, which has received funding from the Y.M.C.A. and Y.W.C.A. for the training of peer counselors. The Spark program is the largest peer project in the country, with services at 107 high schools.

Spark is a good example of how peer counseling grew out of the need for teens to share and work out common problems. In 1971 a group of New York educators (funded by the *State Department of Drug and Substance Abuse Services*) created a drug-prevention program because heroin addiction was then epidemic. They learned that teens got the message best when sharing each others' life stories. So Spark set up "rap groups" under the direction of adult counselors so that the counselors might start training the students to do some of the things that the counselors do, always under supervision.

A proposal needs to include evaluative procedures described in specific terms so that funding agencies can see readily the integrity of a project. Some evaluative procedures are identified in Chapter IX.

In writing the proposal, keep in mind needs, attitudes, and values that are supported by the local community. For example, the title of a proposal might be "Youth Listener Program" rather than Peer Counseling, depending upon prevailing attitudes in the community to be served.

GAINING ADMINISTRATIVE SUPPORT

Administrative support can be gained in many ways. Inviting a supervisor to read short articles, attend programs, visit peer counseling projects, or attend meetings on peer

Itemized Budget for August 1988 through July 1989

| | | Source of Funds | |
		Funding Agency	Local School
I.	**Salaries**		
	Project Director (1)	$ 25,000.00	$ 10,000.00
	Associate Director (2)	15,000.00	5,000.00
	Administrative Assistant ½ x 10 mos	10,000.00	-0-
	Research Assistant ¼ x 10 mos	5,000.00	-0-
	Community Workers ¼ x 10 mos	600.00	700.00
	Clerical Staff (1 full time)		
	Secretary 100% x 12 mos	8,000.00	2,000.00
	Graduate Assistant $350/mo x 10 mos	3,500.00	-0-
	Student Clerical Workers		
	$3.50/hr, 3 hr/wk x 36 wks	378.00	-0-
		$ 67,478.00	$ 17,700.00
	Fringe Benefits (11.27% S & W)		
	Retirement	$ 6,709.77	-0-
	Hospitalization	2,000.00	-0-
	Social Security (6.7%)	4,205.45	-0-
		$ 12,915.22	$ -0-
II.	**Contractual Services**		
	Consultants		
	$500.00 per day x 25 days	$ 12,500.00	$ -0-
	Rental for Equipment	500.00	100.00
	Travel for Consultants		
	$50.00 per day x 25 days		
	(May be put in Travel section)	1,250.00	-0-
		$ 14,250.00	$ 100.00
III.	**Travel**		
	Domestic		
	Figure transportation, 200 miles, 4 cars		
	22¢ per mile	$ 176.00	$ -0-
	Per Diem		
	$50.00 (in state) x 15 days	750.00	-0-
	$60.00 (out of state) x 14 days	840.00	-0-
	Trips (not overnight)		
	(Daily rate) $25.00 x 17 days	425.00	-0-
		$ 2,191.00	$ -0-

Figure 6.2. Sample budget for a large project proposal.

Figure 6.2. Continued.

	Source of Funds	
	Funding Agency	Local School
IV. Commodities		
Things that are expendable (May need to be itemized)	$ -0-	$ 500.00
V. Equipment		
Equipment to be purchased (List all equipment to be purchased)	$ 5,000.00	$ 1,000.00
VI. Communications		
Postage	$ 1,500.00	$ -0-
Telephone—long distance	2,500.00	200.00
	$ 9,000.00	$ 1,700.00
VII. Indirect Costs (Overhead of Institution)	$ 7,841.00	$ 4,000.00
TOTAL	$113,675.22	$ 23,500.00

counseling will increase the probability of administrative understanding and support for the ideas the trainer will be presenting. "Coffee Klach" diplomacy is another method of laying supportive groundwork with administrators prior to submitting a formal proposal. These informal get-togethers reveal areas of opposition, dissonance, confusion, or support which enable one to submit a proposal that accounts for possible administrative areas of objection or confusion.

By anticipating administrative and staff objections or problems, a trainer is in a better position to respond to objections, to clarify confused areas, and generally to meet the needs of supporting personnel. Gaining administrative support by meeting their needs as well as possible increases a program's chance of gaining outside rapport.

STAFF SUPPORT

Successful programs require the support of staff as well as administration. In attempting to develop new programs, concepts, and ideas, gaining consensus from the group with whom the trainer will work is extremely difficult. To set consensus as a goal before initiating a peer counseling program would be a mistake. A more effective way to begin a program is to identify those staff members that can be depended upon for support and interest. If a trainer seeks people who are sympathetic to the goals and attitudes of his/her program, positive reinforcement will occur in the program development. A greater chance of success is assured if the trainer works with one or two people who support his/her program than if the trainer must convince ten skeptics of the value of a program before it has an opportunity to sell itself. A successful program staffed by a small group of dedicated persons will more likely gain a wider support base from other staff members than any other program.

To get the maximum support possible, trainers must involve those who are interested in all stages of program development. This involvement includes soliciting ideas, proposal writing, program development, publicity, logistics, and all other aspects of the total project. In this way, supporting personnel have a vested interest in the success of the program. Other staff members who may not have time for program development or implementation still deserve to be kept informed on the progress and procedures of the program. The Figure 6.3 is an example of a published information sheet give to staff members.

COMMUNITY SUPPORT

An often neglected but vital part of any program development is gaining and maintaining strong community support systems. Support from the community leadership and population is a necessity for programs that serve agencies and churches as well as those that serve schools. Several methods can be used so that community groups can be involved in or be made aware of peer counseling projects.

YOUTH LISTENER PROGRAM

Goals

1. To train youth listeners in communication skills.

2. To teach youth listeners in skills in career awareness.

3. To provide students with an opportunity to talk with another peer that has been trained in listening skills.

4. To help students looking for career information.

5. To help students with academic problems.

6. To assist new students with academic problems.

7. To assist the youth listener in personal growth.

Selection

1. Students volunteer to be youth listeners through cadet teaching.

2. If the counselor in charge of training thinks the student will not be effective, the student is asked to drop.

3. Grade point average for cadet teaching.

Training

1. Basic training—30 hours, which include attending, empathy, open-ended questions, genuineness, confrontation, problem solving, confidentiality, referral sources, career center, and awareness activities.

2. Advance training—weekly meetings either individually or in groups, to set goals, evaluate programs, and obtain further guidance and scheduling.

Figure 6.3. Example of an information sheet given to staff members regarding Youth Listener Program.

One method is to organize an advisory committee composed of key community leaders who will lend a solid base of support for the program. An advisory board may serve as a consulting group, a reaction group for ideas, or as assistants in program development. Persons chosen for the advisory board do not have to be trained or experienced in effective education, but they need to have attitudes, experiences, and philosophies that would enable them to understand the concepts of peer counseling. Other groups that can be employed for help include student groups and political system groups (e.g., school boards, church boards, federal agencies, and city councils).

Letters and visits to other social service agencies also will help gain acceptance of the program from other professionals in the area. Examples of groups that can be contacted are crisis centers, social welfare agencies, Y's, professional helping organizations, and private agencies. If these groups are made aware of the peer counseling program, they can lend support, training, and public relations for development.

Graphic materials are an important adjunct to community support groups and need to be developed regardless of what other activities are instituted. Through the use of brochures, awards to peer counselors, thank-you letters, posters, business cards, and other graphic presentations, the scope of the program can be publicized to the individuals and groups.

Newspaper publicity, staff bulletins, spot radio announcements, and radio interviews are additional ways in which a program can be presented for public knowledge and support. Publicity is necessary during all stages of development but is vital when the program is operational. Speaking at community service groups, using slide presentations, video tapes if available, demonstrations, and audience participation experiences all work to increase the scope of public knowledge about a peer counseling program.

HOW TO FIND POTENTIAL TRAINEES

People to be trained can be secured in a number of ways. The alternatives described in this Source Book and Manual are by no means complete or exhaustive. In the schools, special courses can be small units within a standard course. Students in study hall can be participants for training sessions, or training groups can be started with students from several classes at once.

In using special courses, students can apply for entrance through application or interview. The purpose of the interview is to inform trainees of the nature and demands of the training and responsibilities of peer counseling. In addition, the trainer is able to interact initially with the participants and form a subjective opinion concerning each applicant. The courses should have special titles such as "The Art of Helping," "Communications Training," "Leadership Training," or other descriptive titles. These special courses can be a short workshop type or longer semester courses depending upon the school's scheduling flexibility.

On the other hand, the trainer may want to work through standard courses such as English, social studies, or psychology. The training procedure that is most effective with this model is co-teaching. The term co-teaching means placing two in-structors in a class with different roles. In this process, students are able to select either the peer counseling training or participation in the regular class activities. Each instructor would work with one group. Additional space is required by the co-teaching procedure, and that situation could be a problem if physical facilities are overcrowded. When selecting a co-teacher with whom to work, choose a person who is supportive of the peer counseling concept and possesses a flexible personality.

Regular attendance is a greater problem when students are taken from study halls or other classes. These alternatives have enough disadvantages to warrant being a low priority for selection as training times.

Finding trainees in community agencies, such as crisis centers and churches, is more difficult than in schools. Schools are fortunate enough to have a captive pool of people, while agencies or churches must rely on outside community re-sources. With agencies, trainees must commit time and effort to attend training sessions which require time in addition to their regular tasks. Because of the limitations of a ready population, agency trainers need to be creative in devising advertising and selling techniques. Newspaper articles, word of mouth, speeches at community groups are all effective ways to advertise for potential peer counselor trainees. With churches or community agencies, establishment of an advisory is very important. In addition to the previously listed responsibilities, a board can be very helpful in implementing advertising procedures in a peer counseling program.

Informational meetings for people interested in peer counseling training are a necessary step in program development before the start of training. In this meeting, the trainer has an opportunity to

1. establish training session times by taking into account the needs of the trainees which is more effective than an arbitrary predetermined schedule,

2. give a brief description and demonstration of the proposed training experience,

3. explain the peer counseling responsibilities, and

4. meet with parents or spouses to explain programs.

If trainees are under sixteen years of age, inviting parents or guardians to attend the informational meeting is wise.

WHO IS TO BE TRAINED?

Any person interested in receiving peer counseling training deserves the opportunity to be trained. Communications training which utilizes effectively humanistic concepts and structured models for training procedures can be beneficial to everyone. Whether a person uses the skills in peer counseling activities or not, the experiences gained will be useful. Carkhuff (1969) has supported this opinion in his research and field experience and other research has supported the fact that people experience positive behavior changes as the result of interpersonal communications training (Gray & Tindall, 1974).

Salespersons, students, parents, teachers, businesspersons, prison guards, agency clients, and people in a wide range of human activities are using the skills they have learned. Therefore, training can be meaningful and helpful for all people interested. The limiting factors will be adequate funds, staff, and physical facilities.

If staff and/or funds are limited, several methods are available for obtaining information about individuals prior to selection. The methods may include one or more of the following:

1. interview method,

2. formal application,

3. pretesting, and/or

4. staff or peer referrals.

The **interview** selection process consists of a pre-training interview, the object of which is to assist the trainer in selection of potential participants. The criterion for selection is one that the trainer will develop. Research (Scott & Warner, 1974) has shown that one criteria for selection is about as good as another. Several students in Scott and Warner's literature search show that people who generate warmth and attentive behaviors, whatever warmth is, usually are more effective as the result of their training (see Chapter IV).

Formal application is another screening device which can identify superficial information in addition to the applicant's willingness to commit his/her time to the training and his/her attitude toward helping people. (See Appendix C).

By using a communication exercise as a **pretest,** the trainer is able to get a feel for the readiness and skill level of the people applying for the program. A communication exercise pretest is included in the *Peer Power Book 1*, Exercise 1.1. However, the trainer is encouraged to develop his/her own pretest to fit situations relevant to the population.

Often institutions will have a **sociogram** in which they ask students, employees, teachers, administrators, and supervisors, whom they think are good helpers—those persons who seem to be good listeners and are interested in helping them. From this list, potential paid helpers can be asked to apply (see Appendix E).

Other **staff members and peers** are often in a position to refer people to the trainer as trainees. These sources are not available as frequently as others but are very valuable resources. Referrals from other staff members should be encouraged as a matter of good public relations. Also, their awareness of trainees with a good potential is often helpful.

One must avoid making the entry into a training program difficult or complicated or both. The purpose is to train many people rather than only a few. Adolescents, especially, will tend to shy away from any program that runs the risk of making applicants to a program appear ineffective, stupid, or uncomfortable. A complicated or strict entrance requirement easily could defeat an otherwise good program. Teenagers and lay adults who are volunteering their service often are not willing to complete stringent screening devices.

SELECTION OF PEER COUNSELORS

Even though training may benefit and ideally should be available to everyone, all interested people do not make effective peer counselors. Therefore, one of the professional trainers' responsibilities is to make the final selection of peer counselors. The trainer is to assume this responsibility for two very important reasons: (1) public apprehension is reduced concerning possible peer counselors' inappropriate counseling behaviors if their selection is made by a responsible professional, and (2) ultimate responsibility for peer counselors rest solely with the trainer. Effectiveness of the program depends upon well-trained and well-selected participants. Trainers cannot absolve their responsibility to the population their trainees will service by avoiding the decisions of selection.

Trainer, peer, self, and staff evaluations of trainees, in addition to post-testing, are methods of final selection. Effective selection is improved if as many procedures as feasible are used before final selection is made.

Qualities of subjective humanistic conditions in trainees often are the major selection criteria. The characteristics of warmth, interest, acceptance of others, tolerance of divergent value systems, and high energy level are qualities which weigh heavily in the selection process. These humanistic qualities are as important for the trainees to possess as are the skills they will be learning in training.

The characteristics of the population to be served are very important for the trainer to know. The importance of the characteristics in the helping process was clarified by Kohlberg (1971, p. 13) when he stated, ". . . . that development is not effective in relating to people whose moral development is widely varied from theirs." Because of this condition, the trainer must be cognizant of any wide variation between peer counselors' value systems and the value systems of the people whom they serve. For example, upper socio-economic class trainees will be ineffective, generally, with ghetto residents.

Evaluation of trainees by their peers and other staff members can augment the trainer's evaluation criteria. Evaluation input by other staff members and the trainees' contemporaries must be tempered by the fact that their information regarding trainee's behaviors and/or attitudes may be limited. For evaluation purposes, the same communication exercise in *Peer Power* exercises that was used as a pretest can function as a posttest.

Trainees undergo self-evaluation during the training process, and as a result, some decide not to become peer counselors. A trainee's self-appraisal usually is consistent with the trainer's appraisal. This kind of self-evaluation should be encouraged throughout the training process and can become one valid criteria for final selection.

Additional training or working with more competent peer counselors is suggested procedure for those people who are considered marginal or ineffective in their helping skills. Some institutions meet with individuals and send letters saying that they have not been accepted into the peer helping projects.

The trainer may make the decision on how to use the peer helpers. For example, those peer helpers with good group skills will be "small group" leaders. Those with good one-on-one listening skills may work with at-risk youths. Business and industry may want to use recovering alcoholics trained as peer helpers to reach out to substance abusers. To use peer helpers in projects when they do not have the skills is a disservice to the peer helper as well as the peer helpees.

The final decision to retain or drop a trainee who cannot function effectively is the responsibility of the trainer. To drop a person from the program after all efforts to raise skill levels have been tried often is a difficult task. However, the trainer has the responsibility to do so because an ineffective person can affect others negatively in helping situations (Carkhuff, 1969).

Start one or more new basic training groups when the first group completes their training and moves to advanced training sessions. Attrition through various conditions will deplete the ranks of peer counselors unless new training groups can fill in for those who have dropped out for any reason.

POPULATION TO BE SERVED

Peer counselors have been effective with a widely diversified group of people, from working with indigent welfare recipients, to working as elementary school tutors (see Chapter 4). The number of ways that peer counselors can serve has not yet reached a limit. One thing that research has show is that peer counselor programs are most effective when peers and professionals are responsible for counseling functions as conjoint workers. Using nonprofessionals for undesirable tasks has proven to be both unethical and ultimately destructive to the program.

Many ways are possible for nonprofessionals to be used in helping other individuals. These uses include the ones shown in Figure 6.4. This list is not exhaustive but identifies some ways in which peers can help various populations in different settings.

Functioning As	Setting
Rap leaders	Crisis Centers
Tutors	Teen Centers, Schools, Adult Learning Centers
Outreach personnel	Schools
Discussion leaders	Veterans Centers
Political leaders	Welfare Offices
Peer ministers and youth ministers	Church Groups
Individual counselors	Other Organized Groups
New student orientators	Schools
Leaders	Support Groups
Special friends	Elementary Schools

Figure 6.4. Illustrative ways that nonprofessionals are used to help other individuals and within what settings.

EVALUATION

An evaluation system needs to be designed to change the program and give feedback to the trainer. Suggested evaluation includes evaluating the skills learned by the peer helpees, evaluation of the projects that they undertake, and evaluation of those who receive the services of helpees. Evaluation of the entire program is important.

Should the time and resources be available, good research would assist in this growing field. Suggested designs might be provided by the *National Peer Helpers Association* or the schools of education and psychology of the local universities and colleges.

TRAINING ARRANGEMENTS AND
COUNSELING FACILITIES

The physical requirements for training peer counselors include a room that can be private and away from the mainstream of activities during training. Movable furniture of a comfortable nature is desirable, and adequate informal lighting is necessary. Facilities for audio-visual equipment are necessary additions to the training room.

Peer counseling facilities need to be pleasant, warm, and representive of the attitude and feelings of the group being serviced. For example, a school may have several "rap" rooms throughout the building that are gaily decorated and comfortable. Flexible, comfortable furniture should be part of the decor.

Chapter

TRAINING MODEL AND PROCEDURES

The rationale for a disciplined form of training is derived from the initial concepts developed by micro-teaching and micro-counseling (Ivey, 1971) and the research in training helpers by Charles Truax and Robert Carkhuff (Truax & Carkhuff, 1967; Carkhuff, 1969). The use of a training structure based on these two models provides a framework for relatively precise behavioral skills and allows for the intensive practice required to learn the skills thoroughly.

Training procedures which initially deal with small isolated segments of that skill are more effective in skill building outcomes when these segments are taught specifically and practiced until mastered. In this way, an increase occurs in the probability of the skills becoming used, integrated, and implemented quickly and effectively by the trainee.

The training procedure in *Peer Counseling* and *Peer Power* is not meant to be a recipe which will produce highly competent helping persons. Instead, in the design is described a focused process which forms a skeletal foundation for training upon which individual trainer and helper is able to combine his/her own individual thoughts, ideas, and personality characteristics. No design is a best fit for all trainees, systems, or facilities, and this one can be modified to fit individual circumstances without losing its training qualities or characteristics.

SKILL-BUILDING PATTERN

To increase effectiveness, the trainer is to follow six essential behaviors with each training module. These behaviors are as follows:

1. *explanation of and need for skills,*

2. *modeling of skill to be taught,*

3. *practices of skill,*

4. *feedback to trainees from raters,*

5. *homework and discussion of experiences of doing and rating, and*

6. *prepare for next behavior.*

Graphically displayed the pattern for skill building would be as shown in the Figure 7.1. The steps consist of three processes: "tell," by the trainer, "show," by the trainer, and "do," by the trainees. For effective training, the pattern for skill building should be consistent throughout the training program.

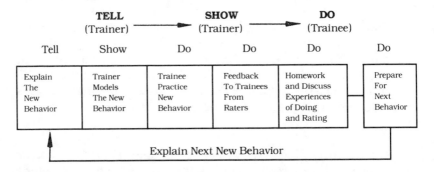

Figure 7.1. Skill building pattern for training modules.

EXPLANATION OF AND NEED FOR SKILLS

Explaining the skill is essential in the teaching procedure. The explanation provides motivational incentives necessary to turn on trainees, intellectually and emotionally, toward their new learning. The trainer cannot expect a commitment from the trainees to learn new behaviors unless they are able to see the personal benefits of those behaviors.

In other words, show informationally or demonstrate experientially how the new behaviors will be directly or indirectly helpful to each trainee. With younger trainees, an effective method is to have them experience the skills that they will be learning in relationship to their world in order that each skill be meaningful. Adults, on the other hand, can be motivated by a combination of research citations and personal experiences. Modeling and explanation behaviors are essential in introducing each training module.

MODELING OF SKILL TO BE TAUGHT

Learning theorists have identified that modeling is a singularly effective way to teach. In teaching communication skills, the use of frequent modeling by the trainer is "the" most effective single teaching procedure that can be used.

To ask a trainee, whether child or adult, to take public risks with new behaviors is a frightening idea. Therefore, the trainer is to take the initial risks when presenting the new behavior for two reasons:

1. The modeling gives the trainee some visual experiences in behaviors that he/she will be asked to imitate, thus making it easier to mimic or parody others when practicing previously unknown experiences.

2. Carkhuff (1969) and associates have shown in their research that a trainee cannot be more effective than trainer. Therefore, trainers must be able to function at higher levels of effectiveness than trainees in order for them to improve their skills.

Trainer modeling of desired behaviors can be done through the use of techniques such as demonstrations, role-playing, or playing of video tapes made of the desired behavior. The modeling is most effective if done immediately after introducing the skill to the trainees. Combining an explanation of the skill to be learned with the immediate modeling of the behavior is a very potent teaching process. The trainer is to teach the skill and immediately model it so that a visual demonstration is available for the trainees to mime in their attempts in trying new behavior. Trainers can demonstrate poor skills to assist trainees in discrimination, but the modeling behavior must include the effective skills so as to reinforce them.

Trainer modeling of the skills to be taught not only provides trainees with a visual design but also demonstrates the impact of the skill directly. Trainees may read about a skill and hear about a skill, but demonstrating is the most effective way to convey the skill to be learned. Discussion concerning each demonstration should follow it.

PRACTICE OF SKILL

Practicing the skills is crucial in order to integrate the new behavior into present listening and communication style. Because the skills are broken into such small segments of new behaviors, their initial impact when practiced is often found to be mechanical and awkward. Practice is the key to making the skill integrated and smooth. In the training sessions, practice allows for immediate feedback and can assist trainees in being able to modify their initial attempts at various skills. In addition, trainees should practice the skills outside of the sessions. Only through constant use of the skills will they replace the old skills which have become habitual. With practice, the mechanical aspects will become extinguished, and as more skills are added and integrated, the new behaviors become useful in interpersonal relations. The mechanical aids of video and audio tapes provide feedback which is efficient in aiding trainees to become more aware of their own skill development.

The use of video tape equipment is extremely helpful in the training process. At least two ways exist to use video equipment. One way is to develop modeling tapes for each skill that the trainer is teaching. The video tape modeling is sometimes better than the on-the-spot demonstration of the skill. For example, you may not want to develop tapes that show low, medium, and high levels of attending behavior. For best results, use a skilled counselor in the modeling tapes for skill building. You may want to use peers with the stimulus tapes used in the module for genuineness.

A second way of using video tape equipment is to tape the participants as they practice the skills and then to play back the tape for review. This form of learning is extremely helpful to the participant. Audio taping also is very helpful.

Throughout the trainee exercises, the group size and number of trainers will change from module to module. The reason for this variance is that some modules involve more skill building than others.

FEEDBACK TO TRAINEES FROM RATER

An important aspect of the learning process in the design is for the trainee to be able to discriminate between effective and ineffective or destructive communication skills. Discrimination of facilitative behaviors precedes the trainee's ability to communicate those behaviors. By rating others' communication skills while in training, trainees learn the difference between effective and ineffective communication in practice as well as in theory. Practice during training can be provided by having trainees identify positive and negative skills and the rationale in each others' audio or video tapes made during practice.

By requiring trainees to rate the behaviors of other trainees, they are taught to discriminate and to communicate the reasons for their ratings to the person being observed, thereby increasing their ability to understand the differences in behaviors and skills and also to learn to articulate the feedback. Knowing the difference between various communication patterns enables trainees to monitor their own behavior when they are required to practice the skills. The usual procedure for rating and discrimination skill training is to form groups of three to five members. One person functions as the helper and one as the helpee. The others in the group function as raters. Each person in the group is required to participate by assuming the role of helper, helpee, and rater within the practice session. The rating and feedback process is an integral part of each skill practice session and training is of little value without it.

After teaching, modeling, and having the trainees practice a new skill, the trainer is to take time to have the trainees discuss their experiences within the group. The discussion after the teaching and training is vital because discussion provides a significant feedback to the trainer as to how well the skill is being perceived intellectually and emotionally. Discussion topics often provide an opportunity for the trainer to do further teaching, to check out how the ideas are being integrated by trainees, and to respond to questions necessary to clarify misunderstandings.

HOMEWORK AND DISCUSSION OF EXPERIENCES OF DOING AND RATING

Assigning homework will be a carry-over activity in learning the new skills. The trainees will be asked to integrate the skill further by practicing each skill away form the training sessions and, in some instances, by completing written assignments such as diaries or observation sheets.

When the trainer evaluates the session after each training session, an evaluation can be made on each of the six skill-building behaviors—explanation of skill, modeling, practice, discrimination, homework, and discussion—to determine which section was weak or strong. If a session has not gone well, one of the six behaviors has been omitted or poorly presented.

PREPARE FOR NEXT BEHAVIOR

Following the session evaluations, which included individual skill evaluation, the trainees prepare for the next behavior which is receiving the explanation of a new behavior. The explanation of the new behavior will be the beginning of the teaching module again.

FORMAT FOR TRAINING PROGRAM

Each module is presented in a uniform manner to facilitate trainer understanding. Each module, when presented, follows the same informational structure. In this way, the trainer will be able to structure each training session. The structure is as follows:

1. Module title

2. Definition of the skill to be taught

3. Behavior goals

4. Appropriate population

5. Group size

6. Approximate time required for the training

7. Physical setting and materials

8. Procedures

9. Evaluation Process

10. Measuring outcomes

Stating the goals in behavioral terms aids in the evaluation process for each skill. This practice is helpful for the trainer to use in explaining the training process to others.

Group size is an important determinant of the rate of learning and the style of teaching. For example, if a trainer has two or three co-trainers, the learning process is cut almost in half. If twelve or more trainees are in the training group, two trainers are important when the group moves into the practice pattern. Also, if video tape equipment is used for modeling or for feedback for trainees, two trainers will increase the efficiency of the training.

In each phase of the training is listed an ideal physical setting and a list of materials needed such as trainee exercises and audio-visual equipment. Training is facilitated if the trainer is organized concerning material and does not waste time setting up video equipment or audio tape equipment. Training is more effective if tape recorders and video tape are available for the trainees and trainers to use.

The time required for each skill will vary, depending on the number of people being trained. The exercises are based on training up to twelve trainees in a group. If a disciplined structure is maintained, the procedures will take the amount of time suggested.

The step by step procedures for each skill are described fully. Alternate procedures for different ages and different groups are pointed out. The order of procedures has been field tested many times, and variations have been attempted. The order presented in this *Peer Counseling* book is the one which has been found to be most effective. This procedure obviously is not the only procedure that can be used for training groups, but it is a workable plan that has been successful many times.

The evaluation process can be used with the trainees or the trainers. The evaluation method may take the form of narrative comments, observations, and completion of rating sheets. All of the different methods of evaluation will be used—trainer, self, rater.

The outcomes of each step will be discussed. These outcomes may be in the form of changes in the trainee, the trainee's environment, or an institutional change.

Throughout the module section of the trainer's manual, space is available for the trainer to write comments, evaluate personal training skill, and make notes of effective ways of teaching. The intent is for the trainer to add personal creative teaching methods and counseling techniques to strengthen the training format.

Each trainer has different needs concerning the training processes. By keeping notes, a trainer will be better able to enter into meaningful dialogue with other trainers relating to communications, skill training, and peer counseling training. Through this dialogue, all can gain skills. Hopefully each trainer will record his/her unique ways of training and arrive at evaluation procedures meaningful for the techniques applied.

THE TRAINING PROGRAM

The training program is divided into modules which are designed to cover all 8 basic communication skills. Skills are to be introduced one at a time, with each new skill being introduced to trainees only after they have practiced and become proficient in one skill before proceeding to the next. Each skill is cumulated on the previous skill(s) learned. After completion of *Book 1* (Basic Skills) they are ready to undertake peer helping projects. Selection of specific modules from Book 2 may form the basics for the advanced training. In some institutions it is called a practicum. The design shown in Figure 8.1 should be followed exactly in introducing the skills. However, procedures of accomplishing goals can be created by each trainer to meet the needs of trainees.

Figure 8.1. Program design of eight basic communication skills in peer counseling.

TIME LINES OF THE TRAINING MODULES

An approximation of the amount of time that needs to be allotted for each module has been included to facilitate scheduling requirements for the entire training program. Modifications can be made in the suggested time schedule to facilitate the maximum growth of the trainees with whom one is working; however, with the first group of trainees, the recommendation is that one adhere to the suggested time schedule. Figure 8.2. is an outline of the schedule for the 24 training modules.

The total time requirement will depend upon several factors such as ability and/or prior experiences of trainees, time block for each training session, and opportunity for practice and preparation between training sessions. Because training conditions will vary from location to location, the training program is organized into Modules with subdivisions (Exercises) that can be taught individually or combined to meet local conditions.

The minimum time block for a training session is 30 minutes with 45 to 75 minutes being preferable. At the start of each Module in this book is given an approximate time span for each Exercise within the Module. Ability and prior experience of trainees may necessitate changes in the times shown.

The overall approximate times by Modules are provided in Figure 8.2. For planning the training program, times can be used for guides. As certain Exercises are grouped for being taught in the same Module, the total time span probably will be less than when each Exercise is taught separately.

PHYSICAL ARRANGEMENTS AND EQUIPMENT

The physical arrangements for a peer counseling training program can be very simple or elaborate. The essential room size is for one large enough for role playing to occur simultaneously in as many clusters as one-third the enrollment in each training session. The room accoustics are important because of the interaction desired among trainees during the training sessions.

Module Number	Module Title	Time Span in Minutes		Age
		Training Session	Homework	
	Book 1 (Developing 8 Peer Helper Skills)			
1	What is Peer Counseling?	90 - 135	15 - 20	All
2	Introduction to the Program	45 - 60	20 - 30	All
3	Let's Look at Helping	120 - 160	60 - 120	All
4	Attending Skill	120 - 160	45 - 60	All
5	Communication Stoppers	45 - 60	45 - 60	All
6	Empathy Skill	290 - 500	155 - 240	All
7	Summarizing Skill	90 - 150	80 - 215	12 - Adult
8	Questioning Skill	80 - 170	105 - 180	12 - Adult
9	Genuineness Skill	165 - 275	140 - 235	12 - Adult
10	Assertive Skill	300 - 360	150 - 180	12 - Adult
11	Confrontation Skill	75 - 110	45 - 65	12 - Adult
12	Problem-Solving Skill	180 - 240	130 - 225	12 - Adult
13	Putting Peer Counseling Into Action	60 - 120+	60 - 90+	All
	TOTAL FOR BOOK 1			
	in minutes	1660 - 2500+	1050 - 1720+	
	in hours	28 - 42+	18 - 29+	
	Book 2 (Applying Peer Helper Skills)			
14	Drugs and Alcohol	430 - 505	205	12 - Adult
15	Wellness/Stress	400 - 480	260	12 - Adult
16	Enhancing Self Esteem	380 - 450	230	12 - Adult
17	Leadership Training	330 - 390	85	12 - Adult
18	Facilitating Small Group Discussion	330 - 520	105	12 - Adult
19	Leading Classroom Discussion	510 - 630	260	12 - Adult
20	Peer Helping Through Tutoring	330 - 580	360	12 - Adult
21	Recognizing Eating Disorders	330 - 480	205	12 - Adult
22	Suicide Prevention	180 - 270	150	12 - Adult
23	Coping With Loss	240 - 270	120	12 - Adult
24	Ethical Considerations	390 - 520		All
	TOTAL FOR BOOK 2			
	in minutes	3850 - 5095	1980	
	in hours	64-85	33	

NOTE: The time is further subdivided by Exercise, which can be taught individually or combined where needed.

Figure 8.2. Approximate time schedule for training session time and for homework time for each module.

Chalkboard is nice but not essential if flip pad or flannel board is available. Some means of writing notes large enough for viewing by all trainees is important.

Video and audio equipment for recording and playback are nice but not essential. Trainees often are able to benefit from video viewing of previously prepared tapes of skills being taught and of tapes made of themselves during role playing.

Furniture requirements are only for a movable chair for each trainee, trainer, and visitor (if any). Generally, the chairs are arranged in a circle during times when trainees are together as a group and moved to smaller groupings as clusters of two to four are formed for interaction and role playing.

Materials needed are a Peer Power book for each trainee and pen or pencil for each. Each trainer will need a Peer Counseling book and chalk for writing on chalkboard or other means of capturing and summarizing ideas during discussions and presentations.

NUMBER AND AGE OF TRAINEES

The number of trainees in any given program is limited by number of trainers, persons (potential trainees) available, facilities, and need of peer counselors once the training program is completed. A very minimum number at one time to facilitate the interaction suggested in many of the Exercises. The maximum number with one trainer probably would be 12 with 6 to 9 being more ideal. When the number of trainees exceeds 12, we suggest a second trainer so as to have two groups or one trainer forming two groups and meeting with them at different times.

The age span of trainees is very large. Older people often want to help others and often feel inadequate in skills to do so. Retirees can benefit as well as middleaged persons or students in junior and senior high schools, colleges, and universities. Youth club members in organizations such as Y's, churches, scouts, and farm groups often want to learn more about helping peers. No maximum age exists, and the minimum age is more dependent upon the person than the age; however, age 10 to 12 is probably the generally accepted minimum for using this material. The reading and/or interest level of the *Peer Power* book may be a factor to consider when selecting persons for a training program. Tindall & White (1989) are developing a book to be used at the elementary level.

FORMAT OF TRAINING SUGGESTIONS

In Chapter 8 are presented by each Module and Exercise the purposes, introductory information, training procedures in sequential order, and homework assignment for trainees between training sessions. The information supplied is above and beyond that supplied in the *Peer Power* book. The trainer will find the information in Chapter 8 supplements that which trainees have in their book. The two books—*Peer Power* and *Peer Counseling*—provide essential information and exercises for the total training program. The trainer will need to have both books and each trainee is to have the *Peer Power, Book 1* and/or *Book 2.*

MODULES
for
BOOK 1

INTRODUCTORY
PROGRAM

WHAT IS PEER COUNSELING?

The first module will be devoted to explaining the program to the trainees and to concerned others. A pretest will be an integral part of the introduction module.

Purposes

1. To inform interested persons of the peer counseling program.

2. To solicit their interest.

3. To gain a commitment to participate as trainees.

Approximate Time

Explanation—30 to 45 minutes for program explanation

Exercise 1.1—30 to 45 minutes

Exercise 1.2—30 to 45 minutes Homework—15 to 20 minutes

Physical Setting

Have potential trainees sit in a circle. All others, such as parents of potential trainees, sit outside the circle.

Materials

Peer Power: Book 1, Introductory Program, one for each potential trainee

Pencil or pen for each trainee

Introduction to Module

During the first group sessions, the trainer may want to invite not only the potential trainees but also their parents or a significant other who may make "significant" differences in the trainee's attitude and behavior throughout the program. Important assets of the program are having all persons know what is the training program, what are the competencies to be learned, and what are the ways in which one can work with others after completing the program.

In discussing the program, you will be able to draw on information throughout this manual. Sharing with the group will help to expand their concepts of a peer counseling program and may help them form their concerns into questions.

Training Procedures

1. Explain to trainees the purpose of the program. At this point avoid lengthy details. Some of the purposes that need to be explained are as follows:

    a. to learn about self.

    b. to train individuals (peers) to help others (peers) with social, educational, emotional, and/or vocational concerns.

    c. to train "rap" leaders (one function of peer counselors).

    d. to explain other roles for peer counselors. Refer trainees to material in *Peer Power* on "Roles of Peer Counselors," Chapter 3. Help trainees to list examples of where and how peer counselors may contribute to their peers. Examples would include

    Schools

    > —helping new students adjust to school
    > —helping during registration
    > —helping tutor younger students
    > —helping newcomers within community to adjust
    > —helping peer find a social group or agency
    > —helping with prevention programs
    > —helping with at-risk youth
    > —serving as rap leaders
    > —serving as classroom presenters

    Agencies

    > —helping in crises centers
    > —helping in orientation of new workers
    > —helping in community outreach programs

    Religious Institutions

    > —helping in church school teaching
    > —helping in leadership groups
    > —helping in outreach programs
    > —helping in peer ministry
    > —helping with substance abuse

—helping with family problems
—helping with prevention
—helping with health issues (AIDS, drugs, alcohol, smoking)
—helping with wellness issues

2. Answer all participants' questions. (Parents of trainees under 16 years of age are encouraged to attend this orientation.)

3. Begin building trust among trainees and set guidelines for confidentiality. The following points might be discussed:

a. What is meant by confidentiality?

b. What rights do individuals have concerning confidentiality?

c. Why is trust important in a group being trained as listeners and helpers?

d. What are norms for groups?

e. Can participants who are drug free serve as role models?

Evaluation Process

1. The trainer can determine how well those at orientation sessions understand the program by responding to all audience questions after goals and procedure for meeting those goals have been explained.

2. The trainer can analyze the Pretest sheets (Exercise 1.1) and determine in part the skills level of the potential trainees.

3. From Exercise 1.2, determination can be made about reasons potential trainees have for taking the Peer Counseling Training Program.

Measuring Outcomes

1. Establish that everyone in attendance at the orientation session understands the goals of the program. This is accomplished by the trainer answering all questions of participants, parents, and others in attendance.

2. The extent to which the Communication Exercise is completed by trainees, including scoring, establishes the beginning levels of discrimination and communication skills of the trainees. Trainees' scores indicate baseline skills of trainees.

EXERCISE 1.1
PRE-TESTING YOURSELF
COMMUNICATIONS EXERCISE

Purposes

1. To gain through a pre-test the personal interest of potential trainees.

2. To understand their levels of competency.

3. To gain insight as to the extent to which they might commit themselves to the training program.

Homework for Trainees
Prior to Group Meeting

1. If the trainer has met with each potential trainee individually, and has had a chance to distribute the *Peer Power* book, then he/she should ask each to read the first part of the book over to the Pretest Exercise 1.1.

2. If the potential trainees have not had *Peer Power* book prior to first group meeting, then no homework would be indicated.

Introduction to Exercise

The Pretest will provide a means for you to assess each trainee's communication skills in terms of empathy based on discrimination and response. You can discuss the items and the trainees' answers with them after the completion of the Pretest by them. The same items will be used as a Posttest at the end of the training program. Therefore, save the Post-Test sheets for comparison with Posttest results later.

Training Procedures

1. Have trainees open *Peer Power* book to Exercise 1.1 entitled, "Pretesting Yourself: Communication Exercise." The purpose of the communication exercise is for the trainer to assess each trainee's skills in discrimination and response.

2. Refer to Exercise 1.1 in *Peer Power: Book 1, Introductory Program,* for explanation of directions and rating scale.

3. Use examples to help the potential trainees better understand the rating scale. The following are examples you could use of conversations between a helpee and a helper together with an analysis of each of the helpers responses:

Person	Response High Rating "H"	Analysis
Helpee:	"I'm having a problem with Betty."	
Helper:	"Betty is really upsetting you."	Heard the problem. Provided feedback. Responded to feelings Helped person know feelings.

Medium Response "M"

Helpee:	"I'm not to blame, she is."	
Helper:	"Let's not talk about what she does."	Heard Helpee. Encourages addi- tional talk. Expresses willing- ness to listen.

Low Response "L"

Helpee:	"Yeah, she is always nagging me."	
Helper:	"What do you do to cause that?"	Not helpful. Makes helpee as sume the blame.

4. Explain the rating scale as being based upon the degree of empathy in the response.

   a. Responses rated "H" included accurate paraphrase for both feeling and meaning of the helpee's statement.

   b. Responses rated "M" included accurate paraphrase for either feeling or meaning but not both.

   c. Responses rated "L" included neither accurate feeling nor meaning.

5. Ask the trainees to rate the responses for the first five statements, 1 through 5, in the *Peer Power: Book 1*, using "L" for Low, "M" for Medium, and "H" for High.

6. Discuss the responses for the first five statements. The following level of responses for Statements 1 through 5 are accepted generally by experts.

Statement	Rating	Response	Statement	Rating	Response
1	L	1a	4	L	4a
	L	1b		H	4b
	M	1c		L	4c
	H	1d		L	4d
2	L	2a	5	M	5a
	H	2b		L	5b
	M	2c		H	5c
	L	2d		L	5d
3	H	3a			
	L	3b			
	M	3c			
	L	2d			

Optional: Omit the discussion and have the potential trainees proceed with Training Procedure Number 7.

7. Ask the trainees to proceed in the Pretest with Statements 6 through 10. Ask each to write what he/she would consider to be a helpful response to the statement.

8. In Statements 6 through 10, check each for an accurate empathetic response including feeling words and paraphrasing of the content. Use ratings "L," "M," and "H" as provided previously.

9. Have the trainees turn in the Pretest sheets upon completion. The Pretest will be readministered at the end of the training sessions as a Posttest. The trainer can compare the pre- and posttest results to determine behavioral changes in discrimination and communication skills.

10. Analyze the sheets from the Pretest so as to establish a base line for your training program.

11. Where necessary, talk with the individual whom the trainer is concerned about readiness for training program.

**Homework for Trainees
after Group Meeting**

1. Ask trainees to do Exercise 1.2 and submit the material to trainer at next meeting.

   Optional: Ask trainees to do Exercise 1.2 following completion of the Pretest (Exercise 1.1). Collect the sheets during the meeting.

2. When Exercise 1.2 is collected, ask the trainees to do the Homework as listed in Exercise 1.2.

EXERCISE 1.2
YOUR REASON FOR TRAINING

Purpose

To learn the potential trainee's personal reasons for learning peer counseling skills.

Introduction to Exercise

The reasons for individuals' enrolling in the Peer Counseling Training Program can help one understand their motivation. The exercise is designed to have the potential trainees examine their reasons and to share these with you.

Training Procedures

1. Have the trainees discuss in the group meeting the answers they gave to the three questions.

2. Help the trainees gain a feel for what the training can do for them personally as well as being useful in helping others.

3. Collect Exercise 1.2 sheets.

Homework for Trainees
After Group Meeting

1. Ask the trainees to read the introduction to Module 2.

2. Ask the trainees to study Exercise 2.1 and to come to the next meeting prepared to complete that exercise.

INTRODUCTION TO THE PROGRAM

Purposes

1. To help trainees learn to know each other.

2. To develop new listening behaviors.

3. To begin relating to others.

Approximate Time

Exercise 2.1—45 to 60 minutes in group session Homework—20 to 30 minutes

Exercise 2.2—60 to 120 minutes in group session

Materials

Peer Power: Book 1, Introductory Program, one for each trainee.

Chalkboard, eraser, and chalk

Optional: Felt tip pen and newsprint or large flip note pad

Name tags (can be small pieces of paper and pins)

Introduction to Module

In this module, the trainer will be able to model for the trainees the behavior in the initial stages of relating to others. The trainees will be able to initiate a relationship with the trainer and each other—persons with whom they will be working over an extended period.

As the trainees talk with each other, you can help them sharpen their listening behavior. As they introduce each other, you will be able to analyze their listening behaviors, their willingness to talk in front of others, and other characteristics that will be useful in planning the balance of your training program.

Training Procedures

1. Be prepared to take the trainees through the entire module at one training session (group meeting).

2. Have the meeting in a room that is conducive to interaction among trainees and large enough for the trainees to move about freely. It should have movable chairs, sufficient heat and ventilation, and adequate lighting.

3. Be prepared to return Exercise 1.2 sheets to trainees and whenever possible give written personal comments to each trainee.

Evaluation Process

1. You can determine the potential for a good learning group by the way trainees interact with one another during the introductions.

2. Listening behavior and recall ability of trainees can be determined by having trainees recall in the group as much information as they can about each of the other trainees.

Measuring Outcomes

The outcome of Module 2 probably can better be determined at the next group meeting by having trainees at the beginning of the next training session identify other members by name and by relating any information they can about each other.

One measure of outcome is whether or not every trainee knows the name and other information with regard to each of the other members of the group.

EXERCISE 2.1
KNOWING OTHERS

Purposes

1. To help trainees know one another.

2. To initiate relationships with others.

Introduction to Exercise

This exercise can best be done with all potential trainees for a given training program being together. The interaction of sharing with each other and getting to know one another, generally, is a low level of threat and is a good process to start the program. If one or more trainees cannot proceed at this level, you may need to work with the person or persons individually and while doing so may decide whether or not the person is to stay in the training program at this time or whether the person(s) will need other assistance before being able to obtain sufficient benefit from the Peer Counseling Training Program.

Training Procedures

1. As the trainees come into the room, hand each a name tag; ask each to write his/her name on it, and have each attach the name tag to front, upper left side of clothing.

2. Introduce self (as trainer) to a partner (a trainee). In so doing, model the behavior desired in trainees when asked to introduce themselves. Some of the specific information in the introduction could include name, family members, things enjoyed, things that irritate, and things desired to change. The leader may want to write the specific information to be shared on the chalkboard, newsprint, or pad.

   Note for Trainer: For the trainer to model the introduction procedure and to use high level effective communication skills at all times is absolutely necessary.

3. Have each trainee select a partner that he/she does not already know or know well. Have each partner share important things about self for approximately three minutes with the other partner.

4. After the sharing between partners has taken place, have each person introduce partner to the group. The introductions will be sequential, moving around the group with each pair of trainees introducing each other before moving to the next pair. The introductions will include as much material as the person giving the introduction can remember from the sharing experience. As introductions are given, have the person speaking stand directly behind the person being introduced and place both hands on the other person's shoulders. The person being introduced will remain seated and silent.

5. Have each trainee complete Exercise 2.1 in *Peer Power: Book 1, Introductory Program*, then move to Step 6.

   Optional: Move directly to Step 6 and have the Exercise 2.1 completed as Homework.

6. Discuss after completing the introductions. The focus of the discussion is to be related to how trainees feel about the introduction exercise.

Homework for Trainees
After Group Meeting

1. Complete Exercise 2.1 to be submitted to the trainer at the next meeting. Even if the trainees wrote on the Sheets during the group training meeting, they may want to add information to the sheets.

2. Ask the trainees to read the introduction to Module 3 and complete the Exercise 3.1.

   Optional: Depending on length of training sessions and frequency, one may want to complete all of Module 3 at the next training session. If so, have trainees complete both Exercises 3.1 and 3.2.

EXERCISE 2.2
SHARING ABOUT MYSELF

Purposes

To help the trainees know one another and to initiate relationships with others. This is an alternative for Exercise 2.1.

Introduction

Please refer to Exercise 2.1.

Training Procedures

1. Ask the trainees to come into the room, hand them the book and have each of them fill it out.

2. Introduce self (as the trainer). Begin going through the form, and always start first in terms of the questions.

3. The trainer may want everyone to respond to each question, one at a time. This could take up to two hours depending on the group.

4. Hold a discussion about the exercise. The focus could be about the introduction exercise.

Homework for Trainees
After Group Meeting

Read the introduction to Module 3 and complete Exercise 3.1.

LET'S LOOK AT HELPING

Purposes

1. To help the trainees explore several different characteristics of helping behaviors.

2. To help the trainees identify ineffective helping behaviors that are used widely.

3. To help the trainees become aware of effective helping behaviors.

Approximate Time

Exercise 3.1—45 to 60 minutes in group meeting

Exercise 3.2—45 to 60 minutes in group meeting

Exercise 3.3—45 to 60 minutes in group meeting

Homework—60 to 120 minutes including time spent in helping two others

Materials

Peer Power: Book 1, Introductory Program, one for each trainee

Chalkboard, eraser, and chalk

Optional: Felt tip pen and newsprint or large flip note pad

Introduction to Module

In Module 3, have the trainees focus on helping—exploring the helping behaviors in others and then in themselves. One can increase their concerns about which kinds of behavior are effective and which ones are ineffective.

Training Procedures

1. Based on time format for training sessions, decide whether all of Module 3 will be taught in one session or in two sessions.

2. Review the Training Procedure steps for each exercise and prepare training format.

3. Collect the Exercise Sheets from Module 2.

Evaluation Process

1. Evaluate the training during the training sessions by what input is being given by the trainees—extent of interaction by all students, kinds of comments being made, whether or not Exercise Sheets are completed ahead of training session time, and the excitement (enthusiasm) with which trainees participate.

2. Determine whether or not trainees are moving toward creating a positive healthy learning environment by the manner in which they discuss the two exercises, e.g., are they discussing behaviors or are they fearful of sharing with each other? Are they concerned with the topic of helping or are they more interested in who?

Measuring Outcomes

The outcomes are to be measured in terms of the effectiveness of the training module in enabling trainees to identify and discriminate effective and ineffective helping behaviors by checking the appropriate qualities of their entries in *Peer Power: Book 1*, Exercises 3.1 and 3.2.

EXERCISE 3.1
EXPLORING HELPING BEHAVIORS

Purpose

To have the trainees become aware of helping behaviors that they like and/or dislike in others.

Introduction to Exercise

This exercise can be done best after the trainees have had time to identify individuals with whom they have enjoyed talking and sharing problems—after the trainees have completed Exercise 3.1 sheets. The group session is built around sharing those experiences and then extracting the positive and negative helping behaviors.

As a trainer, one can take an active role not only in getting the trainees to share, but also in helping them identify helping behaviors. From the list that the group members make, you can assist them in extracting the positive behaviors which they can practice.

To some extent, recording and discussing the behaviors they don't like can be meaningful. Spend some time in listing the undesired (ineffective) helping behaviors and the comparable ones to use instead. Often trainees need contrast (effective and ineffective) in order to remember better.

Training Procedures

1. Have trainees identify with whom they talk (kind of more than name—younger or older people, close friends or speaking acquaintances) about their problems.

2. List the identified people on chalkboard, newsprint, or pad.

3. Have trainees list the verbal and nonverbal behaviors of the people the trainees identified as helpful and give reasons for identifying the behavior as helpful.

4. Have trainees brainstorm personal characteristics of the people the trainees find helpful.

5. Have trainees develop a definition of a helpful person.

6. Discuss how trainees presently help others.

7. List on chalkboard, newsprint, or pad the characteristics or behaviors which make the people (helpers) effective listeners.

8. Discuss effective helping behaviors.

   a. Attending behaviors of the trainee
   b. Effective listening behaviors of the trainee
   c. Responding behaviors of the trainee
   d. Initiative behaviors of the trainee
   e. Problem solving

9. List on chalkboard, newsprint, or pad the characteristics or behaviors which the helpers had that the trainees did not like.

10. Help trainees identify behaviors to overcome or replace the undesired (ineffective) behaviors.

11. Collect Exercise 3.1 Sheets.

Homework for Trainees
After Group Meeting

1. Ask the trainees to practice the helping behaviors they identified before the next training session.

2. If a time period exists between Exercise 3.1 and 3.2, then ask the trainees to complete Exercise 3.2 before the next session.

EXERCISE 3.2
HOW DO I HELP?

After the trainees have identified what they like in others who help them (Exercise 3.1), the trainees generally enjoy practicing the behaviors during the next day or week as they help others. The practice enables them to transfer the list of behaviors from a "talk-about" to an action level. After trainees have experienced doing or attempting to do the behaviors, they often can verbalize better what they need in order to become the kind of person they would like to be.

Training Procedures

1. Have the trainees to cluster with three in a cluster.

2. Ask the trainees to discuss in the cluster which desirable helping behaviors identified in Exercise 3.1 they were able to utilize in helping others.

3. Ask them to identify the helping behaviors that were most meaningful as they used them.

4. Ask them to be prepared to share with the total group after 10 minutes.

5. After 10 minutes, regroup and have the trainees discuss what was gained in the clusters.

6. Use the chalkboard, newsprint, or pad to summarize what is presented, and then record the new list that they extract with your leadership.

7. Collect Exercise 3.2 Sheets.

8. Return Exercise 3.1 Sheets with written comments.

    Optional: If no time existed between Exercises 3.1 and 3.2, then Exercise 3.1 Sheets are to be returned when Exercise 3.2 Sheets are completed.

EXERCISE 3.3
PRACTICE IN HELPING

Purposes

To give trainees a helping experience early in the training without any evaluation.

Introduction to Exercise

Ask the trainees to practice some helping skills. It is important for them to use the behaviors they have identified in Exercises 3.1 and 3.2. They need to try to use those behaviors.

Training Procedures

1. Have trainees divide into groups.

2. One person presents the issue, one person is the listener, one person gives the listener feedback. Change roles until all members of the group have had an opportunity to play each role.

3. Discuss the experience.

Homework for Trainees
After Group Meeting

1. Ask trainees to review Module 4.

2. Ask trainees to bring to the next meeting Exercise 4.1 Sheets already completed.

3. Ask the trainees to come prepared to do Exercise 4.2 during the next training session.

ATTENDING SKILL

Attending behavior relates most directly to the concept of helper respect for the helpee, which is demonstrated when undivided attention is given to the helpee.

Purposes

1. To teach the trainees the difference between effective and ineffective nonverbal attending skills.

2. To teach the trainees to be able to discriminate between effective and ineffective nonverbal attending behaviors.

3. To teach the trainees to communicate effective nonverbal attending behaviors.

Approximate Time

Exercise 4.1—45 to 60 minutes in group session Homework—45 to 60 minutes

Exercise 4.2—20 to 60 minutes in group session

Exercise 4.3—45 to 60 minutes in group session

Exercise 4.4—30 minutes in group session

Exercise 4.5—45 minutes in group session

Materials

Peer Power: Book 1, Introductory Program, one copy for each trainee

Optional: Video tape to be used to model skills taught or to tape the practice sessions of the trainees.

Training Procedures

Be prepared to do the demonstrations required to teach Module 4 as explained in Exercise 4.1, Training Procedures.

Evaluation Process

One can check on trainees' abilities to discriminate between effective and ineffective attending behaviors as they role play and by reviewing the Flow Sheets.

Measuring Outcomes

1. The module goals are met when the trainees show high levels of attending behaviors. This can be subjectively measured by observing the attending behaviors of trainees when they function as helpers.

2. The lesson will be successful when all trainees are able to rate good attending behaviors accurately.

EXERCISE 4.1
EXAMPLES OF NONVERBAL
COMMUNICATION BEHAVIORS

Purpose

To demonstrate with the trainees effective and ineffective nonverbal attending skills.

Introduction to Exercise

Attending behavior is very important in peer counseling and all positive interpersonal communications. Trainees are generally willing and eager to learn more about attending skills. Through video tapes and/or demonstrations one will be able to increase their awareness of various attending skills and how the skills can be used more effectively.

The attending skills can be learned by young and old; however, because skills are ones with which they are not familiar, one will need to proceed step by step with sufficient examples and time for the trainees to organize their new experiences into their memory of previous experiences. Also, give them opportunities to participate and interact.

Training Procedures

1. Demonstrate (model) by video tape or role play (with trainer doing the modeling during the training session) nonverbal, nonattending behavior, such as not giving eye-contact, nervous hand and body mannerisms, and not squaring the helper's body to face the helpee. Upon completion of the demonstration the trainees report their feelings generated by the nonattending behavior of the trainer or model in video tape.

2. Have the trainees pair off and role play so as to experience nonverbal attending behavior as just modeled by the trainer. Trainees should change roles so that each has a chance to role play both helpee and helper role. Upon completion of the role-playing exercise, both partners report feelings generated by a helper's nonattending behavior.

3. Demonstrate on video tape or model minimal attending behaviors. Minimal attending behavior means giving the helpee eye contact and no other nonverbal cues of attending. Verbal behavior can be used without emphasis by noncommittal words such as "um, yes." Upon completion of the demonstration, the trainees report their feelings generated by the minimal attending behavior of the trainer.

4. Have the trainees pair off and role play so as to experience the minimal attending behavior just modeled by the trainer. Trainees should change roles so that each has a chance to role play both helper and helpee. Upon completion of the role-playing exercise, both partners report feelings generated by a helper's minimal attending behavior.

5. Demonstrate on video tape or model attending behaviors. Attending behaviors include direct and consistent eye contact, leaning slightly forward in an open position, squaring the body to face the helpee, and showing through facial expression that the helper is listening attentively. Verbal behaviors can be used which are consistent with the concerns of the helpee but without emphasis.

6. Have participants pair off and role play so as to experience the attending behavior just modeled by the trainer. Trainees should change roles so that each has a chance to role play both helpee and helper. Upon completion of the role-playing exercise, both partners report feelings generated by a helper's attending behavior.

7. Use additional technique for increasing the trainee's awareness of nonverbal communication, such as playing the camera game. Explain to the trainees that many a person's judgments about people are influenced by what he/she "sees" as opposed to really "knowing" the true picture. The camera game consists of the following:

   a. Each trainee selects a partner and faces that partner.

   b. Both partners close their eyes and think about their partner. Inform trainees that after a few seconds, they will open their eyes upon command and look directly at their partner to observe dress, hair style, posture, eyes, sex, age, and as many characteristics as they can observe about the partner.

   c. Have trainees close their eyes and think about what they saw and what conclusions can be drawn by what they saw. (For example, seeing a smile might lead a person to conclude that his/her partner was a happy person.)

d. Have trainees share with the group what they saw and the conclusion drawn from what they saw.

e. Have the trainees close eyes and think about someone they know who reminds them of their partner.

f. Have the trainees share with their partner the type of person about whom they have been thinking.

8. Explain to the trainees that in the next training session (Exercise 4.2) they will be role playing the attending skills and providing each other with vital information on how they perform. Rating material entitled Flow Sheets will be provided to help trainees provide the feedback to each other.

9. Collect Exercise 4.1 Sheets.

10. Return Exercise 3.2 Sheets (and Exercise 3.1 Sheets if not previously returned) with written comments and make any verbal comments at the same time that will help the trainees' motivation and personal growth.

Homework for Trainees
After Group Meeting

1. Ask each trainee to come prepared at the next training session to role play a concern (problem). Inform trainees that the role playing is to be done in clusters of three and that the purpose is to provide experience for their partners to practice attending skills.

2. Ask trainees to review Exercise 4.2 and come prepared to use the Exercise Sheet during the training session.

EXERCISE 4.2
BECOMING AWARE OF
MY ATTENDING BEHAVIOR

Purpose

To help trainees become aware of effective and ineffective nonverbal behavior.

Introduction to Exercise

This exercise will help you gain a better understanding of how one feels with different attending behaviors being shown to one by another person.

Training Procedures

Follow the directions given in *Peer Power: Book 1*, Exercise 4.2.

Homework for Trainees
After Group Meeting

Observe people's attending behaviors and the effect those behaviors have on other people. Then report your observations at the next meeting.

EXERCISE 4.3
REACTION TO ATTENDING
AWARENESS ACTIVITY

Purpose

To assist the trainee in an awareness of attending behavior.

Introduction to Exercise

This exercise will give you experience in verbalizing the results of nonattending, minimal attending and attending behavior.

Training Procedure

1. Have trainees fill out the information in the exercise.

2. It may be helpful to discuss this with the group.

Homework for Trainees
After Group Meeting

Observe the nonverbal behavior of others and report to the next training session.

EXERCISE 4.4
BECOMING AWARE OF OTHERS
NONVERBAL BEHAVIOR

Purpose

To help trainees tune into the nonverbal behavior of others.

Introduction to Exercise

This exercise can be a very moving experience. It is best to discuss the experience for a long period of time.

Training Procedures

1. Divide into two's.

2. Follow directions in *Peer Power: Book 1, Introductory Program.*

3. Discuss the experience at the completion.

Homework for Trainees
After Group Meeting

Be observant after leaving the nonverbal signals of others.

EXERCISE 4.5
RATING THE HELPER

Purpose

To provide experiences for trainees to practice attending behaviors and learn how to evaluate the quality of the attending skills.

Introduction to Exercise

This entire training session is devoted to having trainees role play concerns so that attending skills can be practiced. These trainees will have their first experience in feedback. Often they need assistance in providing feedback in a constructive manner that will be helpful to the receiver as well as to the person who does the rating.

Training Procedures

1. Divide trainees group into clusters of threes (triads.) One person should assume the role of the helpee, one person the helper, and one the rater.

2. Have trainees refer to Exercise 4.2, "Rating the Helper," in *Peer Power: Book 1, Introductory Program,* and explain to the trainees how the rating process operates.

3. Demonstrate the role playing, including helpee and helper activities, and the rater's job, including the marking of the Flow Sheet, and the feedback process. This procedure introduces the task of the rater. In order to explain the rater's task, the trainer will demonstrate by assuming the role of the helper. When the trainer in the role of helper responds to the helpee, the raters will evaluate the trainers attending behavior according to the format in Exercise 4.2, second page, entitled "Attending Skill: Rating Flow Sheet."

4. Model with several responses and discuss after each two or three responses how the rater would mark on the Flow Sheet. Model until all trainees understand the rating process and the marking of the Flow Sheet.

5. Direct trainees to practice the skills of attending, rating, and providing feedback by repeating the model demonstrated by the trainer.

6. Discuss after the first role playing in the clusters what occurred and how trainees felt. Supply additional information to facilitate the learning process.

7. Have trainees to exchange roles so that each trainee has a chance to role play all three roles.

Optional: Trainees can be video taped in groups of three as they practice their attending skills. Play these video tapes back to the large group with the audio turned off. Have the group rate the attending behavior of the helper.

8. Move from cluster to cluster to assist the trainees.

9. Discuss, as a group, what occurred and what they learned.

10. Collect Exercise 4.2 Sheets.

11. Return Exercise 4.1 Sheets with written comments.

Homework for Trainees
After Group Meeting

1. Ask trainees to read introduction to Module 5, *Peer Power: Book 1, Introductory Program.*

2. Ask trainees to complete Exercise 5.1 before the next training session.

COMMUNICATION STOPPERS

Purpose

To assist trainees in better identification of what might occur during communication that might interfere with or stop the communication process.

Approximate Time

Homework and Exercise 5.1—45 to 60 minutes on reading Introduction to Module 5 and completing Exercise 5.1

Training—45 to 60 minutes in session.

Homework and Exercise 5.2—15 to 20 minutes of time outside training session

Optional: Second training session, if trainees need it, is to learn the material and to become more of a cohesive learning group. Time required will depend upon the training needed.

Materials

Peer Power: Book 1, Introductory Program, one copy for each trainee

3 x 5 index cards

Pen or pencil for each trainee

Introduction to Module

Communication stoppers are helper behaviors, which, although they appear to be helpful, are really responses that are negative in effect and retard helpful interpersonal relationships. Helping the trainees recognize the communication stoppers and learn new behaviors to use in their place can be very meaningful. Eleven different kinds of communication stoppers are identified. Through illustrations of each kind, one will be able to help trainees increase their awareness of ineffective, self-defeating behaviors to avoid.

Training Procedures

1. Teach the entire Module in one session.

2. If you find that the trainees need more practice on identification of communication stoppers and, if your training schedule will permit, use a second session to continue the teaching techniques recommended.

Evaluation Process

You can determine the trainees understanding by the responses gained during the training session. The tendency may be for one or two trainees to take the initiative in answering, thus enabling some trainees to not become as involved as is desirable. Concern for the evaluation process will cause you to assure active participation by all trainees and increased involvement by individuals whose skills need improvement.

Measuring Outcomes

1. Degree of accuracy in discriminating stoppers can be determined by role playing, Exercises 5.1 and 5.2, and other techniques used in training session.

2. Degree of accuracy in identifying helpful responses can be determined by the responses provided to participants' problems in one of the training techniques.

EXERCISE 5.1
COMMUNICATION STOPPERS EXERCISE

Purpose

To help trainees learn the different kinds of communication exercises and to be able to recognize them when used.

Introduction to Exercise

Memorizing the eleven kinds of communication stoppers is not the emphasis, but rather to increase the trainees' recognition of the wide scope of activities frequently used that are ineffective in communications is what you can achieve. The definitions, examples, and training session activities will enable the trainees to improve their communication behaviors.

The eleven communication stoppers are defined in the *Peer Power: Book 1, Introductory Program*, Exercise 5.1, with an example provided for the trainees. The eleven kinds, definition of each, and an example (different from that provided in Peer Power Book 1, Introductory Program) are as follows:

1. Directing, ordering—to tell someone to do something in such a manner that gives the other person little or no choice.

   Example: "Get home at 9:00."

2. Warning, threatening—to tell the other person that if the behavior continues, then certain consequences will happen.

   Example: "If you are not home at 9:00, you can't go out the rest of the week."

3. Moralizing, preaching—to tell someone things he/she ought to do.

   Example: "You should always do you homework."

4. Persuading, arguing—to try to influence another person with facts, information, and logic.

   Example: "If you drop out of school, then you can't find a good job."

5. Advising, recommending—to provide answers for a problem.

   Example: "If I were you, I would quit being Jim's friend and be Joe's friend."

6. Evaluating, criticizing—to make a negative interpretation of another person's behavior.

   Example: "You got in so late; you must have been up to no good."

7. Praising—to make positive evaluation of another person's behavior.

   Example: "That is the most beautiful idea I have ever heard; you are great!"

8. Supporting, sympathizing—to try to talk the other person out of his/her feelings or to deny another person's feelings.

   Example: "Just wait, things will be better tomorrow. Your boyfriend will change."

9. Diagnosing—to analyze the other person's behavior and communicate that you have their behaviors figured out.

   Example: "You're just paranoid about your loss."

10. Diverting, bypassing—to change the subject or to not talk about the problem presented by the other person.

    Example: "I know you are having trouble with your mom, but all I want to know is do you want to go to the movie?"

11. Kidding, teasing—to try to avoid talking about the problem by laughing or by distracting the other person.

Example: "Why don't you just blow up your car since it doesn't work well."

Training Procedures

1. Ask the trainees to refer to Exercise 5.1 Sheets as you explain and illustrate the eleven kinds of stoppers of communication.

2. Ask the trainees to provide examples for each stopper as you teach it.

3. After discussing each stopper, model the behavior so as to enable the trainees to see, hear, and feel the effects.

4. Have trainees to role play in diads after stopper is modeled so that each trainee experiences the use of the communication stopper in both the helper and helpee roles, i.e., one trainee presents a problem. His/her partner responds with the stopper. Then, the two reverse roles. Trainees are guided to discuss the feelings each person experienced after the stopper was communicated.

   NOTE: Eleven role-playing situations are to occur with each being done following the modeling of that specific communication stopper.

5. Distribute 3 x 5 index cards and ask each trainee to write one problem on a card. Tell trainees how the card will be used (Step 6).

6. Collect the cards after the problems have been written and select cards to which the trainees are to give responses.

   a. Read a card and ask each participant to write a response on paper. The response is one which the trainee feels would be a helpful response for him/her to give as a helper.

   b. Reread the problem and have different trainees read responses as they wrote them.

   c. Ask trainees to identify the stoppers in the responses.

   d. Ask group members if they would continue talking about the problem if that response were given to them by a helper.

7. Optional Strategies

   a. Have trainees view the filmstrip, "Interpersonal Experiences" and identify stoppers.

   b. Rate responses in terms of helpfulness.

(1) Have students write a problem on a 3 x 5 card. Students turn in problem to trainer. Then the trainer reads three problems. Trainees write their response to each problem. Trainees submit to the trainer their written responses.

(2) The trainer reads the problem and several responses, asking the trainees to rate these responses in terms of helpfulness:

High (H) for when the response was **very helpful.** Medium (M) for when the response was **helpful.** Low (L) for when the response was not **helpful.**

(3) The trainer always rates the statement along with the trainees. Each person, including the trainer, is encouraged to explain his/her rating.

8. Collect Exercise 5.1 Sheets.

9. Return Exercise 4.2 Sheets with written comments.

Homework for Trainees
After Group Meeting

1. Ask trainees to complete Exercise 5.2 Sheets and submit them at the next training session.

2. Ask trainees to read introduction to Module 6.

3. Ask trainees to review Exercise 6.1 and come to the next session prepared to do it.

EXERCISE 5.2
IDENTIFYING COMMUNICATION STOPPERS
IN CERTAIN RESPONSES

Purpose

To provide practice for trainees to identify the kind of communication stoppers in comments.

Introduction to Exercise

Exercise 5.2 is designed for being done outside of the training session. Several statements are provided so that trainees can analyze the communication stoppers and identify the kind according to list supplied in Exercise 5.1.

Training Procedures

1. Discuss with trainees the answers they recorded and why. The answers as we have them are as follows:

Answers	Stoppers
11	1. Kidding
10	2. Diverting
9	3. Diagnosing
8	4. Sympathizing
7	5. Praising
6	6. Criticizing
5	7. Advising
4	8. Persuading
3	9. Moralizing
2	10. Threatening
1	11. Ordering

2. Collect Exercise 5.2 Sheets.

Homework for Trainees
After Group Meeting

Assignments have been made at close of Exercises 5.1 and 6.1.

EMPATHY SKILL

Purpose

To enable trainees to learn and use empathy—accurately perceiving the meaning and feelings of the helpee and then communicating the understanding to the helpee.

Approximate Time

Exercise 6.1—30 to 60 minutes in training session
Homework—15 to 30 minutes

Exercise 6.2—30 to 60 minutes in training session
Homework—15 to 30 minutes

Exercise 6.3—30 to 60 minutes in training session
Homework—10 to 15 minutes

Exercise 6.4—30 to 60 minutes in training session
Homework—20 to 30 minutes

Exercise 6.5—30 to 60 minutes in training session
Homework—20 to 30 minutes

Exercise 6.6—30 to 60 minutes in training session
Homework—10 to 15 minutes

Exercise 6.7—30 to 60 minutes in training session
Homework—10 to 15 minutes

Exercise 6.8—30 to 60 minutes in training session or total Exercise may be as homework requiring 60 to 90 minutes of homework

Exercise 6.9—30 to 45 minutes in training session
Homework—10 to 15 minutes

Materials

Peer Power: Book 1, Introductory Program, one for each trainee

Introduction to Module

Module 6 consists of several exercises and will require three or more training sessions. Empathy skill requires not only knowledge but also practice.

Empathic behavior is the skill of listening to others with understanding. The helper accurately perceives the meaning and feelings of the helpee. Generally, trainees would not have high ratings in empathic behaviors prior to the training sessions, therefore, Module 6 takes on new emphasis because empathy is so important in peer counseling.

Training Procedures

Session Number	Suggested Activities Each Session for Different Possible Number of Sessions		
	3 Sessions	4 Sessions	5 Sessions
	Introduce	Introduce	Introduce
First	6.1 6.2.	6.1	6.1
Second	6.3 6.4 6.5	6.2 6.3 6.4	6.2 6.3
Third	6.6 6.7 6.8	6.5 6.6	6.4 6.5
Fourth		6.7 6.8	6.6 6.7
Fifth			6.8

1. Review training time, length of each session, and ability of trainees to learn new material.

2. Devise approach to Module 6, so as to divide the eight exercises into convenient groupings, i.e., introduction to Module 6 and Exercise 6.1 covered in one session, Exercises 6.2 and 6.3 in another, or consider whether the procedure should be slower (then do only 6.2) or faster (then perhaps do 6.2, 6.3, and 6.4) in one session.

Evaluation Process

Evaluate whether or not the trainees are learning the skill by the way they respond during the cluster and group discussions and how well they are doing on the Exercise Sheets, which can be collected at each training session and reviewed between sessions.

Measuring Outcomes

1. Identify the degree of accuracy in discriminating the effectiveness of helpers' responses in all Exercises within the Module.

2. Identify the degree of accuracy in helpers' responses to feeling and meaning in all Exercises within the Module.

3. Determine the accuracy in homework responses to Exercises which identify discrimination and communication of empathy.

EXERCISE 6.1
EMPATHY SKILL
DISCRIMINATING AND RESPONDING BY PARAPHRASING

Purpose

To enable trainees to discriminate and respond by paraphrasing the helpee's concerns without changing the meanings of those concerns as expressed and felt by the helpee.

Introduction to Exercise

Paraphrasing will need to be explained as well as the purposes for using paraphrasing. The use of paraphrasing can be taught best by modeling and having trainees to practice through role playing. Use of films, filmstrips, prepared video tapes, and/or trainer modeling are effective means of introducing the paraphrasing.

Trainees may be concerned only about words used by the helpee. Stress the importance of understanding the feeling expressed and the intended message as well as the words in order to paraphrase accurately the concerns as expressed and felt by the helpee. This will take time to learn and will require repeated experience with meaningful feedbacks.

Training Procedures

1. Discuss what is meant by a paraphrase and give examples such as:

   Example: "My parents don't let me go anywhere I enjoy going."

   Paraphrase: "Your parents don't let you go places you like to go."

2. Refer trainees to Exercise 6.1, second page, and have them write helper response for the first helpee statement.

3. Have trainees share individually their response and discuss the response with constructive feedback.

4. Have trainees repeat Step 2 and 3 for the second helpee statement, second page, Exercise 6.1. As responses are shared, have the trainees rate the response according to the rating scale for paraphrasing, provided in Exercise 6.1, *Peer Power: Book 1.*

5. Show previously prepared video tape of low, medium, and high paraphrasing. (If no video equipment, Step 5 may be omitted.)

6. Model paraphrasing behavior by the trainer being a helper to a trainee who presents a problem. The group individually rates trainer's response as high, medium, or low according to the rating scale for paraphrasing.

7. By moving around the total group circle, have each person serve as a helper to the person next to him/her while the other trainees in the group rate the helper's response. Have the trainees explain their ratings. The trainer should rate last.

   NOTE: In teaching paraphrasing, the trainer would be wise to explain the need for the helper to repeat silently the exact words in order to assure self-understanding before putting the response into an accurate paraphrase comment.

8. Continue moving around the circle until the trainees are fairly consistent in their ratings with other trainees.

9. Ask trainees to form clusters of three and follow the directions provided in Exercise 6.1 and to complete the Exercise. (As trainer, move from group to group and assist where needed.)

10. Collect Exercise 5.2 and 6.1 Sheets.

11. Return Exercise 5.1 Sheets with written comments.

EXERCISE 6.2
FEELING WORDS

Purpose

The purpose of this exercise is to enable trainees to learn additional feeling words and to increase their awareness of feeling words.

Introduction to Exercise

In Exercise 6.1, the trainees improved their paraphrasing, and one may have started them to understand their feelings. Often individuals are unable to think of feeling words, and unless they have the vocabulary, it will be difficult to learn the feeling part of empathy. This exercise will at least give them a vocabulary.

Training Procedures

1. Ask the trainees to read the list of feeling words.

2. Brainstorm, using the whole group, additional words. Have the trainees write them.

3. Have the trainees look at the exercises and respond using a feeling word from the list.

4. Ask each person to give a statement, and the person next to him/her responds using one of the feeling words.

Homework for Trainees
After Group Meeting

1. Govern the homework assigned according to the Exercises planned to cover in the next training session.

2. Have trainees complete Exercises 6.3 and 6.4 or whatever Exercises planned to be covered in the next training session.

EXERCISE 6.3
EMPATHY SKILL
RESPONDING TO FEELINGS

Purpose

To enable trainees to understand and respond to helpee's feelings.

Introduction to Exercise

In Exercises 6.1 and 6.2, the trainees improved their paraphrasing, and one may have started getting them to understand and include in their responses an understanding of the helpee's feelings. During Exercise 6.3 the emphases are upon understanding and responding to those feelings. The trainee needs to hear all of the meaning expressed by the helpee. Even though stress may be upon words expressed by the helpee also, assist the trainees in being aware of understanding feelings by how the words are expressed, i.e., tone differences, quality variances, rate of speech, and body movements for emphases.

Training Procedure

1. Discuss what is meant by feelings.

   Optional: Distribute a list of feeling words so that trainees can better understand what is meant by feelings.

2. Discuss importance of not only listening for words but also listening for feelings.

3. Teach the helper to respond to a helpee's statement in the following manner. "You feel _____ because _____" This response paraphrases accurately the feelings and the meaning of the helpee's statement.

   Example—Helpee: "This has been a very rough week."

   Helper: "You feel (tired, exhausted, worn out) because it's been a very rough week."

4. Model the behavior being taught. Trainees then rate trainer's responses based upon accurate feeling and meaning.

   Optional: Show previously prepared video tape of behaviors to be taught.

5. Have trainees to share responses to helpee statements in Exercise 6.3. As one trainee shows a response, have others discuss the feeling expressed by the response, e.g., teach them how to provide meaningful feedback to the trainee (helper) who shared the response.

6. After the trainer has modeled the behavior, have two trainees role play in the total group where one trainee is given the task of being a helper to another trainee (helpee). The helpee is to make one statement, the helper one response, and then the response is rated by the group. The rest of the group rates "high (H)," "medium (M)," and "low (L)," and gives feedback to the helper. Each trainee is required to give a rating of "high (H)," "medium (M)," or "low (L)" to the helper's response according to the rating in Exercise 6.6, *Peer Power* book.

7. As trainees develop the facility for discriminating feelings, provide them with alternative response patterns such as:

   You sound
   You're angry
   It bothers you

8. Have trainees identify other alternative response patterns.

9. Emphasize that the helper's communication should accurately perceive the position of the helpee relative to his/her immediate feelings and the reason or conditions which are generating those feelings. Example of being accurately aware of the helpee's position.

   Helpee's thought—"I see the dog."
   Helpee's statement—"Will the dog bite?"
   Helper's thought—"She is afraid of the dog."
   Helper's statement—"You're afraid the dog will bite you."

10. Optional: Have trainees role play in triads with one member taking role of helpee and making a statement, another member being helper and paraphrasing the statement so as to have responded to meaning and feeling, and third member providing feedback after the response. (This may be postponed until Exercise 6.4 is taught.)

Homework for Trainees
After Group Meeting

1. If time elapses between Exercises 6.3 and 6.4, ask trainees to record five statements they hear made by others that have feelings expressed. Following each statement, write the response they, as helper, would make to that statement. Be prepared to discuss with the other trainees and to have trainees submit the material to you at the next training session.

2. Assign the Exercises in *Peer Power: Book 1, Introductory Program* that are to be covered at next session.

EXERCISE 6.4
EMPATHY SKILL
FEELINGS AND EMOTIONS

Purpose

To enable trainees to examine how different words may be used to express similar meanings and how "strength" of a word can communicate different feelings and emotions.

Introduction to Exercise

Exercise 6.4 is an extension of Exercise 6.3. The trainees need to review words that express feelings and emotions and to examine how different words with similar meaning can communicate different feelings and emotions. The Exercise contains examples of words and the trainees will be able to brainstorm many more so as to expose the trainees to a pool of words for their use in paraphrasing meaning expressed by helpee.

Training Procedures

1. Discuss the purpose for Exercise 6.4 and the importance for the trainees.

2. Review with trainees their responses to Exercise 6.4 Sheets and their reasons for different responses given.

3. Have trainees "brainstorm" feeling words and distinguish between feeling words that show different levels of emotion.

    Example: gentle—strong—very strong—annoyed—irritated—"ticked off"

4. Have trainees role play in triads the concepts being taught. Have trainees take roles so that one is helper, one is helpee, and one is providing feedback (rater). Have them to change roles and do the role play three times so that each of the roles is performed by each trainee.

5. Collect Exercises 6.3 and 6.4 Sheets.

6. Return Exercises 5.2 and 6.1 Sheets with written comments.

Homework for Trainees
After Group Meeting

1. Assign the Exercises in *Peer Power: Book 1* that are to be covered at next session (will need to have at least Exercise 6.5 completed).

2. Ask trainees to review the Exercises and come prepared to do them at the next session.

EXERCISE 6.5
EMPATHY SKILL
DESCRIBING FEELINGS

Purpose

To increase trainees' ability to respond to the hidden and surface feelings of the helpee.

Introduction to Exercise

Feelings as expressed may be obvious (surface feelings) or all of the feelings may not be expressed or may be withheld intentionally. The underlying or hidden feelings are very important in peer counseling and Exercise 6.5 is done to help trainees focus on both hidden and surface feelings. A helper to be effective must respond accurately to hidden feelings. Prepare a list of feelings words and distribute to trainees.

Training Procedures

1. Discuss hidden and surface feelings and help trainees understand why they exist, the importance of the helper responding to both, and how the helper may recognize hidden feelings.

2. Discuss the responses trainees have for the Situations in Exercise 6.5. Have one trainee to give his/her response and others identify words used to respond to the different kinds of feelings.

3. Use a technique to demonstrate hidden and surface feelings and involve the trainees in the responses.

   a. **Example:** Boy about to fight.

   The trainer plays the role of a boy going to fight another boy. The activity works best when the trainer goes around the room in progression, having each group member respond to one of trainer's feelings.

If a trainee makes an accurate response, proceed to next person, express another feeling and wait for response. When a trainee gives inaccurate response or uses another category, coach the trainee to improve. Do not hold standards that are too high at early stage of listening skills.

This exercise is excellent to demonstrate difficulty in developing empathic responses and is an opportunity to point out some pitfalls and errors.

b.   **Example:** Boy angry with another boy.

The trainer plays the role of a boy who is angry with another boy in a math class and has determined to do something about his anger.

Feelings the trainer will use in the dialogue are to be used in sequence.

"There is this kid in my math class that really bugs me."

"He always picks on me and calls me names."

"I think I'm going to punch him in the nose the next time he calls me a name."

From this point forward, the trainer responds flexibly to the helpee's response and develops discussion of the problem along these lines:

"Concerned about what might happen to me."

"Concerned about what the teacher will do."

"Concerned about what the principal will do."

"Concerned about what parents will do."

"Concerned about what other boy will do."

"Maybe boy is just trying to bug me."

"Maybe I can ignore him."

c.   **Example:** Worker creating a fight with co-worker. (Note to Trainer— follow same instructions as boy about to fight.)

The trainer role plays an assembly line worker about to fight another assembly line worker.

"There is this guy on the line that really bugs me."

"He is always calling me names and smarts off to me."

"I think I am going to punch him in the nose the next time he calls me Nigger."

From this point, the trainer responds flexibly to the helpee's response and develops the problem along these lines:

"Concerned about what might happen because he is much bigger."

"Concerned I might get fired."

"Concerned what will happen to family."

"Concerned about whether I could get another job because I do not have high school diploma."

"Maybe he has some hang up."

"Maybe I can ignore him."

4. Collect Exercise 6.5 Sheets.

5. Return Exercises 6.3 and 6.4 Sheets with written comments.

Homework for Trainees
After Group Meeting

1. Assign the Exercise in *Peer Power: Book 1, Introductory Program* that are to be covered at next session. (Exercise 6.6 needs to be studied but no written work to be prepared.)

2. Ask trainees to review the Exercises and come prepared to do and/or discuss them at the next session.

EXERCISE 6.6
EMPATHY SKILL
PARAPHRASING FEELING: RATING THE HELPER

Purpose

To improve trainees' ability to determine the effectiveness of paraphrasing feelings.

Introduction to Exercise

In the previous exercises trainees had to role play and provide feedback to each other. By now they should be ready to focus attention on how well they can determine whether or not a helper's response is effective in paraphrasing feelings and emotions.

Assist the trainees in focusing their feedback on the behavior instead of the person (helper). Have them feedback what was done rather than what helper was trying to do. If person who provides the feedback is able to suggest another way and why, then have those suggestions made but only after feedback on what actually was done. The focus is not what was observed (i.e., helper behaviors seen and heard) by the rater rather than inferences (i.e., interpretations and conclusions) made by the rater even though the inferences are based on what was observed.

Training Procedures

1. Point out the importance of the rater and what can be learned by doing the rating and by being rated.

2. Listen to and respond to feelings and concerns expressed by the trainees about rating.

3. Model two helper responses before rating. (Suggested that trainer take the role of helper during the modeling.) To rate more accurately the level of helper responses, a series of two or more helper responses is often needed, thus enabling the rater to hear and see helpee statement and other behavior following the helper's first response. In modeling the responses use two helper responses and then rate. The pattern is as follows.

   Helpee: Statement of concern made.

   Helper: Paraphrased response to show helpee that helper understands the concern and the feelings and emotions associated with the concern.

   Helpee: Follow-through statement which often is a further self-exploration, a repeat of the first statement, or a less revealing statement than the first one.

   Helper: Additional paraphrasing.

   Rater: Provides feedback on observations (seen and heard) of helper's behaviors in responding to concerns including feelings and emotions.

   Example: Helpee: "This has been a very rough week."

   Helper: "You feel (tired, exhausted, worried) because it has been a rough week."

   Helpee: "Yes, but the weekend is coming up and I'm excited."

   Helper: "Even though the week has been rough you feel excited about the weekend."

4. Have the trainees rate the trainer during the modeling.

5. Repeat the modeling until the ratings by the trainees are almost all the same for each role play.

6. Ask the trainees to form triads and follow the directions for completing Exercise 6.6, Part A.

7. Move from cluster (triad) to cluster assisting where needed.

8. Have trainees discuss as a total group after each role play in the triads the concerns and feelings they have.

9. After completing three role plays in the triad (i.e., each trainee has role played helpee, helper, and rater), introduce three helper responses where the pattern is helpee, helper, helpee, helper, helpee, helper, and then feedback by rater. The purpose is to work toward helper being able to use what is being learned not only to respond to each helpee statement but also to make a series of responses which will lead to complete peer counseling sessions. Model the three response patterns.

10. Have trainees to continue as directed in Steps 6, 7, and 8 and complete Exercise 6.6, Part B.

11. Collect Exercise 6.6 Sheets.

12. Return Exercise 6.5 Sheets with written comments.

Homework for Trainees
After Group Meeting

1. Assign the Exercises in *Peer Power: Book 1, Introductory Program* that are to be covered at next session. (Exercise 6.7 needs to be studied but no written work to be prepared.)

2. Ask trainees to review the Exercises and come prepared to do and/or discuss them at the next session.

EXERCISE 6.7
ATTENDING AND EMPATHY
RATING THE HELPER ON ATTENDING AND EMPATHY

Purpose

To have trainees have experience in doing both skills of attending and empathy.

Introduction to Exercise

The trainees have practiced attending skill (Module 4) and empathy skill (Module 6) and should be ready to combine the skills in responding to situations. The Peer Counseling Training Program is designed to teach a skill and then combine that skill with previously learned skills.

The teaching technique utilized is trainees interacting with each other through role playing and feedback from one another and the trainer. Rating Flow Sheet is provided to facilitate recording feeling words and ratings of helper's response in terms of feelings, paraphrased meanings, and attending.

Training Procedures

1. Explain the purpose and procedure for Exercise 6.7.

2. Respond to and have trainees discuss concerns they have as a result of reviewing Exercise 6.7.

3. Remind trainees that Rating Scale for Attending Behavior was in Exercise 4.2 and Rating Scale for Empathy Response is in Exercise 6.7.

4. Review the job of the rater. Each response made by the helpee: (1) Feeling word, (2) Quality of feeling word (how accurate), (3) Accuracy of responding to helpee's meaning, and (4) Level of attending. (Refer to Rating Flow Sheet in Exercise 6.7, Peer Power Book 1.) An example of words and their respective ratings for the Rating Flow Sheet would be as follows:

Feeling Words		Feeling	Meaning	Attending
a.	Concerned	high	high	high
b.	Worried	medium	medium	medium
c.	Upset	medium	medium	medium
d.	No feeling word	low	low	low

5. Ask the rater to rate all three responses before feedback is given to the helpee.

6. Encourage the helpee to use the same problems in sequential practice interchanges. This process develops depth, consistency, and direction toward problem solving and cuts down the necessity of presenting a new problem each time. Guide trainees to use the same concern for each of their four initiating statements.

7. Demonstrate the process by taking the role of helper and having the total group to rate trainer and discuss their ratings after each role play.

   Optional:

   a. Show video tape example of High, Medium, Low-three responses.

   b. The trainer may work with video tape and replay tape for group.

   c. The trainer may provide helpers with example of problems if participants have none of their own.

8. Ask the trainees to cluster in triads and follow the directions for completing Exercise 6.6.

9. Move from cluster to cluster and provide assistance where needed.

10. Stop the role playing periodically and have the trainees to share and discuss their experiences.

11. Collect Exercise 6.7 Sheets.

12. Return Exercise 6.6 Sheets with your written comments.

Homework for Trainees
After Group Meeting

1. Assign the Exercises in *Peer Power: Book 1, Introductory Program* that are to be covered at next session. (Exercise 6.8 needs to be studied and Homework completed prior to next session. The directions are within the Exercise.)

2. Ask trainees to come prepared to discuss Exercise 6.8.

EXERCISE 6.8
EMPATHY SKILL
FACILITATIVE AND NON-FACILITATIVE DIALOGUE

Purpose

To enable trainees to grasp the extended dialogue between helpee and helper and to recognize the differences between a facilitative and a non-facilitative helper.

Introduction to Exercise

Exercise 6.8 is designed so that it can be used during a training session or totally as a Homework activity. The trainees through studying the two Dialogues will be able to understand how the helper can assist the helpee to probe into an expressed concern.

The directions for analysis of Dialogues I and II are for trainees to identify communication stoppers which occur in Dialogue II. The trainee is then directed to explain how the two differ which hopefully will cause the trainee to analyze own behaviors and consider how to improve own helper behaviors.

Training Procedures for Use
During Training Session

1. Have trainees complete Exercise 6.8 as Homework prior to training session.

2. Dramatize the two Dialogues by having trainees read the Dialogue.

3. Discuss the two Dialogues and the response labels which the trainees chose for each helper response. The responses as we key them are as follows:

	Dialogue I			Dialogue II	
Item Number	**Response Letter**	**Kind of Response**	**Item Number**	**Response Letter**	**Kind of Response**
6.	a	advising	39.	o	open-ended questions
8.	a	advising	41.	m	empathic responding (H)
10.	g	moralizing	43	r	underlying feelings
12.	h	persuading	45.	r	underlying feelings
14.	d	diverting	47.	m	empathic responding (H)
16.	g	preaching	49.	m	empathic responding (H)
18.	p	paraphrase words	51.	r	underlying feelings
20.	n	paraphrase words	53.	m	empathic responding (H)
22.	f	kidding	55.	m	empathic responding
24.	d	diverting	57.	r	underlying feelings
26.	h	preaching	59.	m	empathic responding
28.	n	minimal responding	61.	m	empathic responding (H)
30.	h	persuading	63.	m	empathic responding (H)
32.	j	supporting	65.	m	empathic responding (H)
34.	d	diverting	67.	m	empathic responding (H)
			69.	m	empathic responding (H)
			71.	r	underlying feelings
			73.	o	open-ended questions
			75.	m	empathic responding
			77.	j	supporting
			79.	o	open-ended questions

Homework for Trainee
After Group Meeting

1. Assign the Exercises in *Peer Power: Book 1, Introductory Program* that are to be covered at next session. (Exercise 6.9 is to be completed before the next training session.)

2. Ask trainees to review the Exercises and come prepared to do and/or discuss them at the next training session.

3. Hear and respond to trainees' concerns pertaining to Empathy Skill, Module 6.

4. Collect Exercise 6.8 Sheets.

5. Return Exercise 6.7 Sheets (and Exercise 6.6 Sheets if not previously done) with written comments.

EXERCISE 6.9
EMPATHY SKILL
CHOOSE THE BEST EMPATHY RESPONSE

Purpose

To provide the trainees with experience in choosing the best response from among three possible responses for each situation.

Introduction to Exercise

The Exercise will enable one to examine how well the trainees can select best response from among possible ones. The Exercise requires a minimal amount of time to complete the selection, but discussion among the trainees can be extensive and interesting.

Training Procedures

1. Discuss with the trainees the outcomes desired from them doing the Exercise.

2. Discuss the responses they have for the three Situations and include in the discussion the three questions raised in Direction Number 4. The best response for each situation as we have each keyed is as follows:

Situation A: Response 2   Situation B: Response 1   Situation C: Response 1

3. Discuss the trainees comments from their Homework to Analysis of Dialogues I and II, last page of Exercise 6.8.

4. Collect Exercise 6.8 Sheets.

5. Return Exercises 6.7 Sheets with your written comments if not done previously.

Training Procedures
If Used as Homework

1. Have trainees complete Exercise 6.9 outside of training session.

   Optional: Assign trainees in clusters of two or three to do Exercise 6.9 together outside of training sessions. The purpose is to enable them to discuss and share with each other the various points.

2. Collect Exercise 6.9 sheets at next training session.

3. Return during the next training session Exercise 6.7 Sheets with written comments if not done previously.

Homework for Trainees
After Group Meeting

1. Ask trainees to read introduction to Module 7 prior to next training session.

2. Ask trainees to review Exercise 7.1 and come prepared to do the Exercise during the next training session.

SUMMARIZING SKILL

Purposes

1. To enable trainees to learn summarizing skill which involves listening to helper's concerns.

2. To learn to summarize not only with helpee's words but also adding in such a manner that the helpee will gain new insight and added dimensions of awareness to the problem.

Approximate Time

Module 7—Introduction, 5 minutes for Homework

Exercise 7.1—60 to 90 minutes in training session Homework—20 to 30 minutes

Exercise 7.2—30 to 60 minutes in training session Homework—1 to 3 hours

Optional: No training session for Exercise 7.2

Materials

Peer Power: Book 1, Introductory Program, one copy for each trainee

Chalkboard and chalk or flip pad and felt pen

Optional: Video equipment with previously produced video tape containing examples of the behavior being taught

Introduction to Module

Developing summarizing responses is a skill that involves, listening completely to the helpee's concerns and then summarizing the problem in the helpee's own words while adding to the summary new insight into the helpee's problem. The helper attempts to shed new light and adds additional dimensions of awareness to the problem by using initiative responses.

The helper must be very attentive to the helpee. In Module 6 trainees practiced and developed their attending and empathy skills. The trainees, who are participating well in the training program and who demonstrate promise of being effective peer counselors, are able, at this stage of their development, to capture important thoughts and feelings expressed in the extended interchange. They need now to be able to feed back to the helpee the most important parts plus enabling the helpee to gain new insights. Summarizing skill will enable the trainee to do so.

Training Procedures

1. Review training session time to determine whether Exercise 7.2 is to be done as Homework only or as Homework plus a training session.

2. Review the total Module 7 before starting to teach it.

3. Prepare for the demonstrations and/or the video equipment use.

Evaluation Process

The effectiveness of the training process can be determined by the trainees' interaction in the techniques being employed. Their involvement, level of participation and concerns expressed can help determine what is occurring within them.

Measuring Outcomes

1. Measure summarizing responses by trainees' responses during demonstrations and during their role playing in triads.

2. Measure effectiveness in understanding and analyzing summarizing responses by Flow Sheets in Exercise 7.1.

3. Measure application of skills by Exercise 7.2 Sheets.

EXERCISE 7.1
SUMMARIZING:
RATING THE HELPER RESPONSES

Purposes

To enable trainees to study examples of, practice making, and evaluate summarizing responses.

Introduction to Exercise

In Exercise 7.1, *Peer Power: Book 1, Introductory Program*, is provided an example of an extended dialogue that contains summarizing responses. By having the trainees review the dialogue they will be able to understand better the extended dialogue process and how the summarizing responses can assist. The example dialogue can serve as a model.

In addition to the dialogue, the trainees probably will benefit from demonstrations with discussions. Following each demonstration, have helper ratings made by the other trainees, and then discuss the rating made by each and the bases for the rating, thus enabling trainees to observe an extended dialogue and response summarization, make a rating, and discuss the dialogue and rating.

Exercise 7.1 is designed to involve trainees and to provide modeling and feedback so that each trainee will develop the summarizing skill. The training session may be entered by some trainees with fear; however, the fear can be overcome through modeling and sufficient practice in the total group before asking them to role play in triads.

Training Procedures

1. Discuss summarizing skill, its use, and the purposes.

2. Review examples of a stem for a helper's summary response. Examples would include the following:

    a. What I hear you really saying is . . .

    b. It seems to me what you're saying is . . .

    c. The real meaning behind what you're saying is . . .

    d. The real meaning behind what you're feeling is . . .

    e. The important points seem to be . . .

3. Review the Extended Dialogue in *Peer Power*, Exercise 7.1, and assist the trainees with the concerns they have relating to the dialogue.

    a. Assist the trainees in listing the points expressed by the helpee.

       (1) Helpee is angry at his/her teacher for saying and doing two different things.

       (2) Helpee's boss makes a promise to him/her and then changes his/her mind.

       (3) Even the helpee's mom pushes him/her.

       (4) The helpee is fed up with school.

    b. Help the trainees learn about initiative responses which can and should be used at times where summarizing with helpee's words could be used. The initiative response is a means of assisting the helpee in gaining increased awareness of the problem and insight into alternatives. An example of an initiative response that could be used in place of helper response Number 14 in the Extended Dialogue example would be the following:

"What I hear you saying is that you don't like being controlled, and you feel angry because you have no control over yourself. You would like to say to everyone that you can do what you want to do, and you will by quitting school."

4. Discuss the Rating Scale for Summarizing Responses which is provided in the *Peer Power: Book 1*, Exercise 7.1.

5. Demonstrate an extended dialogue with a summarizing response and have each trainee rate the summarizing response. Discuss the ratings and the bases for them.

6. Model an extended dialogue, but just before making the summarizing response, stop the modeling and have the trainees identify the major points listed by the helpee (make a list on the chalkboard or flip pad). Then have the trainees each to write a summarizing response which they would give. Share and discuss the written responses. Have trainees provide feedback to the helper (trainee who has just shared his/her written summarizing response).

Optional: By means of video, play an extended dialogue and stop the video just prior to summarizing response. Have trainees do the activities in Number 6 and then play the video response.

7. Cluster the trainees in triads and have them follow the Directions in Exercise 7.1. Move from cluster to cluster and assist where needed.

Optional: Video tape one or more clusters during the role play and then play back the video for their review and comments.

8. After the trainees have completed the first extended dialogue, have them to share their feelings and concerns.

9. Continue the activities in the triads until each trainee has been in each role—helpee, helper, and rater.

10. Collect Exercise 7.1 Sheets.

11. Return Exercise 6.9 Sheets with written comments.

Homework for Trainees
After Group Meeting

1. Ask trainees to complete Exercise 7.2 before next training session.

2. If no training session time is to be spent on Exercise 7.2, then the Homework is assigned following Exercise 7.1.

3. If training session time is spent on Exercise 7.2, then ask trainees to complete Exercise 8.2 before the next training session.

EXERCISE 7.2
USING YOUR NEW SKILLS
YOUR DIARY

Purpose

To have trainees practice their new skills with persons they know other than members of the training program and to have trainees analyze what and how they did.

Introduction to Exercise

The trainees have learned and practiced three basic communication skills—attending, empathy, and summarizing. Trainees took the Peer Counseling Training Program with the intent of helping others. Now is a good time in the stage of development for trainees to practice their skills with other people.

The Exercise is designed to have trainees use their learned skills as they associate with others in everyday life. As they use the skills, trainees are directed to keep a diary in which they analyze what and how they did. Therefore, the Exercise is primarily homework, and if training session time is spent, the time would be spent on sharing what was done, the experiences and feelings trainees have, and on assisting them in improving their skills.

Four purposes of open-ended questions are identified in Exercise 8.1 in *Peer Power: Book 1, Introductory Program:*

1. Questions used to begin a conversation.

2. Questions used to elaborate on a point by requesting information.

3. Questions used to give an example to help the helpee understand his/her behavior better.

4. Questions used to focus on feelings of the helpee.

Even though examples of questions for each purpose are provided, additional explanation probably will be needed.

Training Procedures

1. Review during the time of the assignment the purpose of the Exercise and the Exercise Sheets where the information is to be recorded.

2. Make the Exercise primarily homework.

3. If training session time is spent, use the time in having trainees share their experiences, feelings, and written comments. Have trainees assist one another in improving their skills.

4. Collect Exercise 7.2 Sheets.

5. If a training session is held, return Exercise 7.1 Sheets with written comments.

Homework for Trainees
After Group Meeting

1. If no training session time is spent on Exercise 7.2, then the Homework is assigned following Exercise 7.1.

2. If training session time is spent on Exercise 7.2, then ask trainees to complete Exercise 8.1 and review Exercise 8.2 before the next training session.

QUESTIONING SKILL

Purpose

To enable the trainees to improve their questioning skill.

Approximate Time

Module 8—Introduction—5 to 10 minutes

Exercise 8.1—30 to 45 minutes in training session
Homework—30 to 60 minutes

Exercise 8.2—20 minutes in training session
Homework—30 to 60 minutes

Exercise 8.3—30 to 45 minutes in training session
Homework—15 to 30 minutes

Exercise 8.4—No training session time required or the option of 15 to 60 minutes in training session for review and practice of skills.
Homework—60 to 90 minutes

Materials

Peer Power: Book 1, Introductory Program, one copy for each trainee

Optional: Video equipment with previously produced video tape containing example of the behavior being taught.

Introduction to Module

Questioning is an important part of the dialogue between helpee and helper. Doing questioning in a skillful manner so as to be helpful to the helpee requires understanding and practice by the helper.

Module 8 is designed to provide information about questioning skill, the differences between open-ended questions and closed questions, and purposes for which questions can be helpful in the dialogue. The trainees are asked to prepare material (questions) on their own and obtain feedback; role play the behaviors during training session, obtain rater feedback, and practice the skill with friends and record what occurs. The trainer can make the experiences very meaningful for the trainees.

Generally one or two training sessions are needed, plus time to prepare material between sessions. If trainees are quick learners and training sessions are approximately sixty minutes or more, then Exercises 8.1 and 8.2 can be done in one session; otherwise, do one in each of two sessions. Exercise 8.3 is to be done as Homework with training time depending on what you feel is needed to facilitate trainees' development.

Training Procedures

1. Review the total Module 8 to understand the scope.

2. Plan to cover the material in one or two sessions and the determination of how many sessions will depend upon available time for each session and how well these trainees are able to comprehend new material.

3. Proceed as suggested in the specific Training Procedures for each of the Exercises.

Evaluation Process

A determination can be made of how well trainees are learning by analyzing the feedback obtained during the training sessions and from the Exercise Sheets they prepare. If trainees are having difficulty, one may need to use one or more training sessions for review and additional practice before progressing into additional material in *Peer Power: Book 1, Introductory Program.*

Measuring Outcomes

1. Measure trainees' ability to know the difference between open-ended and closed questions by the Homework preparation done for Exercise 8.1.

2. Measure recognition and effectiveness of use by what occurs during role playing, recording, and feedback in Exercise 8.2.

3. Measure application by what occurs in homework when questioning skill is used with friends in completing Exercise 8.3.

EXERCISE 8.1
QUESTIONING SKILL
OPEN INVITATION TO TALK
(OPEN-ENDED QUESTIONS)

Purpose

To enable trainees to learn how to use questioning effectively and to keep the interchange ongoing with the helpee.

Introduction to Exercise

The difference between closed questions and open-ended questions is one of the first things to teach. The open-ended question encourages the helpee to explore himself/herself and concerns held. Through use of the open-ended questions, the helper also communicates a willingness to assist the helpee in the exploration. The wording for use in open-ended questions will need to be taught as well as demonstrating the use of the questions.

The closed question tends to cut off the dialogue by emphasizing factual content rather than feelings. The closed question usually can be answered by a yes or no or with a few words. The helpee often feels when a closed question is asked by the helper that the helper lacks interest in the helpee.

Training Procedures

1. Discuss differences between open-ended and closed questions.

2. Model open-ended and closed questions. Also show how the questions can be used for different purposes. Some purposes and examples are provided in the Exercise 8.1 in the *Peer Power, Book 1, Introductory Program.*

   Optional: Use video equipment to show previously prepared video tape of open-ended and closed questions.

3. Have trainees share and discuss examples of their open-ended and closed questions which they prepared in Exercise 8.1.

4. Discuss the trainees' concerns about open-ended questions and their use.

5. Collect Exercise 8.1 Sheets.

6. Return Exercise 7.2 Sheets (also 7.1 Sheets if not previously returned) with written comments.

EXERCISE 8.2
IDENTIFYING GOOD QUESTIONS

Purpose

To provide experience for the trainees in recognizing good questions.

Introduction to Exercise

First recognize both good questions and poor ones. This exercise can either be used as homework or be done during the training time and discussed as the trainees mark their responses.

Training Procedures

1. Ask the trainees to read and rate each question.

2. After reading the question, pause, and answer it in terms of poor, fair, good, and excellent.

3. Check the appropriate place.

Homework for Trainees
After Group Meeting

1. Have trainees review Exercise 8.3 and come prepared to do as stated in the directions.
2. If Exercise 8.3 is done in the same training session, then there is no homework for this session.

EXERCISE 8.3
QUESTIONING SKILL
RATING THE HELPER

Purpose

To provide experience for the trainees in using and rating open-ended questions.

Introduction to Exercise

Trainees need an opportunity to practice the open-ended questioning skill. While doing so, they should continue using other skills where and when appropriate. Exercise 8.2 is designed to provide this experience and to have trainees assist one another in learning and improving skills. An example is provided of an extended dialogue using open-ended questions and empathy. Trainees can study the example to be prepared for role playing during the training session.

Training Procedures

1. Answer any questions the trainees have regarding the directions given for Exercise 8.3.

2. Have the trainees do role playing in triads and have them complete the Rating Flow Sheet.

3. Move from cluster to cluster and assist where necessary.

   Optional: Videotape one or more of the clusters during role play and replay the tape for the trainee's review.

4. After each extended dialogue is role played, discuss what occurred and assist the trainees in completing the Rating Flow Sheet.

5. Collect Exercise 8.3 Sheets.

6. If homework time existed between Exercises 8.1 and 8.3, then return Exercise 8.1 Sheets with written comments. If no homework time was available, retain Exercise 8.1 Sheets to be returned later.

Homework for Trainees
After Group Meeting

1. Ask trainees to do Exercise 8.4 during the week and submit the completed sheets to you.

2. Ask trainees to review the introductory comments to Module 9.

3. Ask trainees to study the information supplied in Exercise 9.1 and complete the exercise sheets before the next training session.

4. If Exercises 9.1, 9.2, and 9.3 are to be covered in the same training session, ask the trainees to both study and complete Exercise 9.2 at home. They should study Exercise 9.3 but should leave the exercise sheets to be completed during the next training session.

EXERCISE 8.4
QUESTIONING SKILLS DIARY

Purpose

To have trainees practice their questioning skill with friends.

Introduction to Exercise

The exercise consists of activities to be done outside the training session to provide the trainees with practice of questioning skill. As such, no training session time is needed unless the trainer wants to have the trainees discuss their experiences and use the feedback to decide whether or not additional training is needed before continuing on to new exercises.

Training Procedures

1. Following completion of Exercise 8.3, have trainees do Exercise 8.4 outside the training session.

2. If feedback is desired to determine competencies of trainees, discuss Exercise 8.4 sheets in the next training session. Provide opportunities for trainees to improve their competencies in the skills taught thus far before continuing in the *Peer Power* book.

3. Collect Exercise 8.4 sheets at the training session immediately following their assignment.

4. If training session time is used for Exercise 8.4, return Exercises 8.1 and 8.3 sheets with written comments.

Homework for Trainees
After Group Meeting

Continuation of assignment made as homework at close of Exercise 8.3.

GENUINENESS SKILL

Purpose

To enable trainees to learn about, recognize, and use genuineness skill.

Approximate Time

Module 9 Introduction, 5 minutes for Homework

Exercise 9.1—30 to 60 minutes in training session
Homework—30 to 45 minutes

Exercise 9.2—10 to 20 minutes in training session
Homework—30 to 45 minutes

Exercise 9.3—10 to 20 minutes in training session
Homework—5 minutes

Exercise 9.4—30 to 40 minutes in training session
Homework—10 to 20 minutes

Exercise 9.5—15 to 30 minutes in training session
Homework—5 to 10 minutes

Exercise 9.6—10 to 15 minutes in training session
Homework—10 to 20 minutes

Exercise 9.7—30 to 45 minutes in training session
Homework—20 to 30 minutes

Exercise 9.8—30 to 45 minutes in training session
Homework—5 to 10 minutes

Exercise 9.9—no time required in training session
Homework—30 to 45 minutes

Materials

Peer Power Book 1: Introductory Program, one copy for each trainee

Tape Recorder for each three trainees

Chalkboard and chalk or flip pad and pen

Optional: Video equipment with previously prepared video tape of the behaviors being taught

Introduction to Module

In Module 9 the major focus is on genuine responses. The trainees are to be taught how they can share their own feelings about what the helpee is saying or doing and maintain or enhance the relationship by doing so. By enabling the trainees to learn genuineness skill, they can express their feelings rather than conceal feelings or become aggressive.

In addition to learning about non-responsive, non-genuine, and genuine responses, the trainees will be asked to use the other skills also. Opportunities for experience is to be provided for the trainees to integrate all five peer counseling skills taught in the training sessions thus far.

The number of training sessions will depend upon your situation and the abilities of the trainees. We recommend a minimum of three training sessions with the Exercises grouped as shown on the chart in this session, however, the Exercises are each self-contained and can be grouped together differently or taught one in each session.

**Suggested Grouping of Exercises
By Training Sessions**

First Session Complete Exercises 9.1, 9.2, and 9.3

Second Session Complete Exercises 9.4, 9.5, and 9.6

Third Session Complete Exercises 9.7 and 9.8 with Exercise 9.9 to be done outside of training session

Training Procedures

1. Decide on grouping of Exercises for the training sessions. The decision will make a difference in homework assignments and the time available for each Exercise.

2. Follow the sequence of Exercises and the Training Procedures for each.

3. Move from cluster to cluster during role playing to identify points which need additional emphases and perhaps to identify individual trainees who

may require additional assistance, maybe even outside of the regular training program.

4. Arrange for audio or video taping and playback. The trainees can gain much from seeing and/or hearing themselves. The feedback by trainer and trainee-raters can be facilitated by tape playback.

EXERCISE 9.1
GENUINENESS SKILL
A COMPARISON OF NONRESPONSIVE,
NONGENUINE, AND GENUINE RESPONSES

Purpose

To enable trainees to differentiate among the three kinds of responses—nonresponsive, nongenuine, and genuine—and to understand the feelings generally prompted in the person to whom the response is made.

Introduction to Exercise

This Exercise is designed to help trainees learn the difference among the three kinds of responses. By increasing their awareness and by having them prepare responses for different situations, they should be better able to use genuine responses with other people.

Learning the differences among the three kinds of responses may not be easy for some trainees. Examples will need to be given and demonstrations done to enable trainees to understand the importance of genuine responses. Placing the trainees into activities, that cause them to make and/or receive different responses, will assist them in gaining an understanding of the feelings generally caused in the person to whom the response is made.

1. Introduce genuineness skill by discussing different ways that a person lets others know about personal feelings.

2. Ask each trainee to discuss how he/she communicates anger, irritation, and so forth.

3. After trainees are discussing freely, have trainees determine how they handle anger by using the Chart of "Feelings During Three Kinds of Response Behaviors" for reference. The Chart is in Exercise 9.1 in *Peer Power: Book 1.*

4. As trainer, demonstrate different ways of initiating interchange concerning the helpee's feelings.

   Situation: The trainer plays the role of a person criticizing his/her brother. The trainer reads the following statements without telling which kind is going to be illustrated.

a. Nonresponsive Response

Trainer: "You must really like your brother."

Trainee Response: "No, he really irritates me."

Trainer requests that the group identify from the previous dialogue which of the three levels of genuineness the trainer's response modeled.

Trainer repeats modeling responses, using examples of nonresponsive responses, until trainees understand how to identify nonresponsive behavior.

b. Nongenuine Response

Trainer models the nongenuine behavior using the same situation.

Trainer: "You made a dumb statement about your brother."

Trainee Response: "Well, he is dumb! If you only knew."

Trainer repeats the two steps done in 4a.

c. Genuine Response

Trainer models the genuine response using the same situation.

Trainer: "When you criticize your brother, I feel uneasy and just want to leave the room."

Trainee Response: "Well, I'm not mad at him; I just get upset with him."

Trainer repeats the two steps done next in 4a.

5. As trainer, initiate a helper statement after which a trainee is asked to respond with feeling. The other trainees then identify which kind of genuineness is reported by the trainee (nonresponsive, nongenuine, or genuine). Repeat the process several times.

6. Optional: Introduce a role playing situation in which one says the following:

"I, the trainer, will go around the room in progression and make a series of statements, requesting a response from each trainee. As you hear the statement by the trainer and response by a trainee, the rest of you in the group are to decide the following three things—

Will the relationship be maintained as the result of the statement by me?

Is there a good chance the offending person, the trainee, will change his/her behavior?

Was I, the person who sent the message, honest with my feelings?"

Then state the role-playing situation:

"I have invited all of you to my house to listen to records. I have a new white carpet and all of you have muddy shoes."

Next make the following statement to a trainee you select to give a response:

"You dummy, didn't your mother teach you any differently than to walk on carpet with muddy feet!"

a. Response from a trainee . . .

b. Then ask the other group members "Does the trainee response meet the three conditions?"

Repeat the last process by making the following statement to a trainee chosen to give the response.

"Let me tell you a joke about a kid that was inconsiderate to his friend. . ."

a. Response from a trainee . . .

b. Then ask the other group members "Does the trainee response meet the three conditions?"

Discuss the trainee's comments and help them work with their concerns.

7. Collect Exercises 8.3 (if not previously collected) and 9.1.

8. Return Exercise Sheets which have not previously been returned. These may include 8.1, 8.2, and 8.3.

Homework for Trainees
After Group Meeting

1. If Exercise 9.2 is not covered in the same training session as 9.1, then ask trainees to study and complete Exercise 9.2 before next session.

2. If Exercise 9.2 is covered in the same training session as 9.1, then give no Homework between 9.1 and 9.2 because 9.2 should have been completed before start of training session.

EXERCISE 9.2
HOW OPEN AM I?

Purpose

To increase trainees' awareness of how open they are and with whom.

Introduction to Exercise

The openness one has may depend on several things including the situation, the topic, and the person or persons with whom one is sharing. This Exercise is designed to cause trainees to think about what they would share and with whom they would share which kinds of topics.

The closeness in relationship may increase the willingness to discuss a topic. After the trainees have recorded their topics with each of four kinds of persons, they are asked to mark their openness on a Likert type of scale.

Training Procedures

1. Discuss with the trainees the purpose of Exercise 9.2.

2. Have trainees share their feelings and comments from preparing Exercise 9.2.

3. Have trainees discuss the differences in kinds of topics discussed.

4. When trainees are discussing freely, move on to Exercise 9.3.

EXERCISE 9.3
OPENNESS CIRCLE

Purpose

To cause trainees to examine further their extent of openness and with whom.

Introduction to Exercise

The form for doing the Openness Circle Game is provided in Exercise 9.3, *Peer Power: Book 1*. All of the Directions are provided in the following section entitled, "Training Procedures." The game is one which often stimulates trainees' thinking and produces much discussion. The result may cause trainees to examine their own values and openness. Also, trainees may better understand the people with whom they work and their reluctance to discuss some topics and not others.

Training Procedure

1. Ask trainees to open *Peer Power: Book 1*, to Exercise 9.3 and prepare to complete the circle as you give them directions. (Each trainee will need a writing instrument.)

2. Explain the meaning of each of the circles which is as follows:

    Intimate Circle—feelings and experiences I share with closest friend (could be family).

    Friend Circle—feelings and experiences I share with the group with which I spend time

    Acquaintances' Circle—feelings and experiences I share with people I know casually.

    Strangers' Circle—feelings and experiences I share with people with whom I am not acquainted.

3. Review with the trainees what was learned in Exercise 9.2 which generally is that a closed person would share most of his/her feelings and experiences with only intimates. The more open a person is, the more feelings and experiences that person shares with friends, acquaintances, and strangers.

4. Ask the following series of questions and have trainees write the key word from the question on the appropriate area in the circle representing with whom they would share the following information.

    a. With whom would you share the fact that you have shoplifted?

    b. With whom would you share the fact that you have smoked pot?

    c. With whom would you share the fact that you cheat in school?

    d. With whom would you share a deep, personal problem?

    e. With whom would you share a physical problem?

    f. With whom would you share two good things about yourself?

    g. With whom would you share two bad things about yourself?

5. Ask each trainee to tell how many items were placed in each category of the circle. Record number of items on a big circle on chalkboard or flip pad so that trainees can understand how their own circle compares with the composite of all trainees.

6. Ask group to determine who is most closed and open in relationships with others according to placement of topics on circle.

7. Ask the most open and most closed trainees to stand at opposite ends of the room, which represents the extremes of the circle, with an area for those that are somewhat open or closed in the middle. then ask trainees to position themselves between the two extremes by talking with persons standing next to them to compare circles. As the result of the comparison, one trainee may find he/she is more open or closed than the person with whom he/she is talking. If so, change places to represent the newly interpreted position.

8. Point out that those trainees who see themselves as closed may have to work harder at being genuine.

9. Discuss the concerns the trainees have about openness.

10. Collect Exercises 9.2 and 9.3.

11. Return Exercises 8.3 (if not previously returned) and 9.1 with written comments.

Homework for Trainees
After Group Meeting

1. Ask trainees to study Exercise 9.4, then prepare the genuine message requested, and come to the next training session prepared to complete the Exercise.

2. If Exercise 9.5 is to be covered in the next training session, ask trainees to review it and come prepared to do the role playing during the training session.

3. If Exercise 9.6 is to be covered in the next training session, ask the trainees to complete it before the next session.

EXERCISE 9.4
PUTTING TOGETHER A GENUINE MESSAGE

Purpose

To have trainees examine in greater detail the contents of a genuine message and then practice making and analyzing genuine messages.

Introduction to Exercise

The genuine message is sent with an "I" message as opposed to a "you" (non-genuine) message. The four parts of the genuine message are described in *Peer Power: Book 1*, Exercise 9.4, with an example developed to identify the parts. In addition, a Communication Model for the helper to use in putting together a genuine message is provided.

Exercise 9.4 is a means to have trainees examine in greater detail the contents of genuine messages. Space is provided for writing a genuine message with the four parts, and space in chart form is provided to analyze two genuine messages, one from the trainer and one written by another trainee.

Training Procedures

1. Discuss the four parts of the genuine message as outlined in Exercise 9.4, *Peer Power: Book 1*, and work with the concerns expressed by the trainees.

2. Give illustrations of genuine messages and identify the four parts on chalkboard or flip pad in the same manner as trainees are to record in chart form in Exercise 9.4. Have trainees to participate in identification of the four parts.

3. Give the following statement and ask trainees to record the four parts in the space provided in their Exercise 9.4 chart.

   Situation: A friend borrowed $5 a week ago and has not paid it back or made any arrangements to pay it back. An example of genuineness would be: "I am really disappointed in you for not paying me back the $5 or letting me know when you would pay me back and that makes me very hesitant to ever loan you money again because I can't depend on your paying it back."

   Check their recordings which would resemble the following:

How I feel	—really disappointed
What has happened	—not paying me
How this affects me	—makes me very hesitant
Reason	—can't depend on you

4. Place the trainees in clusters of two and ask them to follow Directions 5, 6, and 7 on Exercise 9.4 Sheets.

5. Discuss any concerns the trainees have following their work in clusters.

6. Collect Exercise 9.4 Sheets.

7. Return Exercises 9.2 and 9.3 Sheets with written comments.

Homework for Trainees
After Group Meeting

The homework assignment depends upon the grouping of Exercises to be covered in each training session. If Exercises 9.5 and 9.6 are covered in the same session as 9.4, they should have been assigned previously. If not, assign them for the next session.

EXERCISE 9.5
WHEN TO USE A GENUINE MESSAGE

Purpose

To provide experience through role playing to use genuine messages.

Introduction to Exercise

Exercise 9.5 requires training session time to role play but does not require note taking or prior written work. The trainees need to read the Exercise and be prepared to do it. The entire purpose is to provide experience for the trainees to use genuine messages in the training session where the trainer can observe their proficiency and identify points which may need additional emphases.

Training Procedures

1. Discuss with the trainees the purpose of the Exercise and what the trainer will be doing during their role playing.

2. Cluster trainees in diads and ask them to follow the Directions in Exercise 9.5, *Peer Power: Book 1.*

    Optional: View and discuss a tape determining roles found in Exercise 9.5.

3. Stop the role playing after a short time to discuss their concerns and to share with them what was learned by moving from diad to diad.

4. Close the Exercise with a discussion of their experiences and concerns.

5. Tell the students no Exercise Sheets are to be submitted since no written material was prepared for Exercise 9.5.

EXERCISE 9.6
PRACTICE SENDING GENUINENESS RESPONSES

Purpose

To give trainees experience in writing genuine messages.

Introduction to Exercises

This Exercise enables trainees to study a situation and a non-genuine message and then develop a genuine message. This exercise reviews earlier material and practices and enables the trainer to evaluate from written material whether or not the trainees are learning the behavior.

Training Procedures

1. Have trainees discuss their genuine messages written for Exercise 9.6. The genuine message might be similar to the following:

    Situation 1. "I had to make special arrangements to go to the movies at the time you suggested. I feel you just take me for granted, that I can have the car anytime, and I don't feel like going through the hassle to go to the later feature."

    Situation 2. "I get irritated when you keep bugging me about keeping my room clean without considering my brother's part. I feel like moving my brother out because I get so mad at him."

Situation 3. "I feel so bad since you have been avoiding me for the last few days. It is really frustrating not being able to see you like I used to."

2. Discuss any concerns the trainees still have regarding genuine responses, and do the additional training that may be needed to bring their proficiency up to expected level.

3. Collect Exercise 9.6 Sheets.

4. Return any Exercise Sheets which were collected in a previous training session but have not been returned.

Homework for Trainees
After Group Meeting

1. Ask trainees to prepare for the next training session and to complete the homework where requested in those Exercises which will be covered in the next training session. The suggestion is to cover Exercises 9.7 and 9.8 during the next session.

2. Exercise 9.9 is to be done outside of the training session. It may be assigned to do before doing 9.7 and 9.8 in training session so as to discuss it along with 9.7 and 9.8.

EXERCISE 9.7
UNDERSTANDING HOW GENUINENESS IS USED

Purpose

To have trainees use empathic and genuineness responses in appropriate situations.

Introduction to Exercise

Exercise 9.7 enables the trainees to study more about genuineness and to use them along with empathy responses. Examples are provided including an extended dialogue with analysis.

The trainees are to role play and rate each other so as to provide meaningful feedback for their development. The trainer will be able to learn much about their development by moving from cluster to cluster and assisting where needed.

Exercises 9.7 and 9.8 may be done in the same training session if trainees are making good progress. If trainees are learning slowly or are having difficulty, the suggestion is that a time period elapse between the two Exercises.

Training Procedures

1. Demonstrate the empathy and genuineness responses by means of a dialogue with one of the trainees.

   Optional: Use video equipment to show the behavior desired and stop the video at different places to emphasize various points. Have the trainees take an active role in the discussion of the tape.

2. Discuss with the trainees their concerns about doing Exercise 9.7.

3. Cluster the trainees in triads and ask them to complete Exercise 9.7 according to the directions in *Peer Power* book with the additional verbal directions the trainer will provide. Have a means of either audio or video taping each triad's role playing.

4. Assign role to helpee, helper, and rater, and ask helper to establish the situation by describing the role function that the helpee will initiate (behavior which bothers helper). Ask rater to audio or video tape the role playing interchanges.

5. Ask helpee to role play behavior and ask helper to respond with four dimensions of genuineness skill (True Feelings, Specific Happenings, Reasons, and Effects).

6. Ask the helper to give a genuineness communication and then to follow the helpee's next statement with high-level empathy responses.

7. Tell helper that he/she may choose to continue empathic responses or alternate empathic and genuineness responses. Goals of the helper at this point will be the resolution of the relationship difficulties and maintaining or improving the relationship.

8. During the triad, role playing, and discussion, tell the trainees that the trainer will move from cluster to cluster to observe and facilitate role playing. Following the triad discussion groups, the trainer will participate in the feedback experience.

9. Have the rater after the first role-playing interchanges to play back the tape and stop it at various places. Rater is to ask helpee and helper to describe feelings at the stoping point of the tape. Suggest possible rater questions such as the following:

   —What were your feelings when the helper gave you a genuine response.

   —How did you (helpee) feel at this point in the interchange?

   —What behavior did you (helpee) want the helper to show?

Also the rater is to complete the Rating Flow Sheet provided in Exercise 9.7, *Peer Power: Book 1.*

10. Reverse roles until everyone has had a chance to play each role and an opportunity to tape each set of interchanges and discuss them.

11. Discuss any concerns the trainees have.

12. Collect Exercise 9.7 Sheets.

13. Return any Exercise Sheets collected in previous training sessions.

Homework for Trainees
After Group Meeting

1. If Exercise 9.8 has not been assigned, ask trainees to review it and be prepared to complete the Rating Flow Sheet in the next training session.

2. Ask trainees to review and complete Exercise 9.9 before the next training session if it has not been assigned previously.

EXERCISE 9.8
INTEGRATING COMMUNICATION SKILLS

Purpose

To provide practice for trainees to integrate their attending, empathy, questioning, summarizing, and their genuineness skills.

Introduction to Exercise

Exercise 9.8 follows well on Exercise 9.7 and may be done in the same training session. The trainees have learned five communication skills and need the opportunity to practice using all of them, if appropriate, in an extended dialogue. The experience is provided in Exercise 9.8 with other trainees during a training session so that the trainer can obtain feedback on what needs to be done to increase the trainees' skills.

Training Procedures

1. Discuss with trainees what the purpose of the Exercise is and answer any questions they have.

2. Cluster the trainees in triads, and ask them to take the roles of helpee, helper, and rater.

3. Ask the helpee to take a situation which he/she can role play for an extended interchange.

4. Ask the helper to use the appropriate communication response and to try to use the skills of attending, empathy, open-ended questioning, and genuineness.

5. Ask the rater to complete during role playing the Rating Flow Sheet for Integrating Communication Skills in *Peer Power: Book 1*, Exercise 9.8.

   Optional: Ask the rater to audio or video tape the role play and to use the tape during feedback given by the rater.

6. Move from triad to triad and assist where needed plus observe and listen for points which need to be emphasized.

7. At the end of the first role play and feedback, discuss as a total group the concerns of the trainees.

8. Repeat two more times the Training Procedures Numbers 3 through 7 with the trainees changing roles so that each has played all three roles.

9. Collect Exercise 9.8 Sheets.

10. Return any Exercise Sheets collected in prior training sessions which have not been returned previously.

Homework for Trainees
After Group Meeting

1. If Exercise 9.9 has not been assigned previously, ask the trainees to complete it prior to the next training session.

2. Ask trainees to study the introductory material to Module 10 and then study and complete Exercises 10.1 and 10.2 before the next training session.

EXERCISE 9.9
USING GENUINE RESPONSES

Purpose

To make trainees aware of opportunities for them to use their communication skills in everyday life and to have them record the genuine responses used between training sessions.

Introduction to Exercise

As stated in the purpose, the Exercise is a means to have trainees consider opportunities for them to use their improved and/or new skills in everyday life. Since Module 9 was devoted to genuine responses, the trainees are asked to record the genuine responses between the two training sessions.

The Exercise Sheets when reviewed by the trainer can be an excellent means of determining how well the trainees have mastered the skill, the kinds of conditions in which they use the skill, and which trainees may need special attention. Written comments by the trainer on the Exercise Sheets can be a way of reinforcing the good practices of the trainees and of calling their attention to behaviors that require additional attention.

Training Procedures

1. Have the Exercise 9.9 completed between training sessions.

2. If training is not progressing rapidly due to trainees' learning of the skills, use time in the next training session to discuss the trainees' experiences, their concerns, and their written comments.

3. Collect Exercise 9.9 Sheets at the next training session.

ASSERTIVENESS SKILL

Purposes

1. To enable trainees to learn about, recognize, and use assertiveness skills.

2. To learn assertive skills, both verbal and nonverbal, through the exercises, role playing, and practice.

Approximate Time

Module 10 Introduction—10 minutes reading as homework

Exercise 10.1—60 minutes in training session
Homework—60 minutes

Exercise 10.2—60 minutes in training session

Exercise 10.3—60 minutes in training session
Homework—30 minutes

Exercise 10.4—60 minutes in training session
Homework—30 to 120 minutes

Exercise 10.5—60 minutes in training session
Homework—30 minutes

Exercise 10.6—60 minutes in training session
Homework—30 minutes

Materials

Peer Power: Book 1, Introductory Program, one copy for each trainee

Tape recorder for every three trainees

Chalkboard and chalk or flip pad and pen

Optional: Video equipment with previously prepared video tape of the behaviors being taught

Introduction to Module

In Module 10 the major focus is on assertion, awareness, and assertive responses. The trainees are taught the differences among assertive, nonassertive, and aggressive communication. They also will be asked to decide in which relationships they would like to become more assertive. They are asked to keep a daily log, which is very important in helping them recognize how they are communicating.

The trainees also are asked to practice assertive skills. Assertiveness is actually an extension of genuineness and an integral part of openness and confrontation.

Training Procedures

1. Decide on grouping of Exercises for the training sessions. The decision will affect the homework assignments.

2. Follow the sequence of Exercises and the Training Procedures for each.

3. Move from cluster to cluster during role playing to identify points that need additional emphasis and to identify individual trainees who may require special assistance, perhaps outside of the regular training program.

4. Carefully read the logs and give written and verbal feedback to the trainees.

5. Arrange for audio or video taping and playback. The trainees can gain much from seeing and/or hearing themselves. The feedback by trainer and trainee-raters can be facilitated by tape replay.

6. Assertive behavior may be acquired by watching others model assertive responses. Modeling has an informative function—it shows group members how to be assertive; it gives them permission to behave similarly; it provides information about the consequences of such behavior; it strengthens existing assertive behavior, and it also establishes new skills in assertion.

   For example, watching the trainer model refusing an unreasonable request tells the group members, "This is an unreasonable request" (and helps them to discriminate between reasonable and unreasonable requests). It tells the group what verbal and nonverbal behaviors are appropriate. It shows the trainees how to make the response and lets them know that it is okay to stand up for one's rights.

   Modeling, therefore, produces learning primarily through the dissemination and retention of information. The observers characterize the modeled event symbolically in the form of images and verbal codes, and they store this information for future use (Bandura, 1971).

Note that attention is a necessary prerequisite for learning through modeling. The observer must recognize, differentiate, and attend to the distinctive features of the model's response (Bandura 1971). Several factors can influence an observer's responsiveness to modeling influences.

Research has shown that the most effective models are persons who are highly competent and who have prestige and status. This finding suggested that facilitators (because of their roles and skills) exert a considerable impact upon group members. It also provides another reason to emphasize the need for facilitators to be good role models.

In conclusion, it is important to note that the retention of modeled responses is greatly strengthened when the observer has the opportunity to rehearse and practice the modeled behavior.

7. Role playing is a learning-by-doing strategy and a key focus in the assertiveness training. Role playing may be defined as the behavioral enactment of an interpersonal encounter, but it involves more than merely acting out a scene. It encompasses a behavioral rehearsal of "those specific assertive responses which are to become part of their behavioral repertoire" (Jakubowski-Spencer, 1973a).

Role playing facilitates the acquisition of assertive behavior because it allows the group to practice their assertive skills in a safe environment. It provides valuable information about the assertive role player's behavior through self-observation and the observation of others. It strengthens self-confidence as well as assertive skills. It permits group members to learn from watching each other.

Group members are asked to volunteer incidents that have happened to them in the past or that they think will happen to them in the future.

8. Processing is one way of maximizing the effectiveness of group exercise. It involves taking a close look at what each individual has experienced and how group members interact with each other. The goals of processing are to encourage self-evaluation, to provide a mechanism by which feelings about self and others are shared, to encourage the individual to take risks, to aid in the acquisition of assertive skills, and to help develop feelings of trust and closeness.

Processing can most easily be implemented by asking group members to focus on their feelings, observations, and thoughts and to share them honestly and directly with the group.

Evaluation Process

As trainer, evaluate the process used in teaching assertive behavior skills by the feedback obtained from the trainees and by observations of the trainees' written work and their behavior during the sessions.

Measuring Outcomes

1. Use Exercises 10.1, 10.2, and 10.3 to identify the trainees' assertive skills.

2. Use Exercise 10.4 to evaluate how they are incorporating assertion into their daily lives.

3. Observe and listen during the role playing in Exercises 10.5 and 10.6 to measure the ease with which trainees are using assertiveness in their lives.

EXERCISE 10.1
DIFFERENCES AMONG ASSERTIVE, NONASSERTIVE, AND AGGRESSIVE BEHAVIOR

Purpose

To help the trainees learn the differences among these three important types of behavior. They will learn when it is appropriate to use each different style of communication.

Introduction to Exercise

This exercise is designed to help trainees learn the difference among the three kinds of responses. By increasing their awareness and by having them prepare responses for different situations, they should be better able to use assertive responses with other persons.

Learning the differences among these kinds of responses may not be easy for some trainees. Examples and demonstrations should be given to enable them to understand the importance of assertiveness in responses. Placing the trainees into activities that cause them to make and/or receive different responses will assist them in gaining an understanding of the feelings generally caused in the person to whom the response is made.

Training Procedures

1. Ask the trainees to read the material before the training session begins.

2. Ask the trainees to discuss how significant others behave toward them (parents, teachers, bosses, and so forth).

3. Ask the trainees to discuss how they communicate anger needs, and so forth.

4. Give examples of assertive, non-assertive, and aggressive behavior.

Situation:

Someone has borrowed my fur coat to wear to a dance but has not returned it—

"You are really inconsiderate by not bringing back my coat. If you can't be more considerate, I don't want to be your friend anymore."—aggressive

Says nothing about the coat.—nonassertive

"I'm worried about my coat. You promised to bring it back last week and still haven't. Please bring it back today because I need it to wear to a dance."—assertive.

5. Have each person in the group think about times when they behaved in an aggressive, non-assertive, and assertive manner. What were their feelings and what were the results? The leader may want to model an example.

Examples:

a. Assertive—"I took back a dress that did not have good workmanship. The owner did not want it back, but I was firm about the fact that I had shopped there many times and rarely returned anything."

Feelings: Confidence

Result: The owner returned my money.

b. Nonassertive—"My neighbor asked me to watch her small child. I was busy, but I said yes."

Feelings: Anger

Result: Cool toward neighbor and frustrated because I was so busy.

c. Aggressive—"I yelled at my coworker for not finishing a project on time."

Feelings: Justified at the time and guilty afterward.

Result: The project was completed, but the coworker would not speak to me.

6. Have the trainees name instances when someone was aggressive, nonassertive, and assertive. How did they feel and what were the results?

Homework for Trainees
After Group Meeting

1. Complete Exercise 10.1.

2. Fill out assertive profile.

EXERCISE 10.2
MY ASSERTIVENESS PROFILE

Purpose

To increase the trainees' awareness of how assertive they are in what kinds of situations.

Introduction to Exercise

The assertiveness questions are designed to help trainees think about when they are assertive. They are asked to indicate if they display this behavior almost always, sometimes, or rarely.

Training Procedures

1. Collect homework from Exercise 10.1. Make written comments and return.

2. If the trainees did not take home the profile, ask them to fill it out now.

3. Ask the trainees to follow the directions to score their profile.

4. Have them mark it on the graph.

5. Have the trainees share their scores with the group. Have them share what type of activities affected their scores.

6. Have them discuss in what situations and with whom they are most nonassertive.

EXERCISE 10.3
WHEN SHOULD I BE ASSERTIVE?

Purpose

To assist trainees in further refining their skills in identifying situations in which they want to be more assertive.

Training Procedures

1. Ask for any feedback they may have from Exercise 10.2.

2. Ask the trainees to help refine their assessment skills. Ask them to read directions for filling out the questionnaire.

3. Give the trainees approximately 15 minutes to fill out the questionnaire.

4. Discuss the results by asking some of the following questions:

    a.   Look at the overall questionnaire and identify those areas that threatened you (4,5). Why did they?

    b.   Look at your list and think about making some changes to become more assertive (2,3).

Homework for Trainees
After Group Meeting

1. From the questionnaire, identify three areas in which one may want to make some changes.

2. If one can think of others, please have them listed.

3. Make a list of at least three areas in which you may want to make some changes.

EXERCISE 10.4
DAILY LOG

Purpose

To help the trainees further refine areas in which they want to make changes and to keep a daily log of situations in which they were assertive.

Introduction to Exercise

The areas that will be used to develop the scenes for role playing will be from Exercise 10.3. Ask the trainees to be very specific about their scenes. Ask them to role play some of the scenes. This is the best way to begin to become more assertive. The trainees also will be asked to start keeping a log.

Training Procedures

1. Ask the trainees to write a description of a scene using Exercise 10.3. Have them to include the following:

    a.   The person involved

    b.   When it takes place (time and setting)

    c.   What bothers you

    d.   How you deal with the situation

e. Fear of what will happen

f. Goal (what you would like to see happen)

2. Assist the trainees in writing the scenes to include all of the elements.

3. Ask the trainees to role play some of the scenes.

4. Suggested procedure for role playing.

a. Ask if anyone has a situation or scene on which he/she would like to work (Trainee #1).

b. Ask Trainee #1 to briefly describe the scene, reading the description just written. This will permit others to play the scene.

c. Ask if Volunteer #1 would like to play either part.

d. Suggest the role play begin and encourage the other group members to be careful observers.

e. On completion of the role play, ask the participants to share their feelings and observations about the encounter. Ask the observers to give their comments and observations, then offer own observations. It is important that the trainer praise all approximations of assertive behavior and give focused suggestions for improvement.

f. The trainer may have the same scene played using different trainees or have the original participants change roles.

g. Once Trainee #1 has demonstrated adequate assertive skills with this situation, the role play may be repeated and made more difficult by instructing Trainee #2 to behave in an uncooperative manner.

h. Some group members may initially be reluctant to engage in role playing and may require the trainer's assistance and encouragement to deal with their fears and anxieties. While role playing, it is possible for a group member to "get stuck." In such a case, the trainer may need to coach the role player, provide additional encouragement, suggest a role reversal, or break the role play situation into smaller units.

5. Have trainees break into groups of three, read their scenes, practice role playing, and get feedback from the observer.

6. Ask students to maintain a log for the next few days and turn it in to trainer for comment.

7. Explain that the log is similar to a diary; it is a written description of interpersonal encounters. It should include the individual's perception of what happened, with whom, feelings at the time and afterwards, and the consequences. The purpose of the logs is to:

   a. Increase awareness of the individual's behavior and relationships with others.

   b. Help identify situations and individuals with whom the person had difficulty in interpersonal encounters.

   c. Serve as a progress chart to show the individual's development over the seven-week period.

   d. Allow for additional feedback from the trainer.

8. Group members will turn in their logs at the beginning of the next two training meetings. The task of the trainer is to read each log carefully and provide comments. These comments may take several forms.

   a. Rewarding: Praise all successful attempts at assertion, even small ones.

   b. Encouraging: Show support, understanding, and appreciation for their insights, frustrations, and unsuccessful attempts at assertion.

   c. Challenging: Ask the trainees to think of alternatives.

   d. Confronting: Point out discrepancies.

   e. Check out trainees' perceptions and assumptions.

   f. Suggesting: Ask if the trainees would like to work on the situation in the group.

   Avoid:

   • Preaching

   • Telling the trainees what to do

   • Condescending remarks

   • Punishing remarks

**Homework for Trainees
After Group Meeting**

Make logs for next meeting.

EXERCISE 10.5
ASSERTIVE RIGHTS

Purpose

To review the basic assertive rights and to assist the trainees in saying "no." There may be time to process some of the logs.

Introduction to Exercise

After reading the basic rights, the trainees at times take these rights to the extreme. It is important to discuss this carefully. Many trainees have a difficult time learning to say "no." These exercises will help.

Training Procedure

1. Ask the trainees to turn in their logs and assign logs for the next meeting.

2. Read the basic rights statements.

3. Discuss the Basic Assertive Rights and ask the discussion questions from *Peer Power*.

4. Have the trainees move into groups of two each.

5. Ask one to play the persuader, who says only "yes." Ask for a time when this trainee really wanted to convince someone of something.

6. Have the other member of the diad play the role of the refuser, who says only "no."

7. Ask the two to face each other and use the correct tone of voice.

8. Have them change roles.

9. Circulate among the diads and observe the interaction.

10. Discuss the following questions.

    a. Which role was easier for you? How was it easier?

    b. What did you notice about your ability to say no?

    c. Were you able to keep eye contact?

    d. What did the persuader do that made it difficult for you?

    e. In what situations or with whom do you often find yourself giving in instead of saying "no?"

f. Do you have the right to say "no?" When? With whom? About what?

g. How do apologizing, making excuses, and feeling guilty apply to saying "no?"

Homework for Trainees
After Group Meeting

1. Continue to keep log.

2. Practice saying "no."

EXERCISE 10.6
PUTTING ASSERTIVE SKILLS INTO ACTION

Purpose

The purpose of this exercise is to practice skills learned in assertiveness. Incorporate some of the skills previously learned in Module 9.

Introduction to Exercise

This exercise enables trainees to practice skills of assertiveness in a safe situation. This exercise reviews earlier material and enables the trainer to evaluate whether or not the trainees have learned the skill.

Training Procedures

1. Collect logs and return earlier logs. Ask if anyone would like to practice some of the logs.

2. Have trainees divide into three's. Have each play one of three roles: the person being assertive, the person creating the problem, and an observer (use observation sheet).

3. Change roles until they have all played each role.

4. Circulate around the groups giving feedback.

5. Discuss the experience.

Homework for Trainees
After Group Meeting

1. Keep one more log to be turned in at the next meeting.

2. Practice being assertive.

CONFRONTATION SKILL

Purpose

To enable trainees to learn and use effectively confrontation skill.

Approximate Time

Module 11—Introduction, 10 to 15 minutes for homework

Exercise 11.1—20 to 30 minutes in training session
Homework—20 to 30 minutes

Exercise 11.2—10 to 20 minutes in training session
Homework—15 to 20 minutes

Exercise 11.3—45 to 60 minutes in training session
Homework—10 to 15 minutes

Materials

Peer Power: Book 1, Introductory Program, one copy for each trainee

Optional: Video equipment with video tape of the behaviors to be taught.

Introduction to Module

In talking with or observing others, one often receives conflicting messages. As a peer counselor, each trainee needs to be able to communicate to the helpee the double message and to do so in a manner that will be helpful to the helpee. The skill of communicating the double message is entitled, "Confrontation," and when done properly, enables the helper to express the two messages without creating anger or defensive behavior on the helpee's part or the helper's.

Three general incidents where double messages (discrepancies) may occur and for which helpers may find confrontation needed are the following:

1. Between what is said and what is done by the helpee.

2. Between what the helpee has been saying and what others have reported the helpee as doing.

3. Between what the helpee says and how the helpee feels or looks.

When the confrontation is used, it must be done with skill and in a manner that hopefully will be meaningful to the helpee. The five characteristics of confrontation are listed in introductory material for Module 11 in *Peer Power* book.

The number of training sessions needed will depend upon trainees and the time block for each session. All three Exercises could be taught in the same session if needed. We recommend two training sessions with Exercises 11.1 and 11.2 in the first session and possibly demonstration in preparation for Exercise 10.3 which would be in the second training session.

Training Procedures

1. Decide the number of training sessions and the Exercise to be included in each session.

2. Review the content to be covered and the suggested activities as listed in the *Peer Power* book in addition to those listed in this *Peer Counseling* book.

3. Be prepared to do the demonstration as suggested or have video equipment with previously prepared tape of the behaviors to be taught.

Evaluation Process

As trainer evaluate the process used in the teaching of the skill by the feedback obtained from the trainees and by observations of them during the times when they are asked to use the skill.

Measuring Outcomes

1. Use Exercises 11.1 and 11.2 Sheets to determine how well the trainees can identify correct confrontation responses.

2. Observe and listen during role playing in Exercise 11.3 to measure the ease with which trainees are using confrontation and the other peer counseling skills.

3. Use Exercise 11.3 Sheets to determine how well the trainees use the peer counseling skills and how well they can identify the skills when used by others.

EXERCISE 11.1
CONDITIONS OF CONFRONTATION

Purpose

To assist trainees in learning under what conditions confrontation can be helpful, including the kinds of relationships necessary between helpee and helper.

Introduction to Exercise

Confrontation necessitates a combination of two other skills—empathy and genuineness. This is because confrontation is done to free other individuals to be involved with the helpees while behavior changes are undertaken.

The quality of the relationship between the helpee and helper should be such that the helper can be genuine, exhibit empathy, and summarize. A helper must believe that the helpee will want to do so if made aware of the double messages being communicated.

It also is important for the helper to believe that the helpee has the ability to act upon the confrontation. If the ability is lacking and confrontation occurs, the helpee could be hurt instead of helped. The trainer must help trainees understand conditions that must exist before using confrontation.

Training Procedures

1. Use teaching techniques effective for the trainer to teach the characteristics of confrontation, the incidences where double messages generally occur, and conditions that must exist before confrontation is appropriate.

2. Assist trainees in overcoming their concerns related to confrontation.

3. Discuss with trainees their written material from homework for Exercise 11.1.

4. Collect Exercise 11.1 sheets and Exercise 10.9 if not collected previously.

Homework for Trainees
After Group Meeting

1. If Exercise 11.1 is taught in a training session, separate from Exercises 11.2 and 11.3, assign these two as homework to be completed before next training session.

2. If Exercise 11.1 and 11.2 are to be taught in the same training session, move directly into Exercise 11.3.

EXERCISE 11.2
PERCEIVING CONFRONTATION SKILL

Purpose

To provide written material for the trainees to study and to rate for confrontation skill.

Introduction to Exercise

In Exercise 11.1, trainees learned about confrontation. In Exercise 11.2, they have an opportunity to practice rating written confrontation responses to two different situations. Ratings can be done as homework and discussed during the training session.

Training Procedures

1. Discuss with trainees their ratings for the confrontation responses in Exercise 11.2, *Peer Power: Book 1.*

2. Assist the trainees in learning how to rate confrontation responses.

3. Collect Exercise 11.2 sheets.

4. Return any exercise sheets collected in a previous training session.

Homework for Trainees
After Group Meeting

If trainees have not been instructed to do so, ask them to study Exercise 11.3 and be prepared to complete it during the next training session.

EXERCISE 11.3
ROLE PLAYING FOR CONFRONTATION SKILL
AND RATING THE HELPER

Purpose

To provide practice in confrontation skill.

Introduction to Exercise

This Exercise is designed to provide trainees with practice in confrontation skill through role playing. They are asked to use the other peer counseling skills they have learned when appropriate.

A Rating Flow Sheet is provided in *Peer Power: Book 1*, which will enable the rater to record during the role playing. At the close of the role playing extended dialogue, the rater can provide feedback to the helper. Often the feedback results in interchange between the rater and helper which can provide opportunity for use of the peer counseling skills. The trainer often can learn what needs to be emphasized by observing during the feedback period.

Training Procedures

1. Explain and discuss any aspects of confrontation skill that the trainees do not know. The basic concepts are presented in Module 10 and the related Exercises in *Peer Power: Book 1.*

2. Model the behavior before having the trainees practice. This procedure is important.

   Optional: Use video equipment to show the skill and as a base for discussion.

3. Have trainees form clusters of three for role playing practice and ask them to follow the directions in *Peer Power: Book 1,* Exercise 11.3. Review the steps within the directions to assure that the trainees understand the procedure.

4. In the initial role playing exercises, have the trainees go through three to six interchanges (helper responses with emphasis on confrontation) before they stop to rate the helper.

5. Ask the rater to use the space provided in *Peer Power, Book 1,* following the heading entitled, "Exercise."

6. Repeat the role-playing exercise until all trainees have played each role.

7. Upon completion of each role playing, discuss the experience.

8. Repeat role playing until trainees understand and can use confrontation skill.

9. Have the trainees participate in extended dialogue during role playing in which they integrate the seven skills learned to date. Using the same triad cluster, have the helpee use real situations for an extended dialogue of at least eight helper responses. Ask the rater in each triad to rate the helper on all peer counseling skills learned by using the Flow Sheet for Rating Confrontation and other Communication Skills (copy is in *Peer Power: Book 1,* Exercise 11.3).

10. Following role play, discuss experiences the trainees had and assist them in overcoming their concerns.

11. Collect Exercise 11.3 Sheets.

12. Return any Exercise Sheets collected in a previous training session which have not been returned.

Homework for Trainees
After Group Meeting

1. Ask trainees to study the introduction to Module 12.

2. If Exercises 12.1 and 12.2 are both to be included in the next training session, ask trainees to study the seven steps to problem solving and the related dialogue and come to the next session prepared to discuss Exercises 12.1 and 12.2.

3. If only Exercise 12.1 is to be covered in the next training session, ask trainees to study it before the next session.

PROBLEM-SOLVING SKILL

Helping is worthwhile only if the problems causing people trouble can be solved. Therefore, for help to be effective the help which is provided needs to include a problem-solving component. Problem solving is the action dimension behavior that brings about change. Without the action, dimension exploring and understanding are of little ultimate value.

Purpose

To have trainees understand and demonstrate problem-solving strategies.

Approximate Time

Module 12—Introduction, 5 minutes for homework

Exercise 12.1—30 to 60 minutes in training session
Homework—15 to 30 minutes

Exercise 12.2—30 to 60 minutes in training session
Homework—30 to 60 minutes

Exercise 12.3—30 to 60 minutes in training session
Homework—10 to 15 minutes prior to training session

Exercise 12.4—30 to 60 minutes in training session
Homework—60 to 90 minutes

Materials

Peer Power: Book 1, Introductory Program, one copy for each trainee

Introduction to Module

Effective problem solving is possible only after the helper and helpee have explored and understood all the dimensions of the problem. When this has been accomplished, the helpee is in a position to make some commitments to a behavior change. In the training of helpers we feel that the teaching of a complete problem-solving model is important if the trainees are to learn effective skills. Only after trainees have a thorough knowledge of at least one problem-solving procedure, can they be flexible in how to proceed with this part of the helping process.

Each trainee, as a peer counselor, can listen with ease at this point in the training to problems and concerns of others. Helping others to explore and understand is a good start in peer counseling and often is all that is necessary, because a sounding board may be all the peers need. However, many times listening and understanding do not go far enough. A helpee may need to take some action in order to grow. This action behavior can take the form of problem solving. In these situations, unless trainees have each participated in the helpee's solving of his/her own problems, the listening is not really helping.

Many ways are available to solve problems. Having trainees use the communication skills learned is one of those ways. When listening is not enough, trainees will need some other problem-solving techniques. The Problem-Solving Skills Module is when you provide new ways for trainees to help others arrive at problem-solving action. Special emphasis will need to be made that trainees are not to solve helpees' problems for them, rather the intent is to facilitate helpees taking action.

The problem-solving model to be used includes the following seven general procedures which are listed as the seven steps in problem solving:
action. Stress that probably not all of these skills will be used each time, but the different techniques are useful after having done a good job of exploring and understanding and after they (the trainees) are ready to take the final step toward behavior change. In addition, learning the problem-solving skills will benefit each trainee whenever he/she wants to change behavior and needs ways to make this change.

In Module 12 is presented one detailed and structured model which incorporates many of the generally accepted concepts for good problem-solving behaviors. The purpose of the module is to develop a complete but simple training model that can be incorporated into an effective peer training program without going into a highly complicated and technical process.

The problem-solving model to be sued includes the following seven general procedures which are listed as the seven steps in problem solving:

Step 1. Exploring the Problem
Step 2. Understanding the Problem
Step 3. Defining the Problem
Step 4. Brainstorming All Alternatives
Step 5. Evaluating Alternatives
Step 6. Deciding the Best Alternative
Step 7. Implementing the Alternative

In this module each step is defined, and its purpose is explained. In addition, teaching procedures include an example of how the process operates, and in this way, one can walk the trainees through the complete module before they practice the process on their own. These procedures are outlined in *Peer Power: Book 1*, Module 11. The examples in the manual are duplicated in *Peer Power: Book 1*, for trainees to use as the model is being taught.

The Exercises to be covered in each training session will depend upon time block and the practice and teaching needed by trainees. We recommend a minimum of two training sessions. Exercises to be taught in each session might be as follows, and choose the pattern best for your conditions:

Session Number	Exercise(s) to be Included in Session if		
	2 sessions	3 sessions	4 sessions
First	12.1 and 12.2	12.1 and 12.2	12.1
Second	12.3 and 12.4	12.3*	12.2
Third		12.4	12.3
Fourth			12.4

* An alternate plan would be to do 12.1 in first session and 12.2 and 12.3 in second session.

Training Procedures

1. Read through the seven steps in the problem-solving model presented in this book in Exercise 12.1 including the definition of terms before explaining the process to trainees. When teaching the process the trainer must understand the total process.

2. Review the format for trainee exercises as presented in *Peer Power: Book 1*, Module 12.

3. In teaching the module, explain the entire seven steps in one session. After the module has been explained in entirety, give examples or role play specific procedures for practice before the model is implemented. Brainstorming, evaluating the alternatives, deciding the best alternative, and implementing the alternatives are steps that need to be practiced with individual examples. Exploring and understanding have been practiced often in previous modules. After role playing the individual steps separately, try putting the whole process together.

4. Follow the sequence of four exercises presented for Module 12.

Evaluation Process

Determine the effectiveness of the training by how well the trainees complete the problem-solving strategies from the exploring stage through understanding to implementing the alternative.

Measuring Outcomes

The goals of the twenty-four modules are reached when the trainees solve their problems by effectively using the strategies taught. The effectiveness of the outcome will be identified during follow-up sessions.

EXERCISE 12.1
PROBLEM-SOLVING PROCEDURES

Purpose

To have the trainees learn the problem-solving procedures.

Introduction to Exercise

In Exercise 12.1 trainees are introduced to the seven steps of problem solving. In addition, in *Peer Power: Book 1*, are lists what the helpee does in each step, and what the helper procedures and skills are in problem solving. The trainer will need to review the information supplied in the *Peer Power: Book 1*, Exercise 12.1.

The material is to be studied by the trainees as homework, but explanation and discussions should take place during the training session to assure understanding. The problem-solving skill is one that trainees generally want to learn. It often requires extended time, however, because their prior experience has not been of developmental process but rather of acts with no examination of the how or why.

Training Procedures

1. Use chalkboard, flip pad, flannel board, or other means to accentuate the steps when discussing each one with the trainees.

2. Identify the peer counseling skills which the helper can use at each step and place these beside the steps. Help trainees understand how each skill could be used at each step.

STEP	SKILL(S) USED
1. Exploring the Problem	empathy, attending, open-ended questioning
2. Understanding the Problem	empathy, attending, open-ended questioning, genuineness, confrontation

3. Defining the Problem	summarizing
4. Brainstorming All Alternatives	open-ended questioning
5. Evaluating Alternatives	open-ended questioning, summarizing
6. Deciding the Best Alternative	empathy, attending, open-ended questioning, summarizing
7. Implementing the Alternative	open-ended questioning, summarizing

3. Illustrate with sample helpee statements and helper responses as each step is explained.

4. Encourage discussion and assist the trainees in overcoming their fears.

5. Return Exercise 11.3 Sheets with written comments.

Homework for Trainees
After Group Meeting

1. If Exercise 12.2 is taught in the next training session instead of the one where 12.1 is taught, ask the trainees to study the dialogue and come prepared to discuss Exercise 12.2 during the next training session.

2. If Exercise 12.2 and 12.3 are to be taught together, ask trainees to study Exercise 12.3 as well, and come prepared to complete it during the next training session.

EXERCISE 12.2
PROBLEM-SOLVING DIALOGUE

Purpose

To familiarize trainees with the dialogue used in the seven steps in problem solving.

Introduction to Exercise

Exercise 12.2 is where one can help the trainees put it together, to use the various skills, and to become familiar with an overall dialogue during the helping process. By the trainees studying the sample dialogue provided, they can come to the training session prepared to integrate skills learned previously.

Training Procedures

1. Review with the trainees the seven steps.

2. Proceed through the dialogue with the trainees and explain the purpose of each step and how the dialogue illustrates the problem-solving step. Trainees have copy of dialogue in *Peer Power: Book 1*, Exercise 12.2. Trainer has dialogue and explanation in the next section of book for trainer.

3. Assist trainees in overcoming their fears.

4. Call attention to the ease with which the dialogue moves from one step to the next.

DIALOGUE AND EXPLANATIONS FOR THE SEVEN STEPS

Step 1. Exploring the Problem

Exploring the problem means to look at the surface dimensions of the concern. This process incorporates some of the skills learned so far. The process includes attending, empathy, summarizing, open-ended questioning, and confrontation.

Sample (Interchange which explores the problem)

> **Helpee:** "I don't know what job to get once I get out of school."
>
> **Helper:** "You're unsure of the kind of job you want?"
>
> **Helpee:** "Yeah, I think I want to get into the medical area, but I am not sure."
>
> **Helper:** "Medical careers turn you on, but you are not sure."
>
> **Helpee:** "That is what I think I am working toward because I have taken nothing but science courses since I have been in high school."
>
> **Helper:** "What jobs in the medical field have you considered?"
>
> **Helpee:** "I have thought about being a doctor, but I don't think I could make it, so I guess I will be a nurse."

Exploring the problem usually takes place during the early stages of the helping relationship but can be reinitiated anytime during the process as new conditions or materials are introduced into the problem. High empathy, attending, and genuineness are the skills most often employed in this initial stage of the helping process.

Step 2. Understanding the Problem

Understanding the problem means to increase the helpee's awareness of how the many aspects of the concern fit together to create the issues that are causing the difficulties. Understanding usually develops when underlying feelings are brought out and dealt with. To understand necessitates involving the helper and helpee in dialogue that attempts to uncover all of the conditions both internal and external that are causing the helpee difficulty. To fully understand a helpee's concern requires use of all of the skills learned so far. Empathy and attending are still the most frequently employed skills learned, but genuineness and confrontation become strong components of the understanding dimension.

Sample (Interchange that understands the problem)

> **Helper:** "You really would like to be a doctor, but it is too much to make it."

> **Helpee:** "Yes, it takes so long to go to school, I don't know whether I have the stamina to make it."

> **Helper:** "You feel uncertain if you have the energy to make it through medical school."

> **Helpee:** "Being a doctor is something I have always wanted to do, and my family has been planning on me going."

> **Helper:** "I hear you saying two things—You really want to do it; you have the support, but you seem to not have the confidence in yourself that you can make it."

> **Helpee:** "Yes, self-confidence is something I hardly ever have. I convince myself that I can't do certain things, and it really hurts when I go ahead and do things."

> **Helper:** "You put yourself down a lot. I guess I feel uncomfortable when you put yourself down, and it causes me to maybe suggest other careers for you that you will have the confidence to do. This concerns me that you may regret it later."

> **Helpee:** "It seems like the more I talk about my lack of self-confidence, others feel sorry for me, and they tell me I can do it. I don't need a pep talk from others."

The ability to fully understand the concern can take place only after the issues have been fully explored. When understanding occurs, helpees become aware not only of where they are but also of where they "want to be." The helpee's desire to bring about personal change is an important aspect of the understanding level of awareness.

Step 3. Defining the Problem

To define the problem means to articulate the issues causing the difficulty in as specific terms as possible. The more precise the terms that can be used to identify the problem the higher the probability that solutions that will work can be found. Defining the problem includes both **deficits** that create the problem and the goals that are **desired.**

The problems (or deficits) and goals can be defined in useful terms after an adequate exploration and understanding of the problem has taken place. Without these first two dimensions, the problem-solving process becomes inappropriate because too many unknown issues, concerns, or attitudes exist that effect the problem; thus the helpee is unable to develop any solution that will work.

Step 4. Brainstorming

The process of brainstorming is generally understood in human relations training. Brainstorming essentially means that all procedures or alternatives that could help solve a problem are introduced without criticism or comment as to their problem-solving effectiveness. An important point to teach is that both the helpee and helper have the responsibility to supply as many brainstorming ideas as possible.

Sample (Interchange which uses brainstorming technique.)

> **Helper:** "Let's look at some ways to find the answers about yourself and feel good about you. I will write the ideas down and keep notes. Let's not evaluate any of the ideas. Let's just keep notes."
>
> **Helpee:** "Well, I could sign up for counseling or take some of those courses on understanding yourself."
>
> (Helper writes two ideas—"counseling" and "self help course."
>
> **Helper:** "You could take a series of tests to see your strengths and weakness as far as ability."
>
> (Helper writes "testing.")
>
> **Helpee:** "I could ask friends what they think about me, or I could just spend time thinking about it."
>
> (Helper writes "ask friends.")
>
> **Helper:** "You could ask your family or teachers how they see your abilities."
>
> (Helper writes "ask family or teachers.")
>
> **Helpee:** "I could sign up for one of the Human Potential Groups at school."
>
> (Helper writes "Human Potential Groups.")

When teaching brainstorming, have the trainee group choose a simple problem and then practice the brainstorming technique with one member of the group. Writing all of the ideas generated by the group is helpful. In this way each trainee has the opportunity to experience how the process operates. When teaching the trainees to brainstorm, one can teach them to write each idea. Later when they have practiced the process, it will not always be necessary to write each idea. However, to write the brainstorming thoughts so they can be appraised in total upon completion of the activity usually is valuable. One of the final steps in problem solving is to reduce all of the ideas generated in brainstorming to one or two workable alternatives and having them written facilitates the evaluation of the final choice patterns.

Step 5. Evaluating Alternatives

Evaluating alternatives means to link the values and the strengths and the weaknesses of the helpee that relate to the issue with the alternatives generated during the brainstorming activity. A helpee's values that relate to the issues exert a great deal of influence over the final decision-making process. If these influencing values are ignored in choosing a solution, the probability of a successful outcome is reduced considerably.

Since people's behavior and attitude are so strongly affected by the values they hold, linking the affected values with all possible alternatives identified is extremely important in order to arrive at an alternative that will receive full support of the helpee because the solution is compatible with his/her value system.

In teaching trainees to consider those values that will affect the alternatives chosen, having the helper list the helpee's values is important so that the values can be considered along with each of the alternatives chosen in the brainstorming activity.

> **Strengths**—When listing the values, teach the trainees to work with the helpee in identifying his/her strengths that can be brought to bear in solving the problem. As in the case of listing values, an important point is to have the helpee be the one to identify the values, the strengths, and later, the weaknesses that will influence the final alternative chosen. The helper can only suggest possible strengths and weaknesses the helpee may have but cannot establish a value system for a helpee.

> **Weaknesses**—Along with strengths and equally important is to explore the weaknesses that will affect the final alternative chosen. When the values, strengths, and weaknesses which are brought to bear on the final solution are understood, the final decision as to which alternative has the best probability for success can be made. Without incorporating all of the three constructs, the final decision will be less likely to withstand the pressures when implementation is initiated.

With many problems the helper will recognize that the alternatives possible, the values affecting the alternatives, and the strengths and weaknesses of the helpee may be few in number and not require several lists to establish the total picture. However, in teaching the process be sure to have the trainees write alternatives, values, strengths, and weaknesses in order to establish that they know the process and how it operates. Without this step in the training, trainees have a tendency to gloss over the process in their anxiety and their desire to arrive at a solution, but this step is very necessary in arriving at an effective solution.

Before choosing the best alternative, have the trainees identify and underline the helpee's most important value(s) that relate to the problem and the strength(s) that would most easily facilitate a successful solution to the concern.

Sample (Interchange which evaluates alternatives).

> **Helper:** "Let's look at the list of suggested alternatives and then figure if any of your values are applicable to these alternatives. Then let's look at your strengths and weaknesses that are applicable to each alternative. We can do it by making two charts that will compare each of the qualities with which we are working."

Through working with the helpee, the helper and the helpee have identified important values held by the helpee. In the case illustrated five important values were identified—having independence, gaining an education, doing well on tests, having a family life, and having friends. These five values were used in a chart to examine whether or not each alternative would be appropriate for each value held. The "Comparison Chart of Values to Each Alternative" is shown for the illustrative case.

Following the completion of the "Comparison Chart of Values to Each Alternative," the helper used another chart to enable the helpee to examine strengths and weaknesses of the helpee as related to each alternative. The "Comparison Chart of Alternatives to Strengths and Weaknesses" is shown for the illustrative case.

COMPARISON CHART OF ALTERNATIVES TO STRENGTHS AND WEAKNESSES

	Alternatives	Strengths	Weaknesses	Strongest Potential Character
1.	Counseling	Solve things myself	Time (lack of)	Strength
2.	Self-Help Course	Learn quickly	Time (lack of)	Weakness
3.	Testing	Do well on tests	Fear of results	Strength
4.	Ask Family	Communicate openly	Family reaction	Strength
5.	Ask Friends	Leadership	Can't trust	Weakness
6.	Human Potential Group	Like to talk	Time (lack of)	Weakness

Step 6. Deciding the Best Alternative

Deciding the best alternative means that the final decision as to which one or two of the alternatives appear to be the best will be chosen from the brainstorming alternatives, the developed list of values and the identification of strengths and weaknesses of the helpee. In teaching this step of problem solving, a series of questions can be used to develop a check list of data that will enable the helper and helpee to compare each alternative to a single set of criteria. Thus, each solution is compared to the same conditions, and the decision as to which alternative appears to be the most effective solution is more easily made.

**Check List to Evaluate
Each Alternative Identified**

1. Do I have all of the data available?

2. Is the alternative specific?

3. Is the alternative conceivable?

4. Is the alternative believable?

5. Does the alternative coincide with many of my values?

6. Does the alternative help me to grow as a person?

7. Is the alternative controllable?

8. Is the alternative what I want to do?

Completing the check list will usually eliminate all but two feasible alternatives. Have the helpee circle the alternatives that are usable. Trainees need to be taught that a commitment by the helpee to act on one of the alternatives is the next necessary step to solving the helpee's problem.

Sample (Interchange which decides the best alternative.)

Helper: "Underline the top value and best strength."

Helper: "There are several choices, but it looks like your best choice might be Human Potential Group and a self-help course."

Helpee: "Yes, because I enjoy learning about myself and learning in general. I am not afraid to talk about myself, and I learn quickly."

Helper: "Let me ask you some questions about your decision. Is the alternative specific? Is it clear?"

Helpee: "Yes."

Helper: "Does the alternative coincide with your values?"

Helpee: "Yes."

Helper: "Will the alternative help you grow as a person?"

Helpee: "Yes."

Helper: "Is it something that is in the realm of your control?"

Helpee: "Yes."

Helper: "Do you want to do it?"

Helpee: "Yes."

Step 7. Implementing the Alternative

The final step in this problem-solving model is to implement the alternative that (1) satisfies the most appropriate helpee values; (2) uses and implements the most important strengths, and (3) minimizes the helpee's deficiencies. This requires that the trainees be taught how to implement a plan of action using the alternative chosen.

A plan of action incorporates several necessary phases which assist in its development. Assuming that one alternative has been chosen as most appropriate and stands the best chance of effectively solving the problem, the helpee must ask and respond to several action questions.

1. What are my goals which need to be met in order to solve this problem?

2. What is the first action necessary to put the plan into operation?

3. What are the next activities that are necessary in the plan and in what sequence must they take place in order to reach my goal?

4. What obstacles are in the way toward reaching the goal?

5. What strengths do I have to overcome the obstacles?

6. Who are the people that will be involved in the plan of action and how will they be involved?

7. What are the time lines needed for me to reach my goals?

8. Where do I put this plan of action into effect?

9. When do I take my first action?

Sample (Interchange which examines implementing the alternative.)

> **Helper:** "Now comes the hardest part of figuring out ways of implementing alternatives. Will the alternative help you meet your goals of understanding yourself now and feeling good about yourself?"
>
> **Helpee:** "Yes."
>
> **Helper:** "What steps must you take to accomplish the alternative?"
>
> **Helpee:** "I can sign up for Human Potential Group with my counselor and probably go see the counselor about a self-help course."
>
> **Helper:** "I really wonder what strengths you possess that will help you overcome your lack of time."
>
> **Helpee:** "Well, I like to learn, and I stick to things once I have decided."
>
> **Helper:** "Will anyone else be involved?"
>
> **Helpee:** "My counselor."
>
> **Helper:** "When are you going to see the counselor?"
>
> **Helpee:** "This week because the Human Potential Group starts soon, and I hope to take the course in the summer."
>
> **Helper:** "Where do you go?"
>
> **Helpee:** "Guidance Center."
>
> **Helper:** "What is your first step?"
>
> **Helpee:** "Talk to the counselor."

Homework for Trainees
After Group Meeting

1. Have trainees study again the sample dialogue if any of the seven steps are not understood.

2. Have trainees review the purposes for each of the seven steps and the means for achieving each.

3. Have each trainee to think of a situation (a problem) which is or has been real to him/her and is one which he/she is willing to role play during the next training session.

4. Ask trainees to review Exercise 12.2 in the *Peer Power* book and be prepared to do the Exercise during the next training session.

EXERCISE 12.3
ROLE-PLAYING PRACTICE
FOR PROBLEM-SOLVING SKILL

Purpose

To provide supervised role-playing practices of the seven steps in problem solving so that trainees will learn how to utilize the seven steps and related information appropriately.

Introduction to Exercise

The trainer will find it difficult to structure precisely this part of the training because the problem solving aspect of helping comes toward the end of the helper/helpee relationship, and each problem takes its own particular route and has it own particular idiosyncrasies. As a result, precise, real situations and procedures cannot easily be planned for teaching purposes. The one effective way to teach this aspect is to develop a role-playing situation that will arbitrarily illustrate all seven steps in problem-solving procedures.

The trainer can best illustrate this module by dramatizing the seven steps through a role-playing situation with one or more of the trainees. In this way, each of the steps is illustrated, even though the role playing is in reality a canned version of how the procedure works. Practice by the trainees will be the best learning condition as to the effectiveness of the training process using the model described. In the role playing experience, the trainer will take the helper role.

Training Procedures

1. Dramatize the seven steps through a role-playing situation with one or more of the trainees.

    Optional: Play a video tape situation that will illustrate the seven steps.

2. Discuss with the trainees each of the seven steps dramatized through role playing.

3. Have the trainees divide into clusters of two and take real problems through the seven steps of problem solving using the worksheets found in *Peer Power: Book 1*, Exercise 11.3. The helper is to complete the sheet during the role playing.

4. Following the completion of the first role-playing situation using the seven steps, have the trainees to come together and discuss the experiences they had. The helper from each cluster of two will be able to contribute by reviewing the notes completed on the work sheets in *Peer Power: Book 1*, Exercise 12.3.

5. Have trainees reverse roles and repeat the experience.

6. Ask the trainees to come together as a total group following the second role-playing situation and discuss the experiences they had.

7. Inform the trainees that Exercise 12.3 Sheets will not be collected at this time, but Homework will be given for the Sheets.

Homework for Trainees
After Group Meeting

1. Ask the trainees to review and revise where appropriate Exercise 12.3 Sheets written during the role playing and to bring the completed Sheets to the next training session.

2. Suggest to the trainees that each one review the role-playing situation for the following purposes (written as desired to state them):

   a. "To gain a feel for what the helper did for 'you' as a trainee when you were in the helpee role."

   b. "To understand your strengths when 'you' as a trainee were in the helper role."

3. Ask trainees to study Exercise 12.4 and complete the Exercise before the next training session.

EXERCISE 12.4
PLAN OF ACTION TO ASSIST
HELPEE IN PROBLEM SOLVING

Purpose

To enable trainees to develop a plan of action containing a sequence of meaningful activities that will assist another person in problem solving.

Introduction to Exercise

In the training sequence a helpful procedure is to have the trainees, as they work with helpees, write a plan of action for each problem-solving situation they encounter. This plan of action should be shared with the trainer for evaluation and suggestions for alteration and improvement. In this way the trainer is able to evaluate the progress of the trainees. Also, the trainer can keep in touch with the problems with which the trainees are dealing and the progress they are making. By requiring a written plan of action, the trainer can be aware of the effectiveness of the training program.

Training Procedures

1. Discuss with the trainees the work sheets in Exercise 12.4, taking each step separately, answering questions which may occur, and helping trainees to become familiar with the procedures of developing a plan of action.

2. Cluster the trainees in triads and ask them to help each other complete their work sheets.

3. Move from cluster to cluster and review plans with the trainees.

4. Sign plans which are approved. (May need to collect the work sheets for review and approval outside of training session.)

5. Write comments on plans which need revision to help trainees learn how to develop adequate plans.

6. Collect Exercise 12.3 Sheets unless Exercise 12.3 and 12.4 were taught in the same training session.

Homework for Trainees
After Group Meeting

1. Require trainees after the training session and after approval of each trainee's plan of action to implement their plans during the week.

2. Ask trainees to come prepared to report progress to the group at the next training session.

3. Ask trainees to study introduction to Module 13 and think about how they might apply their peer counseling skills. If time permits during the homework, ask them to review Exercise 13.2.

PUTTING PEER COUNSELING INTO ACTION

Purpose

To have trainees become peer counselors.

Approximate Time

Module 13—Introduction, 5 to 10 minutes for homework

Exercise 13.1—30 to 60 minutes in training session
Homework—no Homework time needed

Exercise 13.2—30 to 60 minutes in training session
Homework—60 to 90 minutes

Exercise 13.3—Time depends upon plans developed for supervision and consultation with trainees selected for peer counseling

Materials

Peer Power: Book 1, one for each trainee

Introduction to Module

When the trainees have finished the basic training, the question the trainer must answer is "Which trainees are skillful enough to participate actively in peer counseling?" The answer is not easy. For those who are ready, opportunities for doing so must be made available and also supervision and consultation must be available. For those who are not skillful enough, additional assistance will be needed to assure their continued growth.

Answering the question as to which ones are skillful enough requires objective information and professional experience. The answer to the question by some trainees may be different than the answer by the trainer. Certainly the trainer wants as much reliable information as possible before supplying the answer. The Exercise Sheets collected, reviewed, and commented upon in writing throughout the training program become vital. The interactions observed during training sessions have enabled the trainer to work with trainees during training sessions and in some instances outside of training sessions on an individual or small group basis. What the trainer gained during these times becomes background information for answering the question.

Early in the training program, a Pretest was administered. The same items can be administered again as a Posttest. The results from the Posttest can be important; however, remember that the trainees have had the Posttest throughout the training program, and the results may not be reliable as the base for answering the question.

If trainees are encouraged to participate as peer counselors, then plans will need to be made to facilitate their participation. Exercises 13.2 and 13.3 can assist.

Training Procedures

1. Review the total Module and decide which Exercises are to be taught when.

2. Prepare to administer the Posttest.

3. Think through when and how trainees will be informed as to whether or not they are encouraged to become active as peer counselors.

Evaluation Process

The progress of the Peer Counseling Training Program can be determined by the skills learned by the trainees and the number of them who will become involved actively in peer counseling.

Measuring Outcomes

1. Count the number of trainees who become peer counselors.

2. Watch the involvement of trainees in activities where peer counseling skills can be beneficial.

3. Watch progress of trainees in various groups, organizations, and activities.

4. Determine how many trainees follow through with completing "Peer Counseling Feedback Flow Sheets" and seeking supervision and/or consultation.

EXERCISE 13.1
POSTTEST COMMUNICATIONS EXERCISE

Purpose

To have trainees take posttest as one means of determining readiness to participate actively in peer counseling.

Introduction to Exercise

The Posttest items are the same as those of the Pretest used in Exercise 1.1. After the Posttest is administered and scored, the trainer can compare the results both for the group as a whole and for each trainee.

Training Procedures

1. Have trainees take the Posttest, Exercise 13.1 in *Peer Power: Book 1.*

2. Collect Posttest and score it.

3. Collect Exercise 12.4 and review it. Do the same with Exercise 12.3 if not previously collected.

4. Compare results of Pretest with those of Posttest.

5. Review all information available to the trainer regarding each trainee.

6. Decide whether or not each trainee is to be encouraged to participate actively in peer counseling.

7. Discuss with each trainee whether or not active participation in peer counseling should be encouraged at this time and what alternatives exist for that individual.

Homework for Trainees
After Group Meeting

1. Ask trainees to review and complete Exercise 13.2 before the next training session.

2. Ask trainees to review Exercise 13.3 before next training session.

EXERCISE 13.2
ORGANIZING FOR PEER COUNSELING

Purpose

To assist trainees who are to participate actively in peer counseling to organize for doing so.

Introduction to Exercise

Exercise 13.2 is a means of helping trainees get started as peer counselors. The process includes having trainees examine and record their goals and plans of action and do a self-analysis. Criteria are suggested for checking goals. The trainees need homework time for preparing Exercise 13.2 Sheets. They generally can benefit both from interaction with one another during a training session and from talking individually with the trainer.

Training Procedures

1. Discuss with trainees selected to be peer counselors the process outlined in Exercise 13.2 and help them overcome their fears.

2. Cluster trainees in triads and ask them to assist one another in reviewing and completing Exercise 13.2 Sheets.

3. Move among triads and assist where needed.

4. Discuss where trainees can apply their peer counseling skills and develop plan of action for supervision and consultation for the peer counselors.

5. Review Exercise 13.3 with trainees.

6. Collect Exercise 13.2, Part I, Sheets.

7. Return any exercise sheets previously collected.

Homework for Trainees
After Group Meeting

1. Ask trainees to follow the discussed plan for supervision and consultation as they actively participate as peer counselors.

2. Ask trainees to complete Part II, Self-Analysis, of Exercise 13.2.

EXERCISE 13.3
PEER COUNSELOR FEEDBACK FLOW SHEET

Purpose

To provide a means of self-evaluation for each peer counselor and communication between peer counselor and trainer (or supervisor).

Introduction to Exercise

Peer Counselor Feedback Flow Sheets will enable peer counselors to do self-analysis; hopefully, doing so will produce additional growth. Their supervisors can use the flow sheets to make comments to assist the peer counselors and when reviewed periodically to provide a means of determining progress and direction. Flow Sheets also can provide a starting point when consultation is necessary.

Training Procedures

1. Ask peer counselors to complete a "Peer Counselor Feedback Flow Sheet" after each peer counseling contact.

2. Review flow sheet with the peer counselors, and in a supervisory/consultative role assist in their growth and helpees' development.

3. Collect Exercise 13.2, Part II, Sheets.

4. Collect Exercise 13.3 Sheets as they are completed, and return them with comments as soon as possible.

MODULES
for
BOOK 2
APPLYING PEER
HELPER SKILLS

DRUGS AND ALCOHOL ABUSE—
INTERVENTION AND PREVENTION

Purposes

1. To enable trainees to learn some introductory material concerning the problem,

2. to become aware of their own chemical use, and

3. to look at alternative ways for coping with life.

Approximate Time

Module 14—Introduction Homework—10 to 15 minutes

Exercise 14.1—60 to 120 minutes in training session
Homework—60 to 120 minutes

Exercise 14.2—30 to 60 minutes in training session
Homework—20 minutes

Exercise 14.3—60 to 120 minutes in training session
Homework—60 minutes

Exercise 14.4—60 to 120 minutes in training session

Exercise 14.5—15 to 30 minutes in training session
Homework—60 minutes

Exercise 14.6—30 to 60 minutes
Homework—15 minutes

Exercise 14.7—60 to 120 minutes in training session

Exercise 14.8—60 to 120 minutes in training session
Homework—30 minutes

Exercise 14.9—60 minutes in training session
Homework—15 minutes

Materials

Peer Power: Book 2, Applying Peer Helper Skills, one copy for each trainee

Optional: Video equipment with video tape of the confrontation and intervention

Speaker on Alcohol and Substance Abuse

Film on the chemical problem

Book—*Counseling the Alcoholic* by Joseph Perez, Accelerated Development Inc., 3400 Kilgore Avenue, Muncie, IN 47304.

Introduction to Module

Drug and alcohol abuse has been one of the major problems facing Americans today. In part, it is a problem because many individuals lack awareness of how chemicals affect their minds and bodies and thus, have a difficult time learning how to lead a healthy, happy life free of chemicals, suggest activities and relationships that can be helpful, and train peer counselors in the use of confrontation when intervention is necessary for a friend or family member.

Trainers may want to supplement this module with speakers and films concerning drugs and alcohol. They also may want to use the form in Exercise 13.2, *Peer Power: Book 2 Applying Peer Helper Skills,* for setting goals.

Training Procedures

1. Decide number of training sessions and Exercises to be included in each.

2. Review content to be covered and suggested activities as listed in *Peer Power, Book 2: Applying Peer Helper Skills.*

3. Be prepared to do demonstration of confrontation as suggested or have videotapes of behaviors to be taught.

4. If a speaker or film is used, the trainer may want to schedule it in the early part of training. The National Council on Alcoholism has excellent films at reasonable cost.

Evaluation Process

As trainer, one can evaluate the process used in teaching a skill by the feedback obtained from trainees and by observations of their written work and their behavior when practicing the skill during training sessions.

Measuring Outcomes

1. Use Exercise 14.1 concerning the review quiz and puzzle and Exercise 14.2 to identify the effects of chemicals and the awareness of use.

2. Use Exercises 14.3 and 14.4 to examine the process and awareness of alternative approaches to drugs and alcohol.

3. Watch and listen closely during the role playing in Exercise 14.5 to measure the ease with which trainees are using confrontation in terms of intervention.

EXERCISE 14.1
CHECKING MY KNOWLEDGE
OF DRUGS AND ALCOHOL

Purpose

To learn some of the symptoms of alcoholism and drug abuse to become aware of the problems caused.

Introduction to Module

In Exercise 14.1, trainees will learn about the effects of alcohol and drug abuse. They will learn about how serious the chemical problem is, perhaps with someone they know. This exercise is designed to make them aware of these problems.

Training Procedures

1. Discuss with trainees the material presented concerning drugs and alcohol.

2. The trainer may want to show a film or ask a speaker to talk to the group concerning the effects of chemicals.

3. "It's Best to Know" questionnaire is excellent to assess the trainees' personal use or friends' use of alcohol.

4. Ask trainees to complete the "Drug Review Quiz" and "These Contain Drugs," too.

5. The trainees will have a hard time believing the effects of drugs and alcohol and may even challenge the trainer concerning the problem. The purpose is not to get into a debate but to encourage them to do further reading about the problem.

6. Assign Exercise 14.1 sheets for homework.

Homework for Trainees
After Group Meeting

1. Ask trainees to complete Exercise 14.1 by the next meeting.

2. Prepare for Exercise 14.2.

EXERCISE 14.2
STAGES OF ADOLESCENT CHEMICAL USE

Purposes

1. To provide trainees the opportunity to understand that chemical abuse happens in stages.

2. To help adolescents to examine their own use as well as that of others.

Introduction to Exercise

In Exercise 14.1, the trainees learned about the effect of chemicals. In Exercise 14.2, the trainees will learn about their own and others chemical use and how it affects them.

Training Procedures

1. Review the material from Exercise 14.1.

2. Discuss the material in Exercise 14.2 in terms of whether or not the trainees agree with it.

3. Emphasize trust which is very important in proceeding with this exercise.

4. Ask the trainees to identify others whom they know and in what stage they are.

5. Ask the trainees to examine the different stages and decide in which stage they are. If any of the trainees bring up their own problems, they may need to be referred to outside help.

6. Ask them what they learned from the activity.

7. Ask the trainees to turn in their homework from Exercise 14.1.

Homework

Ask trainees to prepare for Exercise 14.3.

EXERCISE 14.3
MY OWN CHEMICAL USE

Purpose

To provide trainees an opportunity to assess their own chemical use.

Introduction to Exercise

In Exercise 14.1, trainees learned about the effect of chemicals. In Exercise 14.2, they learned the stages of adolescent chemical use. In Exercise 14.3 trainees will learn about their own use of chemicals and how it affects them.

Training Procedures

1. Review the material from Exercise 14.1, 14.2 and from the speaker.

2. Discuss the material in terms of whether or not trainees agree with it.

3. Ask trainees to identify others they know who have had a chemical problem.

4. Ask trainees to turn in homework from Exercise 14.2.

5. Ask trainees to examine their own chemical use. Use the exercise as a guide for discussion.

6. Ask them what they learned from the activity.

7. This exercise will be helpful if the training group really trusts each other. They should be trusting by this time.

8. Some trainees may have a problem with chemicals. One might suggest they seek outside assistance.

9. Have the trainees set goals concerning chemical use of how they would like to change their life this week.

Homework for Trainees
After Group Meeting

Ask trainees to work on their goal concerning chemicals for the week.

EXERCISE 14.4
TWENTY THINGS I LOVE TO DO
AND MEANINGFUL RELATIONSHIPS

Purpose

To provide an opportunity for trainees to examine their activities and relationships and to see if they are leading to a healthy, fulfilling life.

Introduction to Exercise

As individuals begin to turn away from drugs and alcohol abuse and look to a healthier lifestyle, or as they begin to look at ways to prevent abuse, it is important to look at the kinds of activities they love to do and the type of relationships they have.

This exercise can be used in two ways: to see if the activities and relationships are helping trainees lead a chemical-free life, and to change the activities and relationships if they represent an unhealthy lifestyle. It is important first to examine these areas.

Training Procedures

1. Refer to the "Twenty Things I Love to Do." Encourage trainees to start filling out their lists by suggesting, "They can be big things in life or little things." One might offer an example or two or perhaps suggest, "You might think in terms of the seasons of the year for things you love to do." As trainer, draw up own list of twenty items. Explain to trainees that it is all right if they have more or less than twenty items on their lists.

2. When the lists are done, tell the students to use the rows of boxes on their papers to code their lists in the following manner.

   a. A dollar sign ($) is to be placed beside any item that costs more than $5 each time it is done.

   b. The letter A is to be placed beside those items the trainee really prefers to do alone.

      The letter P, next to activities that the trainee prefers to do with other persons.

      The letters A-P, next to activities that the trainee enjoys doing equally alone or with other persons.

   c. The letters PL are to be placed beside those that require planning.

   d. The coding N5 is to be placed next to those items that would not have been listed five years ago.

   e. The numbers 1 through 5 are to be placed beside the five most important items. The best loved activity should be number 1, the second best 2, and so on.

   f. The trainee is to indicate next to each activity when (day, date) it was last engaged in.

   g. Place a C beside any activity that includes chemicals.

   h. Use the following additional suggestions for coding:

      R—Those things on the list that have an element of risk to them (physical, emotional or intellectual risk).

      I—Any item that involves *intimacy.*

      S—Any item that can be done only in a particular *season* of the year.

      Q—Any item that you think you would enjoy more if you were *smarter.*

      U—Any item that you think others would tend to judge as *unconventional.*

C—Any item that you think others would tend to judge as **conventional.**

MT—Any item that you think you will want to devote increasingly **more time** to in years to come.

CH—Any item that you hope your own **children** will have on their lists someday.

RE—Any item for which nobody would **reject** you just because you love to do it.

3. Discuss with the trainees their results.

Do they see a pattern?
Ask under what circumstance they like to engage in a chosen activity.
Ask the trainees to look at the items listed in direction 1 think of advantages, pleasures, gains, benefits, or satisfactions they gain from the activity.
Ask them if the activities are chemical-free or is this part of their lives?

4. If desired, to give the trainees this activity after the end of training to see if this is different.

5. Have trainees look at Assessment of Meaningful Relationships and select 10 friends that are most significant to them today. Assess each friend selected according to the requirements of the worksheet.

6. Discuss results.

Did they discover anything about themselves?
Were they surprised?
Were they disappointed in what they uncovered?
How many of the relationships involve spending time with chemicals?

7. Ask trainees to think about their activities and relationships and to set any goals to make changes in either.

Homework for Trainees
After Group Meeting

Ask trainees to work on goals for different activities and relationships.

EXERCISE 14.5
PERSONAL INVENTORY

Purposes

1. To help trainees to consider alternative highs from other activities.

2. To help trainees think of alternative highs for any group to which they belong.

Introduction to Exercise

1. Ask trainees how they are doing with their goals from Exercises 14.2, 14.3, and 14.4 and ask them to set future goals (30 minutes).

2. Ask trainees to list ways they get high other than from chemicals. There is a list suggested, but assist them in coming up with other ways. Ask them to explain these issues in a written form.

3. Ask students to circle any of the stereotypes they fit into, and ask if they would like to change.

4. Help students explore ways in which the group to which they belong can find an alternative high.

5. Help trainees set goals concerning alternative highs and changing stereotypes.

Homework for Trainees
After Group Meeting

Ask trainees to continue working on goals for Exercise 14.4 and to begin working on goals for Exercise 14.5. Examples of alternative highs might be to learn to play tennis, go jogging, plan a dance for the school, ask a good friend to go to a movie, or prepare a gourmet meal.

EXERCISE 14.6
RECOGNIZING PROBLEMS IN OTHERS

Purpose

To help trainees to examine the behavior in others in terms of their chemical use and how this affects them and what they would like to have done. This is helpful when trying to do confrontation.

Introduction to Exercise

Peer counselors are often called on to help when someone wants to confront another person with their chemical use. The following exercise will help the trainee keep a journal.

Training Procedures

1. Discuss the reaction to Exercise 14.5.

2. Have the trainees write things that have happened when a family member or friend abused chemicals.

3. Have the trainees write the date and behavior:

My feelings, my reaction, what I would like to see done. For example:

6/25 /Drank so much passed out at party/Angry, frustrated/Cried/ You're not to drink at parties.

4. From the chart, have them make a plan of confrontation.

Guidelines for Confrontation

1. Confrontation is an individualized plan of action.

2. Confrontation must be done out of love, not malice, resentment, or retaliation.

   a. Must be made when the chemical abuser is not under the influence and at an appropriate time and place.

   b. A genuine statement must be sent: "I feel _____ ."

   c. Circumstances must be stated simply.

   d. Must be calm and caring.

3. Before confrontation is made, you must develop:

A sense of direction.
A sense of confidence.
A sense of well-being.

Homework for Trainees
After Group Meeting

Continue with the chart and plan.

EXERCISE 14.7
PUTTING CONFRONTATION INTO ACTION

Purpose

To help trainees use their skills in confrontation, assertiveness, and genuineness in an intervention activity.

Introduction to Exercise

Peer counselors are often put in the position of being aware that someone is having a chemical problem. It is frustrating not knowing what to do about the problem. Sometimes it is good to work with a professional counselor to help facilitate the confrontation concerning drugs and alcohol. This activity also can be used with a friend or family member.

Training Procedures

1. Discuss intervention and the purpose of intervention. Suggest the option of having a professional counselor present.

2. Ask trainees to divide into groups of three.

3. Ask the group members to choose one of the situations given or one with which they are familiar.

4. Have each trainee play one of three roles: the confronter, the person with the problem, and the facilitator.

5. Rotate around the groups to discuss the activity.

6. As trainer, role play one of the situations.

7. Encourage trainees to use all the skills they have learned thus far.

8. Discuss the experience.

Homework for Trainees
After Group Meeting

Continue to work on their own personal goals and read introduction to Exercise 15.1.

EXERCISE 14.8
FAMILIES AFFECTED BY ALCOHOLISM

Purpose

To focus on the effect of alcohol on the family.

Introduction to Exercise

Alcoholism not only affects the alcoholic but it also affects their family. An important aspect of this exercise is to assist trainees in identifying symptoms and finding some help for the dysfunctional family.

Training Procedures

1. Discuss the intervention and the purpose of the intervention from Exercise 14.7.

2. If possible to obtain, show a film or video on adult children of alcoholics or on addiction is a family affair.

3. Ask the trainees to read the material from this section and discuss each point.

4. Ask the trainees if they identify with some of the roles in the family of an alcoholic.

5. Focus on the differences in the body reaction of a social drinker versus that of an alcoholic drinker.

6. Help the trainees focus on their own family in terms of possible alcoholism.

7. Help the trainees to focus on others by having them role play with one person being the child of an alcoholic and another playing the helper and using the information available.

8. Refer them to the appropriate outside help.

9. Have the peer counselors write for information.

Homework for Trainees
After Group Meeting

Have the trainees write their reaction to the activity.

EXERCISE 14.9
JUST SAY "NO"

Purpose

To help the trainees practice saying "No" to peer pressure.

Introduction to Exercise

Peer counselors are role models for others in terms of leading a healthy lifestyle. This exercise is to be used by the training group; at other times it could be used in groups that the peer counselor facilitates or in a classroom presentation.

The trainees need to be encouraged to identify levels of alcohol use in themselves and others and to identify peer pressures to use alcohol in social, party settings. The trainees need to realize that the danger of alcohol lies in the relative ease in obtaining it and its social acceptability over other drugs. The trainees need to see the positive consequences of nonuse or use in moderation (as an adult), and the negative consequences of misuse, abuse, and dependence. The trainees should be asked to define the difference between use and abuse of alcohol and to express ways of avoiding peer pressure to misuse alcohol.

Terms: Nonuse = Avoidance of alcohol
Use = Use of alcohol in moderation

Training Procedures

1. Discuss peer pressure and its meaning.

2. Discuss the terms nonuse, use, abuse, and dependence. Ask for examples of each.

3. Discuss the concept of peer pressure. Ask for definitions and/or examples. Peer pressure has no age limit. Give them examples of peer pressure in the young and old as well as outcomes such as vandalizing or buying a certain car.

4. Discuss how easily students are exposed to alcohol by asking them about their personal introduction to it. Be sure to bring out the party setting. Talk about parties and what these mean.

5. Discuss how some individuals misuse alcohol at parties. Give examples.

6. Ask the members to discuss the consequences of nonuse and abuse.

7. Ask the trainees how they can put a limit on their use.

8. Divide the group into triads. Ask them to role play a party where all are drinking. One person decides to say "No." Change roles so that all of the members have a chance to play each role.

9. Lead a discussion on consequences.

Homework for Trainees
After Group Meeting

Write how it felt to say, "No."

STRESS MANAGEMENT—
MOVING TOWARD WELLNESS

Purpose

To help trainees become aware of their own stressors and to learn effective techniques for coping with stress and moving toward a lifestyle of wellness.

Approximate Time

Module 15—Introduction Homework—60 minutes

Exercise 15.1—60 minutes in training session
Homework—60 minutes

Exercise 15.2—60 minutes in training session
Homework—60 minutes

Exercise 15.3—60 minutes in training session
Homework—60 minutes

Exercise 15.4—60 minutes in training session
Homework—30 minutes

Exercise 15.5—30 minutes in training session
Homework 30 minutes

Exercise 15.6—30 minutes in training session
Homework—30 minutes

Exercise 15.7—60 minutes in training session
Homework—30 minutes

Exercise 15.8—60 minutes in training session
Homework—20 minutes

Exercise 15.9—60 minutes in training session
Homework—60 minutes

Exercise 15.10—60 minutes in training session

Materials

Peer Power: Book 2, Applying Peer Helper Skills, one copy for each trainee

Chalkboard and chalk or flip pad and pen

Optional: Film on wellness or stress

Introduction to Module

In this module trainees will have an opportunity to learn about stress and wellness. The trainer may want to use the goal setting materials described in Exercise 13.2 to assist in changes in behavior. It is important for the leaders to model kinds of responses that they want the trainees to use. This module is a skill that naturally follows the drug and alcohol module, because it assists trainees in moving toward a healthier lifestyle. This module is simply an introduction to stress management and wellness. For changes to be permanent we would suggest working with a group for a minimum of 12 meetings on changing lifestyles (this could be in weight loss, stopping smoking, exercise). The important thing is to help trainees become aware of how they need to make some changes.

Training Procedures

1. Decide on groups of exercises for the training sessions. The decision will make a difference in homework assignments and the time available for each exercise.

2. Follow the sequence of Exercises and the Training Procedures for each.

3. Arrange for films, if used.

4. Arrange for goal setting sheets to be available to trainees.

5. Model each exercise with trainer expressing their stressors and so forth.

Evaluation Process

As a trainer, evaluate the process used in the teaching of the skill by the feedback obtained from trainees and by observations of written work and of their behavior when they are asked to set some goals.

Measuring Outcomes

1. Use Exercises 15.1, 15.2, and 15.3 to identify stressors, stress reaction, and effective techniques for coping with stressors.

2. Use Exercise 15.4 to look at setting goals for a balanced lifestyle. Use Exercise 15.5 for setting long-range goals.

EXERCISE 15.1
WHAT HAPPENS UNDER STRESS

Purpose

To enable trainees to understand stress and to help them identify events that cause stress in their lives.

Introduction to Exercise

This exercise is designed to help trainees learn about stress and to discuss the issue of stress with their trainer. The trainer may decide to show a film on stress and wellness. The exercise is most beneficial to trainees; it helps them to identify stressors through the personal appraisal form.

Training Procedures

1. Review goals set from Module 14 and assess progress.

2. Review the introductory material to this module and that for Exercise 15.1.

3. Show a film on stress and wellness if available.

4. Discuss the whole area of stress and wellness and, for those who are interested, suggest some of the related books listed in the trainer's manual.

5. Ask trainees to fill out the personal appraisal form to help identify stressors.

6. Discuss the responses.

   Example:

   > When are you feeling most stressed?
   > Around whom do you feel most stressed?
   > What did you learn about yourself concerning your stressors?

Homework for Trainees
After Group Meeting

1. Continue working on goals from Module 14 and setting new goals.

2. Recognize stressors in your life during the next week (day).

3. Read Exercise 15.2 on effects of stress.

EXERCISE 15.2
EFFECTS OF STRESS ON ME

Purpose

To enable trainees to understand the effects of stress on the individual both in a positive and negative manner.

Introduction to Exercise

This exercise is designed to help trainees learn about stress and its positive and negative effects. The idea is to convey that stress can be both positive and negative and to assist the trainees in identifying how stress affects them.

Training Procedures

1. Review goals from Module 14 and assess progress.

2. Review stressors and discuss their discovery of additional stressors.

3. Ask trainees to review positive and negative effects of stress.

4. Have trainees work with a partner to help identify effects of stress on them.

5. Discuss results.

6. Have trainees turn in Exercise 15.2 for trainer feedback.

Homework for Trainees
After Group Meeting

1. Continue to work on goals from Module 14.

2. Begin to identify positive and negative effects of stress on trainee.

EXERCISE 15.3
COPING WITH STRESSORS

Purpose

To assist trainees in examining effective and ineffective techniques for coping with stressors.

Introduction to Exercise

Review Exercises 15.1 and 15.2 and return material handed in. This is a very important exercise and begins to help trainees learn new ways of coping with stress.

Training Procedures

1. List stressors and how they affect the trainee (reaction). The trainer models what they want by using the chalkboard.

2. Have trainees discuss stressors and their effects.

3. Ask trainees to work with a partner to develop how they can handle stress (both ineffectively and effectively).

4. The trainer then asks the group to list effective and ineffective techniques for coping with stress. List methods on a chalkboard and have someone else record them on paper in a form for duplicating for the group. This may assist group members in coming up with effective techniques.

5. Refer to goal setting techniques from Exercise 13.2.

6. Ask trainees to try a new effective coping technique.

Homework for Trainees
After Group Meeting

Work on a goal to change by handling stressor differently.

EXERCISE 15.4
UNDERSTANDING THE DIFFERENCE BETWEEN TENSION AND RELAXATION THROUGH IMAGERY

Purpose

To enable the trainees to know the difference between tension and relaxation.

Introduction to Exercise

This exercise uses imagery to help the trainees visualize tension and relaxation. Please have the room as quiet as possible and the light low. You may want to use some quiet music in the background.

Training Procedures

1. Read the following script in a calm, even voice:

    Please get as comfortable as possible and close your eyes to better feel the contrast between tension and relaxation. If you are worried about other things, please put those aside for a while. Today we are going to practice paying attention to how we feel. Sometimes our bodies let us know how we feel before our minds do. Please do not talk. I will be asking you questions, but think about the answers and keep your answers to yourself.

We are now ready to begin. Please follow my directions exactly and concentrate on what you are feeling. First, close your eyes. Keeping your eyes closed, sit in your chair so that you feel comfortable. Think to yourself, how am I sitting? Are my legs stretched out or are they crossed? Are my arms at my side or folded? Am I sitting up straight or slouching? Think about how you are sitting and how you feel right now. (PAUSE HERE FOR A FEW SECONDS.) Keeping your eyes closed, next make a frown with your face. Frown as much as you can. Frown harder . . . harder. Keep frowning, and as you frown, think about how your face feels. Think about, does it hurt? How do your eyebrows feel? How do your cheeks feel? How does your mouth feel? Okay, stop frowning. Keeping your eyes closed, think about how your face feels now. Does it feel differently than when you were frowning? How do your eyebrows feel? Keeping your eyes closed, think about how your face feels now. Does it feel differently than when you were frowning? How do your eyebrows feel? How do your cheeks feel? How does your mouth feel?

Now, keeping your eyes closed, ball both hands into a fist. Ball the fists as tightly as you can and place your arms down at your sides, keeping your fists balled tightly. Think about how you feel right now. How do your fingers feel? How do your arms feel? How do your shoulders feel? (PAUSE FOR A FEW SECONDS.) Now unball your fists and relax. Keeping your eyes closed, think about how you feel right now. How do your fingers feel? How do your arms feel? How do your shoulders feel? Do you feel differently now than you did when you had your fists balled tightly? Think about how you felt with your fists balled and how you feel now. (PAUSE FOR A FEW SECONDS.)

Now, keeping your eyes closed, inhale and, as you inhale, try to hold in your stomach until it touches your back. Think about how you feel right now. How does your chest feel? How does your stomach feel? Exhale and relax. Think about how you feel right now. How does your chest feel? How does your stomach feel? Do you feel differently now than you did when you were holding your breath? (PAUSE FOR A FEW SECONDS.)

Now, keeping your eyes closed, stretch your legs out in front of you. Curl your toes under as tightly as you can. Think about how you feel right now. How do your toes feel? How do your legs feel? Do they hurt? Now uncurl your toes, unstretch your legs, and relax. Keeping your eyes closed, think about how you feel right now. How do your toes feel? How do your legs feel? Do they hurt? Think about how you felt with your toes curled under and your legs stretched and how you feel now. (PAUSE FOR A FEW SECONDS.)

Now, keeping your eyes closed, make a frown with your face, ball your fists as tightly as you can, and place your arms down at your sides; hold in your breath and hold in your stomach until it touches your back. Stretch your legs out in front of you and curl your toes. Keeping eyes closed, think about how you feel right now. Okay, exhale, but keep the frown on your face, your fists balled, your legs stretched, and your toes curled. Think about how you feel right now. Okay, stop frowning, but keep your fists balled, your legs stretched, and your toes curled. Think about how you feel right now. Okay, unball your fists, but keep your legs stretched and your toes curled. Think about how you feel right now. Okay, now relax your legs and toes. Think about how you feel right now. Keep your eyes closed. Think about how your face feels. Think about how your shoulders feel. Think about how your arms feel. Think about how your fingers feel. Think about how your chest feels. Think about how your stomach feels. Think about how your legs feel. Think about how your toes feel. Keep your eyes closed and relax. Now open your eyes.

2. Have the trainees draw a picture of both relaxation and tension. You may even want them to color the pictures.

3. Ask the trainees to answer questions about the images.

4. Lead a discussion with questions from the trainees' worksheets.

5. Have pictures shared by those who are willing.

6. Try to get the idea of using images to feel relaxed.

7. Lead a discussion on how both relaxation and tension relieve stress.

Homework for Trainees
After Group Meeting

1. Ask the trainees to think about their image of relaxation and imagine this at least twice a day.

2. Read and prepare for Exercise 15.5.

EXERCISE 15.5
BALANCED HEALTHY LIFE

Purpose

To provide an opportunity for trainees to look at how balanced their lives are and to examine how they may want to change their lives.

Introduction to Exercise

Ask the trainees to think about their life and about a balance toward a healthier lifestyle. The trainer will have to use several examples for trainees to understand the concept of "out of balance." Only if we help manage stress at all levels of their lives are we able to move toward wellness.

Training Procedures

1. Review goals from Exercise 15.4 and answer any questions.

2. Explain that today the training will involve looking at the "total you" to see if anything is out of balance.

3. Optional: Ask one trainee to stand in the middle of a circle. Have another representing "diet" move clockwise around the circle. Ask another trainee to move counterclockwise representing "emotional." Proceed until everyone is moving in either a clockwise or counterclockwise direction and then ask the "physical" to sit down. Ask the others to stop and discuss with them the interaction of all areas and what happens when one part stops.

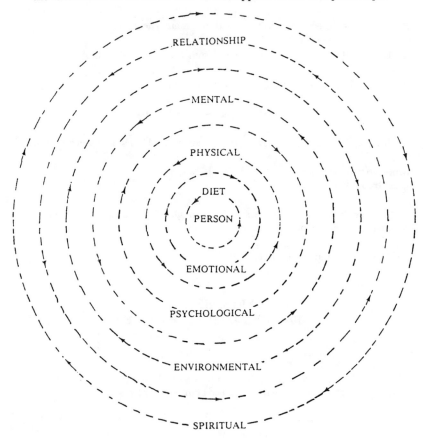

4. Ask them to think about their own lives.

   Are they eating balanced meals?
   Are they feeling good most of the time?

Are they getting adequate exercise (vigorous exercise three times a week)?
Are they feeling okay psychologically?
Are they able to think and concentrate and problem solve?
Are they living in a healthy environment?
Do they have supportive friends and family?
Do they have a spiritual outlet?
Additional questions.

5. Ask trainees to set goals to deal with an area that is out of balance. They should not work on more than one area at a time.

Example:

   "I will exercise three times a week by running two miles each time."

Homework for Trainees
After Group Meeting

1. Ask them to work on goal.

2. Read and complete Exercise 15.6.

EXERCISE 15.6
HEALTH HABITS AS A
MEANS OF REDUCING STRESS

Purpose

To help the trainees get in touch with their life styles and examine ways to change their life styles.

Introduction to Exercise

The way we choose to live our lives has a lot to do with how long we live and how we handle stress and tension. In the trainee book is a checklist to help trainees get in touch with some simple ways to change their lives.

Training Procedures

1. Review the homework from the previous exercise.

2. Show a film or filmstrip that looks at these issues of wellness and healthy life styles.

3. Lead a discussion on the above health habits.

4. Lead a discussion on how to help the trainees change their lives.

Homework for Trainees
After Group Meeting

1. Develop a plan of action in terms of life change.

2. Read and complete Exercise 15.7.

EXERCISE 15.7
THOUGHTS, FEELINGS, BEHAVIOR

Purpose

1. To assist the trainees in understanding the differences among thoughts, feelings, and behavior.

2. To help the trainees understand how thoughts affect feelings and behavior.

Introduction to Exercise

When trainees and/or others are involved in a tense situation, trainees need to understand that they have a choice in terms of how they behave. Their behavior is influenced by thoughts and feelings. Vital for them is to understand that they can change their thoughts and hence their behavior.

Training Procedures

1. Review the homework from the last exercise.

2. Review the differences among thoughts, feelings, and behavior.

$$A = \text{Thoughts}$$
$$B = \text{Feelings}$$
$$C = \text{Behavior}$$

$$A + B = C$$

3. Demonstrate with role-playing situations two alternative ways of thinking and feeling and behavior.

4. Divide the group into triads and continue the role-playing situations along with other situations that they may want to introduce themselves and then ask them to write their thoughts, feelings, and behavior as well as alternative thoughts, feelings, and behavior.

5. While observing the role-playing activities, identify the trainees who have particular strengths in making up dialogues that illustrate accurately the situations. Give assistance to them. Additional practice sessions could be established with the trainees' own examples.

6. Lead a discussion centered around:

    a. Do you see that the way we think about a situation often determines how we act?

    b. Do you understand that we all choose to behave in a certain way?

7. Have the trainees identify strong feelings in their personal life and come up with feelings and behavior.

Homework for Trainees
After Group Meeting

1. Ask the trainees to identify strong feelings and thoughts and write them; have them consider alternative thoughts and feelings.

2. Read and complete Exercise 15.8.

EXERCISE 15.8
EXAMINING YOUR SUPPORT SYSTEM

Purpose

To enable the trainees to understand the need for a good support system.

Introduction to Exercise

This exercise is designed to help trainees learn about support systems and the help it can give them, how to expand their own support system and make opportunities to give their support system a change, and how they can support others.

Training Procedures

1. Review the homework from the previous exercise.

2. Discuss the fact that we all have "people needs" and that no one is self-sufficient, although some need people more than others.

3. Ask the trainees to make their lists of individuals with whom they have contact and what needs they meet.

4. Ask the trainees to call out the needs that they have listed from their right-hand column on the chart, "Your Needs and Your Support System," as you put them on the board.

5. Review the lists and show that they generally fall into the following categories:

Physical Needs: sex, food, shelter
Psychological Needs: caring, understanding, listening, intimacy
Social Needs: belonging, status, group identity, helping others

6. Lead the trainees through a discussion concerning how often they see those individuals whom they feel they need, who makes contact, and is there a pattern?

7. Explore the next section in terms of improving the effectiveness of individual support systems by planning a support system so that one's needs do not go unmet.

8. Discuss the three columns in the chart in their workbooks: listed on the left-column of the chart is the type of support that individuals need; in the second column is one for work and school, and the third column is personal life. Each of the three columns is divided into "Present" and "Possible" columns.

9. Ask the trainees to brainstorm possible individuals who might supply support.

10. Focus on others whom we try to support and what function we play in terms of meeting others' needs.

Homework for Trainees
After Group Meeting

1. Ask the trainees to write a paragraph concerning how to expand their own support system as well as how they can be supportive of others.

2. Read Exercise 15.9.

EXERCISE 15.9
HOW TO BEAT STRESS

Purpose

To provide a long-range plan to handle stress in a healthy manner.

Introduction to Exercise

How we choose to handle stress is an important factor of our well-being. Work with trainees to help them handle stress more effectively. It may be desired to take them through a relaxation exercise.

Training Procedures

1. Review goals from Exercise 15.8 and previous modules.

2. Ask trainees to review the list of how to beat stress.

3. Ask trainees to go through a relaxation activity. Have them sit comfortably with their eyes closed as trainer very slowly reads the following exercise. Ask them to quietly repeat each statement when finished.

Relaxation Phrases

a. I feel quite quiet.

b. I am beginning to feel quite relaxed.

c. The muscles in my toes and feet feel heavy and relaxed.

d. The muscles in my calves, knees, thighs, and hips feel heavy and relaxed.

e. My abdomen, solar plexus, and the whole central portion of my body feel heavy, relaxed, and comfortable.

f. My fingers, hands, arms, and shoulders feel heavy, relaxed, and comfortable.

g. My neck, jaws, eyes, and forehead feel relaxed. They feel comfortable and smooth.

h. The muscles in my whole body feel heavy, comfortable, relaxed, and quiet.

i. Continue silently on your own, feeling this heaviness throughout the body and continuing the relaxation (take 1-2 minutes).

j. I am quite relaxed.

k. My arms (legs) and hands (feet) feel heavy and warm.

l. I feel quite quiet.

m. My whole body is relaxed and my hands (feet) feel warm, relaxed and warm.

n. I can feel the warmth flowing down my arms (legs) into my hands (feet).

o. My hands are warm, toasty warm.

p. Warmth is flowing into my hands (feet); they are warm, very warm.

q. My hands (feet) are warm, relaxed and warm.

r. Continue silently on your own, feeling this warmth in the hands (feet) and fingers (toes) (take 1-2 minutes).

s. My whole body feels relaxed and my mind is quiet.

t. I have withdrawn my attention from the outside world, and I feel serene and still.

u. My attention is turned inward, and I feel at ease.

v. Within my mind I can visualize, imagine, and experience myself as relaxed, comfortable, and still.

w. I am aware in an easy, quiet, inward-turned way.

x. My mind is calm and quiet.

y. I feel an inward quietness.

z. I am at peace; I am at peace.

Continue silently on your own, feeling your own body as relaxed and feeling your mind as calm, quiet, and peaceful (take 1-2 minutes).

The relaxation is now concluded and the whole body is reactivated with a deep breath and the following phrases: (a) I feel life and energy flowing through my toes, feet, calves, knees, thighs, hips, solar plexus, chest, shoulders, arms, hands, fingers, neck, jaws, eyes, and head; (b) this energy makes me feel light and alive; (c) I open my eyes and make contact with the outside world; (d) I feel refreshed and good. (Stretch if desired).

4. Ask the trainees how they felt.

5. Ask them to identify a long-range goal. Have them fill out the long-range goal forms. Have the whole group listen to the goals and as trainer make comments.

6. Ask trainees to turn in the long-range goal forms for review.

Homework for Trainees
After Group Meeting

1. Begin to implement a long-range goal.

2. Read and complete Exercise 15.10.

EXERCISE 15.10
LONG-RANGE GOALS

Purpose

To help the trainees set up long-range goals in terms of changing their life style.

Introduction to Exercise

Help trainees know the importance of developing their goals. Tell them that as a group assistance will be given to set up specific activities for them to do to accomplish development of long-range goals.

Training Procedures

1. Review the homework from the previous exercise.

2. Ask the trainees to address long-range goals for themselves in terms of mental, physical, and emotional aspects.

3. Use the last sheet in their workbooks for this module to expand on their goal(s).

4. Divide the group into twos and review their long-range goal(s).

5. Ask the trainees to have you review those goals.

6. Discuss how a support system could assist them in reaching these goals.

Homework for Trainees
After Group Meeting

1. Read the introduction to the next module.

2. Read and complete Exercise 16.1.

ENHANCING SELF ESTEEM

Purpose

To help trainees assess their self esteem and focus on their strengths.

Approximate Time

Module 16—Introduction
Homework—10 to 15 minutes

Exercise 16.1—60 minutes in training session
Homework—30 minutes

Exercise 16.2—60 minutes in training session
Homework—20 minutes

Exercise 16.3—30 to 60 minutes in training session
Homework—30 minutes

Exercise 16.4—30 to 60 minutes in training session
Homework—30 minutes

Exercise 16.5—60 minutes in training session
Homework—30 minutes

Exercise 16.6—60 minutes in training session

Exercise 16.7—60 minutes in training session
Homework—30 minutes

Exercise 16.8—60 minutes in training
Homework—30 minutes

Materials

Peer Power: Book 2, Applying Peer Helper Skills, one copy for each trainee

Cards 3 x 5

Introduction to Module

Trainer can use enhancing self esteem exercises to help trainees develop positive feelings about themselves, to help them view themselves as capable of developing and changing through examination of their strengths, successes, and values, and to teaching the trainee how to set and act on goals. A helpful resource is the book entitled *Enhancing Self Esteem* by D. Frey and J. Carlock (1984), published by Accelerated Development Inc., Muncie, IN.

It is important for the trainer to be structured, positive, and open, and to encourage and build these important feelings in trainees.

Training Procedures

1. Decide the number of training sessions and the exercises to be included in each.

2. Review the content to be covered and the suggested activities as listed in *Peer Power: Book 2, Applying Peer Helper Skills,* and *Peer Counseling* book.

3. Be prepared to be open and positive.

Evaluation Process

As trainer evaluate the process used in teaching this skill by the feedback you are obtaining from the trainees and by observations of them in the group.

Measuring Outcomes

1. Use Exercise 16.1 to determine whether or not trainees can relate present self-confidence to past events.

2. Use Exercise 16.2 to determine whether or not trainees can understand the effects of both positive and negative messages.

3. Use Exercise 16.3 to get acquainted with and tune into positive thinking.

4. Use Exercises 16.4 and 16.5 to help examine and clarify trainees' values.

5. Use Exercise 16.6 to see if trainees can acknowledge their strengths.

6. Use Exercise 16.7 to set short-term and long-term goals.

7. Use Exercise 16.8 to get feedback from others.

EXERCISE 16.1
ENHANCING SELF-ESTEEM

Purpose

To assist trainees in identifying their level of self-esteem and ways of enhancing their self-esteem.

Introduction to Exercise

The purpose of this exercise is to assess how trainees see themselves in terms of self-esteem. The checklist in this exercise might be good to give again at the end of the module to see whether or not the level of self-esteem has changed for the trainees. The last part of this module is designed to get the trainees to look at areas on which they need to work. You may want to refer them to other modules if they need additional help such as assertiveness training for speaking up.

Training Procedures

1. Review the introduction to see whether or not the trainees agree and have other things to add.

2. Ask the trainees to test themselves on the checklist.

3. Ask the trainees how they would rate themselves in terms of self-esteem. If they answer "Yes" to most of the items, then they need a lot of help. If they answer "Yes" to only some items, then these are the areas on which you can help them work.

4. Discuss ways to enhance self-esteem.

5. Help the trainees to develop individually a plan of action.

Homework for Trainees
After Group Meeting

1. Ask them to observe themselves and how they react to others.

2. Read and complete Exercise 16.2.

EXERCISE 16.2
MESSAGES FROM THE PAST

Purpose

To get in touch with positive and negative messages from the past.

Introduction to Exercise

This is a powerful exercise. As a result of doing it, you may need to do a great deal of discussing and possibly make referrals for some participants.

Training Procedures

1. Review the homework from the last exercise.

2. Discuss the idea that our past influences the present, for example, what individuals whom we have known have said to us. Help the trainees to identify messages from the past that influence them today. "If it is worth doing, it is worth doing right." "You are a bum." "You are dumb." "You are fat."

3. Lead a discussion on how these messages still influence us today.

4. Discuss ways to change some of the messages.

Homework for Trainees
After Group Meeting

1. Be aware of messages from the past.

2. Read and complete Exercise 16.3.

EXERCISE 16.3
STRENGTHS

Purpose

To assist trainees in identifying significant good events in their lives, to help identify strengths, and to build cohesiveness.

Introduction to Exercise

The purpose of this exercise is to help trainees discover or rediscover their strengths, capabilities, and attributes—their own human potential.

"Although you will not be encouraged to take risks in this group, your experience will be most meaningful and productive if you behave as authentically as possible. So try constantly to be honest with the group and with yourself. The training group will be a very helpful resource for each of you."

"If you behave authentically, you might reveal some things about yourself that you don't usually reveal. Therefore, the information that is shared in this module is confidential; it belongs only to this group. Do you agree?" (Clear up any doubts and/or questions about this before proceeding.)

Training Procedures

1. Review goals set from Module 15, the long-range planning and their progress.

2. Read or summarize information from introduction of the module.

3. Each group member will have five minutes to share with the others those significant events of his/her life.

   What were the good moments? The good events? The good relationships? What were your successes? Positive achievements? Rewards? Honors? Or simply good, meaningful, rewarding experiences?

   Just name them without complete sentences to give as many significant ones as possible within the time limit. Each of you will have five minutes.

4. Complete the written exercise for Exercise 16.3.

5. This is usually a very powerful experience.

Homework for Trainees
After Group Meeting

1. Continue working on goals.

2. Continue thinking about positive experiences.

EXERCISE 16.4
PERSONAL COAT OF ARMS

NOTE: Our thanks to Str. Louis, Principal of St. Julian's School in Chicago in 1972.

Purpose

To help trainees publicly affirm things that they believe in and share these with the group.

Introduction to Exercise

The trainer could go into the significance of a coat of arms shield. The idea is to publicly affirm these values and things that are important and to share them with the group.

Training Procedures

1. Review goals from previous meetings.

2. Divide the coat of arms shield into six sections (see figure in *Peer Power: Book 2, Applying Peer Helper Skills*, Module 16). The trainer makes it clear that words are to be used only in the sixth block, all the others are to contain pictures. Stress that it is not an art lesson, only crude stick figures need be used. Review what goes into each section.

3. Ask trainees to share their coat of arms with the group. Encourage questions and comments.

4. Suggest that trainees take the coat of arms home and if they feel comfortable doing so, share it with their families.

5. Discuss experience. "I learned. . . . . . ."

   "I was surprised at. . . . . . ."

Homework for Trainees
After Group Meeting

Continue to work on goals from previous modules.

EXERCISE 16.5
VALUES AUCTION

NOTE: Recognition for the Values Auction is given to W. Clement Stone Foundation, *Achievement Motivation Program*, 111 E. Wacker Dr., Suite 510, Chicago, IL 60601.

Purpose

To publicly affirm values to other group members.

Introduction to Exercise

The values auction can be fun for the participants while helping them clarify their values.

Training Procedures

1. Check on past goals.

2. Read the directions in *Peer Power: Book 2, Applying Peer Helper Skills*, and assist the trainees in going through the activity.

3. Each item is discussed in terms of the value it represents. If their highest bid was $1,000, they would be able to assess this as their most important value.

4. The trainer plays the auctioneer.

5. This is generally an activity that the trainees enjoy.

Homework for Trainees
After Group Meeting

Continue working on goals.

EXERCISE 16.6
STRENGTH ACKNOWLEDGEMENT

Purpose

This exercise is designed to assist the trainees in expressing their strengths.

Training Procedures

1. Review the goals on which the trainees are working.

2. Discuss the fact that focusing on strengths is difficult. The trainer should model the kind of discussion the group wants.

3. Ask for a volunteer to share a self-perceived strength.

4. Ask for comments from others.

5. A desirable procedure is to ask trainees if there is anything keeping them from using their strengths.

Homework for Trainees
After Group Meeting

Continue working on goals.

EXERCISE 16.7
JOURNEY INTO LIFE GOAL SETTING

Purpose

To assist trainees in short-term and long-term goal setting using some of their strengths.

Introduction to Exercise

This exercise is designed to help group members set short-term and long-term goals about something they will do.

Training Procedures

1. Review goals on which trainees are working.

2. Pass out note cards and ask participants to write short-term goals and share them with the group.

3. Ego reinforcement: When all have established their short-term goals say, "Now, look at your goal. Commit the entire statement to memory."

4. Have the group stand up and form a circle with arms around each other.

5. While they are together say, "Remember that we all have our recorders, our 'alter-egos.' These are the only ones who have data about us because they record for us. So, during the week let's each make copies of the personal data our recorders gave us and try to use it."

6. Ask them to write on the cards the following sentence stems and then complete each.

    a.   If I had three wishes, they would be

    b.   Two of my recent significant achievements are

    c.   List one recent, significant failure or unresolved task or problem

    d.   If I were to die, I would want to be remembered for

7. Divide into pairs. With your alter-ego set achievement goals for one year or longer. Talk about them.

8. Ask the trainees to write goals and give them to their partner to check on in one year.

Homework for Trainees
After Group Meeting

Continue working on goals from previous modules.

EXERCISE 16.8
CONCLUSION

Purpose

To gain feedback concerning strengths from others in the group.

Introduction to Exercise

This is a powerful exercise and the trainees should feel very good about the experience. Tell the group to be serious.

Training Procedures

1. Check on previous goals.

2. Distribute cards so that each trainee has a separate card for every other group member.

3. Have each participant write a positive statement about every other trainee. These statements must be strengths or attributes, only good qualities. Tell the group to mean what they say and to be spontaneous. Then have them add an "I urge you to _____ " on the back of each card. This focuses on suggested change.

4. Discuss the cards.

5. Give participants the cards written about themselves.

6. This activity may take one or two training sessions.

Homework for Trainees
After Group Session

1. Work on short-term and long-term goals.

2. Review the cards given to you.

3. Read the introduction to Module 17.

LEADERSHIP TRAINING

Purpose

To enable trainees to examine their leadership style and to develop techniques for leading a group, such as action plans, and planning a meeting.

Approximate Time

Module 17—Introduction
Homework—10 to 15 minutes of homework

Exercise 17.1—60 minutes in training session

Exercise 17.2—60 to 90 minutes in training session
Homework—30 minutes

Exercise 17.3—60 to 90 minutes in training session
Homework—30 minutes

Exercise 17.4—60 minutes in training session
Homework—60 minutes

Exercise 17.5—30 minutes in training session

Exercise 17.6—60 minutes in training session
Homework—30 minutes

Materials

Peer Power: Book 2, Applying Peer Helper Skills, one copy for each trainee

Optional: If this module is used with an existing organization, one may want to use his/her own activities with which to work in Exercises 17.4, 17.5, and 17.6.

Introduction to Module

Many individuals are often called upon to serve in leadership roles who lack skills to do a good job. This is frustrating for the group and for the leader. This module will assist in helping trainees identify their own leadership styles and to learn some practical ideas that will help them be an effective leader.

Training Procedures

1. Decide on grouping of the activities.

2. Decide if it is desired to use own organization.

3. Move from group to group to give feedback.

Evaluation Process

As a trainer, evaluate the process used in the teaching through feedback from participants and from the written work.

Measuring Outcomes

1. Use Exercise 17.1 to measure leadership style.

2. Use Exercise 17.2 to assess discussion group skills.

3. Use Exercise 17.3 to assess time management skills.

4. Use Exercises 17.4, 17.5, and 17.6 to actually set up a plan of action.

EXERCISE 17.1
LEADERSHIP STYLE PROFILE

Purpose

To help trainees assess their own leadership styles.

Introduction to Exercise

Leadership style is learned by individuals discovering the kind of leaders they are, either task-oriented or people-oriented. The following exercises will assist in reviewing the differences between the two.

Training Procedures

1. Discuss the different types of leaders: those that are democratic, laissez faire, and autocratic.

2. The leader may want to role play the different types.

3. Have trainees fill out the Questionnaire.

4. Talk about the importance of combined concern for task and person.

5. Announce that to locate themselves on the Leadership Style Profile sheet, group participants will score their own questionnaires on the dimensions of task orientation (T) and people orientation (P).

6. Instruct the trainees in the scoring as follows:

    a.   Circle the items number for items 8, 12, 17, 18, 19, 30, 34, and 35.

    b.   Write a "1" in front of the circled items to which you responded S (seldom) or N (never).

    c.   Write a "1" in front of items not circled to which you responded A (always) or F (frequently).

    d.   Circle the "1's" which you have written in front of the following items: 3, 5, 8, 10, 15, 18, 19, 22, 24, 26, 28, 30, 32, 34, and 35.

    e.   Count the circled "1's." This is your score for concern for task. Record this number in the blank following the letter "T."

7. Ask trainee to follow directions on the profile sheet. Then lead a discussion of the implications that members attach to their location on the profile.

NOTE: The T-P Leadership Questionnaire comes from T. J. Sergiovanni, R. Metzcus, and L. Burden, (1969). Reprinted from *A Handbook of Structured Experiences for Human Relations Training, Volume I*, J. William Pfeiffer and John E. Jones, Editors, San Diego, CA. Copyright 1984, titled *"T-P Leadership Questionnaire: An Assessment of Style."*

Toward a particularistic approach to leadership style: Some findings. *American Educational Research Journal, 6,* 162-79.

Homework for Trainees
After Group Meeting

1. Think about the types of leadership observed, and decide if they are task oriented or people oriented.

2. Read the information in Exercise 17.2.

EXERCISE 17.2
LEADING A DISCUSSION GROUP

Purpose

To have the experience of leading a small discussion group and getting feedback.

Introduction to Exercise

Leaders are often asked to lead discussion groups. This Exercise will assist the trainee in leading a discussion group.

Training Procedures

1. Ask for feedback from Exercise 17.1.

2. Have trainees divide into small discussion groups.

3. Ask one person to be an observer and use observation form.

4. Move among discussion groups and give leader feedback.

5. Continue until everyone has been both a discussion leader and an observer.

Homework for Trainees
After Group Meeting

Look over Exercise 17.3.

EXERCISE 17.3
WORKING WITH OTHERS

Purpose

To assist the trainees in understanding how they relate to others who are different and can work with others who have different strengths. They also get practice in motivating others in a group meeting.

Introduction to Exercise

The ability to understand and work with others different than ourselves is an important skill to have and use. Individuals often withdraw and are afraid of individuals who are different. This exercise will take through a role-play situation.

Training Procedures

1. Review previous homework.

2. Discuss the concept of individuals whom the trainees know who are different than they.

    a. Do they get along with them?

    b. Are they threatened?

3. Take the trainees first through an example of different types of individuals.

4. Lead a role play with a group of different types of individuals.

5. Using the "Role Play Example" in *Peer Power: Book 2, Applying Peer Helper Skills*, the election, help them think of team members.

Example: Outgoing individuals of different cultures. Someone good with accounting and money. Someone good at setting up an exact plan.

6. Have a group to role-play the example. To do so will necessitate roles for each including identifying the leader.

7. Following the role-playing, discuss the actions of the leader and help the group understand positive aspects and to identify other things that might have been done, if any.

8. Change roles so that all of the members have a chance to lead.

Homework for Trainees
After Group Meeting

1. Have the trainees think of a group that they presently lead and decide how to work with those individuals who are different than they.

2. Have them prepare for the next exercise.

EXERCISE 17.4
TIME MANAGEMENT

Purpose

To help the trainees look at time wasters and look at how they spend their present time.

Introduction to Exercise

Often leaders are ineffective because they cannot get things done. This exercise will help you look at the time management skills of the trainees and suggest ways to change them.

Training Procedures

1. Discuss the different time wasters.

2. Discuss ways that they can change some of their time wasters.

3. Help the trainees look at the long-term and short-term goals that they have such as the following:

Long-term goals
- Going to college
- Being a good parent
- Becoming a pilot

Short-term goals

- Losing weight
- Quitting smoking

4. Ask the trainees to make a list of activities for yesterday.

5. Ask them to account for the approximate time that it took.

6. Ask the trainees to indicate whether the activities were "have to" or "want to." Ask them to notice the balance.

7. Ask whether the activities fit into short-term or long-term goals.

8. Ask the trainees to develop a plan to manage their time differently.

Homework for Trainees
After Group Meeting

Ask the trainees to:

1. Keep a chart of how they spend their time.

2. Keep a journal of how to change time problems.

3. Learn to prioritize activities.

4. Look for a balance of "have to" and "want to."

EXERCISE 17.5
DEVELOPING AN ACTION PLAN

Purpose

To assist trainees in developing their own action plan for a leadership position.

Introduction to Exercise

This activity will help trainees focus on how to establish what needs to be done in certain positions.

Training Procedures

1. Ask for feedback from Exercise 17.4.

2. Have the trainees work in groups of two to develop their own action plan.

3. If they do not have assigned leadership positions or cannot think of one, the trainer needs to assign one.

4. Work with the groups in the development of the plan.

5. Collect the action plans for written feedback.

Homework for Trainees
After Group Meeting

If not done during the session, complete the action plan at home. Complete Exercise 17.6 for homework.

EXERCISE 17.6
PLANNING PUBLIC RELATIONS

Purpose

To assist trainees in following through with their plans for Exercise 17.3 and plan for the public relations aspect.

Introduction to Exercise

Leaders must keep their publics—membership, coworkers, community, organizational officials—informed of plans, needs, and activities. To do so requires careful planning well in advance with responsibilities clearly delineated. Approval must be obtained before implementation of the plan as well as assurance of financial and other necessary resources. The leader is the one to make sure that his public relations aspect is integrated early and throughout the action.

Training Procedures

1. Return material from Exercise 17.5 with comments. These sheets are to be used in Exercise 17.6.

2. Ask trainees to share homework from Exercise 17.6 and share comments that might help each other.

3. Divide the group so that they work in pairs and ask them to assist each other in improving their public relations plans.

4. Demonstrate with a local specific example the different publics and their needs for different kinds of information about an organization or a business.

5. Collect the written plans.

6. Have trainees to share experiences from working on their plans as partners and answer questions.

Homework for Trainees
After Group Meeting

Complete Exercise 17.7 for next meeting.

EXERCISE 17.7
PLANNING A CONFERENCE OR OTHER MEETING

Purpose

To assist trainees to work as a team for planning a conference or meeting.

Introduction to Exercises

Leaders are often called upon to develop and plan a meeting. It is important to be able to do this.

Training Procedures

1. Return material from Exercise 17.4 and make comments.

2. Ask for any problem with homework from Exercise 17.5.

3. Ask trainees to share homework for Exercise 17.5 and make suggestions.

4. Ask trainees to divide into teams of three and plan the conference listed in *Peer Power: Book 2, Applying Peer Helper Skills,* or in their own area.

5. Collect the written plans.

6. Ask teams to share their plan with the entire training group. Offer suggestions.

PEER HELPING
THROUGH TUTORING

Purpose

1. To learn material about motivation.

2. To understand their own ability to tutor.

3. To understand their own study habits.

4. To learn their own way of learning.

5. To learn specific ways of tutoring individuals in problem areas.

6. To learn how to deal with problem areas.

7. To learn how to be a successful tutor.

Approximate Time

Module 18—Introduction, 10 to 15 minutes for homework

Exercise 18.1—60 to 120 minutes
Homework—30 minutes

Exercise 18.2—30 to 60 minutes
Homework—30 minutes

Exercise 18.3—30 to 60 minutes
Homework—120 minutes

Exercise 18.4—120 to 160 minutes
Homework—120 minutes

Exercise 18.5—30 to 60 minutes
Homework—30 minutes

Exercise 18.6—60 to 120 minutes
Homework—30 minutes

Materials

Peer Power: Book 2, Applying Peer Helping Skills, one copy for each trainee.

Optional: Slide, film, or video show on study skills.

Speaker: Ask someone from special education (an L.D. or B.D. teacher).

Introduction to Module

Tutoring can be one of the most rewarding roles a peer can perform. I feel that it is very important that the peer tutor has completed *Peer Power: Book 1* before starting on this module. You may want to expand on this module if this is the only role that your trainees will be performing. You may want to include different material if they will be working with very young children or adults. The exercises and information from this unit also can be used with the tutee. The material is not designed to help tutors who are working with students with severe learning problems. These students may need professional tutors.

Training Procedures

1. Decide the number of training sessions and exercises to be included in this module.

2. Be prepared to demonstrate all the role-playing situations. If you don't feel comfortable, ask a professional teacher to demonstrate some of these role-playing situations.

3. If a speaker is used, time it with the appropriate exercise.

4. The homework portion of this module is important and should be reviewed carefully by you as the trainer.

5. When actually doing tutoring, the management becomes very important in terms of public relations with the cooperating teacher on such issues as the place to do the tutoring and support for the tutor and materials.

Evaluation Process

As a trainer, you can evaluate the process used in teaching a skill by the role playing used by the trainees and the written homework.

Measuring Outcomes

1. Use Exercise 18.5 in terms of integration of skills.

2. Use Exercise 18.6 in terms of tutoring operation.

EXERCISE 18.1
TUTOR: SELF-ASSESSMENT

Purpose

1. To provide the trainees an opportunity to assess their own ability to tutor.

2. To review the introductory material.

Introduction to Exercise

The following assessment can be used before starting the module and at the conclusion. You may want to supplement the introduction section with a slide, film, or video show on motivation or learning.

Training Procedures

1. Review the material from the introduction as well as the reaction of the trainees to the slide, film, or video show.

2. Discuss motivation and Maslow's needs in relationship to where they are as persons (e.g., level of love needs). Use the introduction material to Module 18, *Peer Power: Book 2, Applying Peer Helper Skills.*

3. Discuss the difference between encouraging and discouraging statements.

4. Help the trainees complete the "Self-Assessment Questionnaire" and look at the strengths that they have now as tutors.

5. Help the trainees set goals for improving weaknesses; use the entire group to brainstorm goals.

6. Have each trainee complete the "Goal Sheet." Then talk with them individually and, when the plan is appropriate, sign the "Goal Sheet" to show your approval. (This may need to be completed at the next meeting with the group.)

Homework for Trainees
After Group Meeting

1. Ask the trainees to fill out the goal sheet if not completed and review with them any additional ideas that you may have.

2. Have the trainees prepare for Exercise 18.2.

EXERCISE 18.2
HOW I STUDY

Purpose

1. To help the trainees understand their own study habits.

2. To help the trainees to develop a plan to improve their own study habits.

Introduction to Exercise

Discuss with the trainees that they need to understand their own values and their own ways of studying. Next they can use their strengths to help others, and they can learn new ways to study.

Trainees also may want to use this with their own tutee once a relationship has been established.

Training Procedures

1. Discuss the Trainees' homework assignment.

2. Review the total scores on the "Personal Study Habits Survey."

3. Assist the trainees in seeing their strengths and weaknesses.

4. Assign homework to develop a plan (you may want to spend class time getting them started).

Homework for Trainees
After Group Meeting

1. Develop a plan for change.

2. Bring back for review.

3. Prepare for Exercise 18.3.

EXERCISE 18.3
HOW I LEARN BEST

Purpose

1. To understand the preferred way of learning.

2. To help the trainees apply this information to how they study.

3. To help the trainees apply this to the tutoring situation.

Introduction to Exercise

We all have a preferred way that we learn best. However, we need to develop additional learning styles. Be sure to be clear about these different learning styles and also about developing additional ways of learning. Use lecturer and/or audio-visual materials.

Training Procedures

1. Use "Styles of Learning" found in this exercise to use in your lecture about different styles of learning.

2. Provide examples and have the trainees to brainstorm examples. Have them to share how they learn.

Examples

- Big picture making

- Making connection to something else

3. Have the trainees take and score the "Learning Style Survey."

4. Discuss the results of the survey.

5. Lead a discussion on "Discussion Questions."

6. Make the point that there is no right way to learn.

7. Work with the trainees, showing them how to do their homework.

Homework for Trainees
After Group Meeting

1. Design and plan tutoring a person using each style.

2. Ask the trainees to use this skill in teaching various content areas.

3. Prepare for Exercise 18.4.

STYLES OF LEARNING

Visual Learning. Learns by watching, likes to read, has good imagination, shows emotions facially, usually has neat penmanship, dresses neatly, plans and outlines, takes neat notes, likes order and neatness.

Auditory Learning. Learns by listening, likes to discuss, remembers by reciting, will move lips while reading silently, likes quiet, is distracted by outside noise, displays emotion through intonation.

Kinesthetic Learning. Learns by doing, needs to be directly involved, likes to move around during study, appears impulsive, shows emotion, uses hands when talking, does not tend toward order and neatness.

Examples of visual tutoring:

- Write out an outline.
- Have tutees take notes.

Examples of auditory tutoring:

- Read directions out loud.
- Talk to tutee about work.
- Tape record important things.

Examples of kinesthetic tutoring:

- Hands-on activity.
- Encourage writing
- Trace new words.

EXERCISE 18.4
MAJOR STUDY SKILLS

Purpose

1. To teach the tutor how to use SQ3R method, test taking, note taking, writing skills, and time management.

2. To have the tutors practice using these skills.

Introduction to Exercise

This exercise may take three to four class periods to learn and practice. You may also want to invite a special education teacher to demonstrate some of these skills.

Training Procedures

1. Review the homework from the previous exercise.

2. Review the written material in this exercise.

3. Demonstrate each activity.

4. Have the trainees work in groups of threes: one person is the tutor, one is the tutee, and one is the observer. The observer is to give feedback if the tutor used the information in this exercise.

5. Have the trainees do the other activities identified in Directions 4 through 9.

Homework for Trainees
After Group Meeting

Ask the tutors to write the activities that they were not able to complete in the group work.

Prepare for Exercise 18.5.

EXERCISE 18.5
PROBLEMS IN TUTORING

Purpose

1. To help the tutors learn how to deal with special problems in tutoring.

2. To practice using skills in tutoring.

Introduction to Exercise

This exercise needs to be used to integrate the skills used in *Peer Power: Book 1* and also in the earlier learning of this module.

Training Procedures

1. Review the homework.

2. Demonstrate the following:

   Attending
   Empathy
   Encouraging word
   Contracting

3. Ask the tutors to work in threes. While doing their role-playing ask them to work on attending, empathy, responses, encouragement, and contracting.

4. Stop after completing each of the directions in the *Peer Power: Book 2, Applying Peer Helper Skills*, and discuss and give feedback.

5. Lead a final discussion.

Homework for Trainees
After Group Meeting

1. Have the trainees complete in writing those items in the directions that were not completed in the group.

2. Prepare for Exercise 18.6.

EXERCISE 18.6
PUTTING TUTORING SKILLS INTO ACTION

Purpose

1. To learn the steps involved in putting a tutoring program into action.

2. To practice skills of tutoring.

Introduction to Exercise

You may want to empathize each of the points listed on each step and apply these to your local situation. Also trainees may want to take the self-assessment test again.

Training Procedures

1. Review each of the steps.

2. Apply these to your local situation.

3. Demonstrate a tutoring experience.

4. Have the trainees divide into groups of three and practice tutoring. Have the observer fill out the observation sheet and share it with the trainee who is to then give it to you.

Homework for Trainees
After Group Meetings

1. Set up a first meeting with cooperating teacher and tutee.

2. React to the role-playing situation.

3. Assign reading introduction to the next module.

FACILITATING SMALL DISCUSSION GROUPS

Purpose

To enable trainees to facilitate small discussion groups such as life problems groups (open-ended), subject matter groups (specific topic), and problem-solving groups (tasks).

Approximate Time

Module 19—Introduction
Homework—10 to 15 minutes

Exercise 19.1—30 to 40 minutes
Homework—40 minutes

Exercise 19.2—60 to 120 minutes
Homework—20 minutes

Exercise 19.3—60 to 90 minutes

Exercise 19.4—60 to 120 minutes
Homework—15 minutes

Exercise 19.5—60 to 120 minutes
Homework—15 minutes

Exercise 19.6—60 to 120 minutes
Homework—15 minutes

Materials

Peer Power: Book 2, Applying Peer Helper Skills, one copy for each trainee

Optional: If this module is used with an existing organization, you may want to use your own activities with which to work in Exercises 19.4, 19.5, and 19.6.

Introduction to Module

Many organizations have now gone to participatory management; therefore facilitating group skills is essential. Many companies are using quality circles. Education is spending time with small discussion groups to use in terms of prevention and to help all participants feel that they belong. Churches are using the discussion format to assist their congregation to feel a part of the group and to make decisions.

Training Procedures

1. Decide on the exercises to use for this module.

2. Decide whether or not it is desirable to use your own organization issues.

3. Move from group to group to give feedback.

4. This could be used along with the Leadership Module.

5. Model each discussion before the trainees.

6. Once the peer counselors are trained in facilitating groups, design projects to use in small group work such as from elementary school age to adult to aging.

Evaluation Process

As a trainer, evaluate the process used in the teaching through the feedback obtained from the participants as well as by their written work and evaluation materials.

Measuring Outcomes

1. Use Exercise 19.4 to measure skills in the life problems group (facilitating open-ended discussions).

2. Use Exercise 19.5 to measure skills in the subject matter group (facilitating discussions on specific topics).

3. Use Exercise 19.6 to measure skills in the problem-solving group (facilitating discussions related to tasks).

EXERCISE 19.1
SELF-ASSESSMENT OF
GROUP FACILITATOR SKILLS

Purpose

To help the trainees to assess their own group facilitator skills.

Introduction to Exercise

Group facilitation skills are difficult and involve skills first in basic communication. The following exercise will assist trainees in reviewing their own perception of basic skills.

Training Procedures

1. Discuss each of the areas being assessed and give examples.

2. Mention the following as basic conditions for a good small group discussion:

   a. Clear topic of interest to the group.

   b. Group members who differ in their opinions.

   c. A climate of acceptance so as to promote expression.

   d. A facilitator who gets things going and then serves as a guide.

3. Have the trainees take assessment.

4. Discuss each area and gain ideas from the trainees.

5. Have the group members share their strengths and weaknesses.

Homework for Trainees
After Group Meeting

1. Help the participants find groups in which to participate as homework.

2. Prepare for Exercise 19.2.

EXERCISE 19.2
FUNCTIONS OF A
DISCUSSION FACILITATOR

Purpose

To help the trainees to understand the different functions and activities involved in leading a group and also to practice on small activities.

Introduction to Exercise

Peer counselors are often asked to facilitate small discussion groups. Before leading an entire group, it is good to practice on small segments of group facilitation.

Training Procedures

1. Review all of the functions. Use the list provided in "Group Facilitator Functions" listed in *Peer Power: Book 2. Applying Peer Helper Skills.*

2. Place the functions on chalkboard or flipchart.

3. Have a discussion around each area.

4. Demonstrate as a leader each section.

    Example: Dealing with problem participants. (Number 5 in the "Group Facilitator Functions" list).

5. Have the trainees move into groups of four with one observer and have the facilitator of each group lead the group just on one issue (e.g., starting a group). Have the observer use the feedback form entitled "Discussion Skills Observations." Then have the observer give feedback. Make sure that each group works on all of the issues. Rotate roles in the group.

Homework for Trainees
After Group Meeting

1. Examine checklist from Exercise 18.1.

2. Prepare for Exercise 19.3.

EXERCISE 19.3
LEADING A DISCUSSION GROUP

Purpose

To provide the trainees with the experience of leading a small discussion group and getting feedback.

Introduction to Exercise

Leaders are often asked to facilitate a discussion group. This exercise will assist the trainee in facilitating a discussion group.

Training Procedures

1. Ask for feedback from Exercise 19.2.

2. Demonstrate what you are asking the trainees to do.

3. Have the trainees divide into small discussion groups.

4. Ask one person to be an observer and use the "Observer Evaluation Form."

5. Move among discussion groups and give feedback to the facilitator.

6. Continue until everyone has been both a discussion leader and an observer.

Homework for Trainees
After Group Meeting

1. Look over Exercise 19.1.

2. Prepare for Exercise 19.4.

EXERCISE 19.4
LIFE PROBLEMS GROUP

Purpose

To have the trainees experience leading a rap group (life problems group).

Introduction to Exercise

One of the most valuable benefits of participating in a peer counseling group is the sharing that takes place. This exercise will give participants an opportunity to share their own concerns or some from the stimulus questions entitled "Let's Discuss."

Training Procedures

1. Ask for feedback from the previous exercise.

2. Review the role of facilitator in this type of group.

3. Demonstrate a life problems group.

4. Divide into groups of five, with one being the facilitator, one the observer, and three the participants.

5. Have the observer focus on facilitator skills using the "Group Feedback Forms" provided. You may want to have the observer give the "Group Feedback Form" to the facilitator who in turn will give it to you.

Homework for Trainees
After Group Meeting

1. Have the participants refer back to the skills listed in Exercise 19.1 and evaluate their own effectiveness.

2. Prepare for Experience 19.5.

EXERCISE 19.5
SUBJECT MATTER GROUP

Purpose

To train facilitators to present topical groups.

Introduction to Exercise

Often information that is presented by peers is far more accepted by the group members than that presented by the group leader; therefore it would be helpful for your peer group facilitators to have various topics that they can discuss.

Training Procedures

1. Ask for feedback from Exercise 19.4.

2. Demonstrate leading a group before asking the trainees to lead a group.

3. Have the trainees divide into small discussion groups.

4. Ask one person to be a discussion facilitator and another person to be an observer and use observation form.

5. Move among discussion groups and give the facilitator feedback.

6. Continue until everyone has been both a discussion facilitator and an observer.

7. Focus on the group members.

Homework for Trainees
After Group Meeting

1. Look over Exercise 19.1

2. Prepare for Exercise 19.6.

EXERCISE 19.6
DECISION-MAKING GROUP

Purpose

To help the trainees with experience in leading a small group that needs to perform a task or arrive at a solution.

Introduction to Exercise

Facilitators are asked to help groups make decisions and solve problems. This exercise will assist the trainee with this type of group.

Training Procedures

1. Ask for feedback from Exercise 19.2.

2. Review the steps to problem solving (as outlined in Module 12, *Peer Power: Book 1*) and spend time having trainees discuss and understand brainstorming (see the section on "Brainstorming" in *Peer Power: Book 2*, Exercise 19.6).

3. Demonstrate a problem-solving group.

4. Have the trainees divide into small discussion groups and use one of the "Suggested Decisions To Be Made" or one that you give them.

5. Ask one person to be an observer and use observation form.

6. Move among discussion groups and give the facilitator feedback.

7. Continue until everyone has been both a discussion leader and an observer.

Homework for Trainees
After Group Meeting

1. Look over Exercise 19.1.

2. Prepare for Exercise 20.1.

LEADING CLASSROOM GROUPS

Purpose

1. To enable trainees to learn some introductory material concerning leading classroom groups.

2. To become aware of the different skills needed to lead a classroom group.

3. To give trainees practice in leading classroom groups.

Approximate Time

Module 20—Introduction
Homework—30 to 45 minutes.

Exercise 20.1—30 to 60 minutes
Homework—20 minutes for one week

Exercise 20.2—60 to 90 minutes
Homework—60 minutes

Exercise 20.3—30 to 60 minutes
Homework—30 minutes

Exercise 20.4—90 to 120 minutes
Homework—60 minutes

Exercise 20.5—60 minutes
Homework—30 minutes

Exercise 20.6—4 to 5 hours
Homework—60 minutes

Materials

Peer Power: Book 2: Applying Peer Helper Skills, one copy for each trainee.

Introduction to Module

Peer helpers are often asked to lead classroom groups on various topics. Research supports the idea that health issues when presented by peers have more impact than when presented by professional teachers. Therefore an appropriate activity for peer counselors is classroom groups. It is suggested that the supervisor monitor closely the content of each lesson for accuracy. A good idea also is to have a professional in the classroom during the presentation.

Training Procedures

1. Decide the number of training sessions and exercises to be included in each.

2. Review the content to be covered as well as the suggested activities, as listed in *Peer Power: Book 2, Applying Peer Helper Skills.*

3. Be prepared to demonstrate what you are asking the trainees to do.

4. Be prepared to offer lots of suggestions on developing classroom activities.

5. Decide whether or not you want to use your own classroom lessons on which the trainees might practice.

6. Help the trainees in the planning phase.

7. If you choose, use this exercise along with Module 19, "Facilitating Small Discussion Groups."

8. Once the peer counselors are trained in leading large groups, design projects to use with large groups. For example use with community groups or with elementary, middle, and high school classes on health issues, value clarification, and so forth.

9. Have a professional present when a peer counselor is leading a class.

Evaluation Process

As a trainer, you can evaluate the learning based on the homework that the trainees hand in and also by observing them in their role play activities.

Measuring Outcomes

1. Use Exercise 20.1 before and after the module to check for understanding.

2. Use the observation forms from Exercise 20.6 to check on skill developing.

3. Watch and listen closely during the role playing to measure the ease with which the trainees are able to do this skill.

EXERCISE 20.1
CHECKLIST OF SKILLS FOR CLASSROOM GROUP

Purpose

To learn some of the skills needed for leading a classroom group as compared to one-on-one helping and small group discussion.

Introduction to Exercise

In Exercise 20.1, the trainees will learn the differences among skills needed for a variety of helping roles. They also will become aware of the skills they need to improve.

Training Procedures

1. Discuss the introductory material.

2. Have the trainees review together the "Skills of Helping" chart and discuss each point.

3. Have the trainees particularily take note of those skills unique to a large classroom.

4. Have the trainees mark for each skill whether it is a strength, possessed and feel comfortable in using, or need help to develop.

5. Have each trainee identify possible ways other members of the group might assistance him or her in developing one or more of the areas.

Homework for Trainees
After Group Meeting

Ask the trainees to write a plan of action to improve those areas that need developing.

EXERCISE 20.2
UNDERSTANDING OTHERS

Purpose

To assist trainees in understanding that different learning styles exist in the classroom and that provision for all of the styles need to be considered.

Introduction to Exercise

Any learning situation for all of us depends on the teacher and the learner and the interaction between the two. You as leader need to make sure that some of the activities in the lesson are designed for different types of learning styles.

Training Procedures

1. Discuss the homework from the previous exercise.

2. Preview the appropriate material from the tutoring module. (Number 18).

3. Ask the trainees to complete the "Different Ways to Learn" chart.

4. Have the entire group share so that all areas are covered (put on the board).

5. Brainstorm additional ways of teaching different styles.

Homework for Trainees
After Group Meeting

Ask the trainees to give activity examples of how they would teach a group on "How to Cook Breakfast." Make sure that they have a variety of activities, appealing to different kinds of learning.

EXERCISE 20.3
MOTIVATING OTHERS

Purpose

To understand what motivates us as well as others in terms of learning.

Introduction to Exercise

Motivation is very difficult to understand and trainees will need to recognize this so as not to get discouraged as they try to motivate others. Help trainees understand what motivates them as well as others.

Training Procedures

1. Review the homework from the previous exercise.

2. Lead the group through the "Visualization Exercise."

VISUALIZATION EXERCISE

a. Play soft music in the background (e.g., Steve Halern tapes).

b. Have each person get very comfortable.

c. Relax each part of the body (take them through each body part). Use a visualizing exercise from a book or use a visualizing tape if you have not previously gained proficiency in this exercise.

d.   Imagine a very quiet place that is special (e.g., mountain, ocean).

e.   Imagine that you are learning a new task.

   (1) What got you excited?

   (2) What is happening?

   (3) What was the thing that the leader did that helped you to learn?

   (4) Open your eyes and feel refreshed and relaxed.

3. Have the participants draw and/or write the scene in their image.

4. Discuss the image with the entire group.

5. Write motivators on the board.

6. Get the group to brainstorm examples of motivators.

Homework for Trainees
After Group Meeting

1. Have the trainees think of motivating activities for teaching others how to get along with their peers.

2. Prepare for Exercise 20.4.

EXERCISE 20.4
PUBLIC SPEAKING SKILLS

Purpose

To teach specific skills in public speaking.

Introduction to Exercise

This exercise is not meant to be a complete class in speech. It is designed to focus on specific skills needed for large groups.

Training Procedures

1. Review the homework from the previous exercise.

2. Review the "Public Speaking Skills" listed in *Peer Power: Book 2* as well as others that you think are important.

3. Have the trainees give a five-minute talk on something about which they know a lot. They may use notes.

4. Ask the audience to give feedback concerning public speaking skills. They may use the "Public Speaking Skills" list.

Homework for Trainees
After Group Meeting

1. Ask the trainees to practice in front of a mirror and look at their nonverbal behavior as they talk.

2. Prepare for Exercise 20.5.

EXERCISE 20.5
PLANNING FOR LARGE GROUPS

Purpose

To learn some of the skills needed in planning a lesson.

Introduction to Exercise

If a large group lesson goes well, most frequently the reason is because the leader is organized and has a lesson plan. The art of planning is difficult. Once you have a plan, it is much easier to change it if things are not going well than to have no plan at all.

Training Procedures

1. Review the homework from the previous exercise.

2. Review the steps needed to be taken for planning a lesson.

3. Have the trainees work in triads to design a classroom presentation on "Good Listening Skills."

4. Work with each of the groups to assist in their thinking and planning.

5. Have someone from each group share their lesson plan with the entire group.

Homework for Trainees
After Group Meeting

1. Refine the lesson plan.

2. Prepare for Exercise 20.6.

EXERCISE 20.6
PRACTICE IN LARGE CLASSROOM
GROUP PRESENTATION

Purpose

To provide practice in leading a classroom group with a set lesson.

Introduction to Exercise

To decide how long each activity will take and actually have all of the materials available is a difficult task. Using the two examples included in this exercise, allow each trainee to lead the other trainees in the activity.

Training Procedures

1. Review the homework.

2. Go over the two sample lesson plans provided in the *Peer Power: Book 2 Applying Peer Helper Skills*, and demonstrate.

3. Divide into groups of 4 or 5 members each.

4. Have each person present one of the lessons for the rest of the group.

5. Have one person play the observer role and give the leader feedback.

Homework for Trainees
After Group Meeting

1. Read the introduction to the next module.

2. Prepare for Exercise 21.1.

RECOGNIZING EATING DISORDER PROBLEMS

Purposes

1. To enable trainees to learn about eating disorders.

2. To become aware of their own potential for having an eating disorder.

3. To learn signs of eating disorders in others.

4. To learn some intervention techniques for dealing with a person with an eating disorder.

Approximate Time

Module 21—Introduction, 30 minutes for homework

Exercise 21.1—30 to 60 minutes
Homework—30 minutes for one week

Exercise 21.2—30-60 minutes
Homework—30 minutes

Exercise 21.3—60 minutes
Homework—30 minutes

Exercise 21.4—30 to 60 minutes
Homework—20 minutes

Exercise 21.5—60 to 120 minutes
Homework—30 minutes

Exercise 21.6—60 minutes
Homework—20 minutes

Exercise 21.7—60 minutes
Homework—15 minutes

Materials

Optional: Filmstrip, film, or other audio-visual material on eating disorders.

Optional: Pamphlets from some of the references.

Speaker: Ask someone from an eating disorder program or from OverEaters Anonymous to come and talk with the group.

Books:

Bauer, Anderson, & Hyatt. *Bulimia: Book for Therapist and Client.* Accelerated Development Inc., 3400 Kilgore Avenue, Muncie, IN 47304.

Hollis. *Fat Is a Family Affair.* Hazelden.

Stein & Unell. *Anorexia Nervosa.* Comp Care Publications.

Introduction to Module

Eating disorders are on the rise in this country. Anorexia, bulimia, and compulsive overeating are dangerous illnesses that need intervention. Eating disorders are progressive, addictive diseases in that the behaviors become very compulsive and generally get worse before getting better. Multiple interventions are needed for individuals suffering from eating disorders, sometimes hospitalization, and sometimes outpatient help. Generally the involvement of a dietitian, psychiatrist, medical doctor, dentist, and psychologist are needed in the treatment of eating disorders. This module, along with "Stress Management Moving Toward Wellness" Module 15, might be taught together. You will need to help the peer counselors to learn that they must refer to a professional mental health person if they encounter this problem rather than trying to handle this themselves. Exercises from the module can be used in the classroom presentations and/or small group discussions.

Filmstrips, Films, other audio-visual material, and speakers may be used with this module.

Training Procedures

1. Decide the number of training sessions and exercises to be included in this module.

2. Review the content to be covered as well as the suggested activities, as listed in *Peer Power, Book 2.*

3. Be prepared to do a role playing or video tape of a person with an eating disorder.

4. If a speaker is to be used, the trainer may want to schedule this early in the training.

5. It might be helpful to have the peer helpers order materials from the resources listed at the end.

6. Ask the peer helpers to keep a journal of food intake and also complete their homework assignments.

Evaluation Process

As a trainer, you can evaluate the process used in teaching a skill through the feedback obtained from trainees and by observation of their written work as well as their behavior when practicing the skills during training sessions.

Measuring Outcomes

1. So that trainees might assess their own eating disorder, use Exercise 21.1.

2. Use Exercise 21.2 so that the trainees might judge where they are as a person with eating disorders of an enabler.

3. Watch and listen closely during the role playing in Exercise 21.6 to measure the ease with which trainees are using the techniques learned earlier in the module and skills of empathy and confrontation. You may want to have helpers tape record their role playing and use the tapes for your evaluation process.

EXERCISE 21.1
FOOD CHART

Purposes

1. To provide the trainees an opportunity to keep a food chart.

2. To review introductory material.

Introduction to Exercise

In the introduction of Module 21, the trainees will learn some facts about eating disorders. This would be a good time to show a film or listen to a lecture.

In this exercise the trainees will get in touch with their own eating patterns.

1. Review the material from the introduction as well as the reaction of the trainees to film or speaker.

2. Discuss the material in terms of whether or not the trainees agree with it.

3. Have the trainees keep a food chart for a week.

4. Have the trainees chart their food from yesterday and walk them through the chart.

5. Ask the trainees what they have learned so far from the food chart and the material that they have read.

6. Ask the trainees how they might change their eating behavior.

Homework for Trainees
After Group Meeting

1. Ask the trainees to keep during this whole module a journal of their homework assignments.

2. Ask the trainees to keep a "Food Intake Chart" and bring it in each day of training.

3. Prepare for Exercise 21.2.

EXERCISE 21.2
ASSESSING EATING DISORDERS

Purpose

To provide an opportunity for trainees to examine their own risk for eating disorders and also to recognize eating disorder problems in others.

Introduction to Exercise

As individuals become aware of their own eating disorder risk, many will begin to get professional help to reduce that problem. As peer helpers recognize these risk factors in others they will refer them to professional counselors. What has been found is that often peer helpers are the first to recognize eating problems; hopefully they would refer the person with the problem for professional help.

Training Procedures

1. Discuss the trainees' homework from the previous exercise and review the goals that they have set.

2. Have the trainees answer Yes or No to the "Self-assessment Check List on Eating Disorders."

3. Ask the trainees to share their information from the check list with the group.

4. Have the group members assist each other in suggesting intervention strategies to reduce eating problems.

5. Ask the trainees to think of someone they know and try to assess their potential for an eating disorder.

Homework for Trainees
After Group Meeting

1. Have the trainees continue with their journal.

2. Ask them to write in their journal their reactions to their eating behavior.

3. Prepare for Exercise 21.3.

EXERCISE 21.3
BULIMIA, ANOREXIA, COMPULSIVE OVEREATER
WHERE ARE YOU AS AN EATING DISORDERED PERSON OR ENABLER?

Purposes

1. To help trainees understand that an eating disorder is a progressive disorder.

2. To help trainees understand the concept of co-dependency in eating disorders.

Introduction to Exercise

An eating disorder is a progressive, addictive disease. The behaviors associated with eating are addictive. Unlike alcoholism or chemical dependency, one cannot stop eating. Therefore it is important to examine where the individual is on the disease chart. It is also important to look at the issue of co-dependency and see whether or not the person with an eating disorder is a co-dependent to someone else.

Training Procedures

1. Review the homework journal and food chart from the previous exercise and discuss these.

2. Review the two charts in the *Peer Power: Book 2*, Exercise 21.3.

3. Review co-dependency. If done in the group, skill must be used because of effect upon those trainees who are co-dependents or are close to someone who is.

4. Discuss ways to get out of the co-dependency.

Homework for Trainees
After Group Meeting

1. Ask the trainees to continue keeping their food charts and journals.

2. Focus on the items in Directions 2 through 5.

EXERCISE 21.4
FOOD CHOICE EVALUATION

Purpose

To learn about the four food groups and learn whether or not the trainees are eating food from the four food groups.

Introduction to Exercise

The four food groups are important to know and to be a guide to healthy eating. You may want to have a dietitian talk before this activity.

Training Procedures

1. Review the homework from the previous exercise.

2. Ask the trainees to bring in their food charts and use the information for the last full day.

3. Put the information from the food chart on the "Food Record" and follow directions on food choice evaluation.

4. Review the "Food Selection Changes" and help the trainees set goals for healthy eating.

Homework for Trainees
After Group Meeting

1. Have the trainees do their homework based on suggested questions from the book and continue with the food charts.

2. Prepare for Exercise 21.5.

EXERCISE 21.5
CULTURAL IMPACT ON EATING DISORDERS

Purpose

To help the trainees to understand the cultural impact on eating problems and understand self-worth and body image.

Introduction to Exercise

Men and women are influenced by the media (TV, magazines, billboards), and the relationship between the media and real individuals is very limited, if any.

Training Procedures

1. Review the homework.

2. Allow plenty of time for this activity and bring in popular magazines for both men and women.

3. Ask the trainees to look at billboards and TV commercials.

4. As they are looking at pictures in the magazines, as trainer, point out certain pictures that make the point of the difference between media and real individuals at work, supermarkets, and so forth.

5. Have a discussion on cultural push for thinness and fitness and how this affects individuals' self-esteem.

6. If possible, have the trainees work at an art table cutting out pictures and putting on poster boards with glue. Make sure you have enough poster board and glue for all the participants.

7. Have the trainees to make a collage to describe themselves.

8. Ask each person to present their collage to the rest of the group and have them explain their collage.

9. Discuss at the end how much emphasis is on beauty, body size, and so forth.

Homework for Trainees
After Group Meeting

1. Ask the trainees to turn in an essay at the next training meeting concerning how they view the impact of culture on eating behaviors.

2. Ask the trainees to react to the collage; would they like to be different?

EXERCISE 21.6
PRACTICE IN HELPING A PERSON
WITH AN EATING DISORDER

Purposes

1. To help the trainees to learn intervention techniques for coping with another person with an eating disorder.

2. To help the trainees to learn that they must refer to a professional(s).

Introduction to Exercise

Stress that an eating disorder is a serious issue for peer helpers to deal with and that they must obtain additional help if the person they are dealing with is an eating disorder candidate.

Training Procedures

1. Review and discuss the homework journal from the previous exercise.

2. Review materials learned earlier.

3. Review skills of attending, empathy, questioning, and confrontation.

4. Review observer role.

5. Demonstrate role play first.

6. Ask participants to work together in groups of three.

7. Move from group to group assessing helpers.

Homework for Trainees
After Group Meeting

1. Ask the trainees to continue writing in their journal.

2. Assign outside reading if available.

3. Have the peer counselors get local information concerning help for eating disorders.

4. Prepare for Exercise 21.7.

EXERCISE 21.7
LOOKING AT MYSELF

Purposes

1. To examine how the individual trainees view themselves in relation to all the material they have learned and have been writing about.

2. To set goals for the future.

Introduction to Exercise

Review all the learning and talk about eating disorders' being multi-dimensional.

Training Procedures

1. Have the trainees complete Direction 1 and help them to discuss each one with you and participants.

2. Assist trainees to set new goals relative to their eating behavior and exercise behavior.

3. Have the trainees share their goals with the group.

4. Collect the journals and respond to writing of the trainees.

5. Use the journal for evaluation.

Homework for Trainees
After Group Meeting

1. Read the information in first part of Module 22.

2. Prepare for Exercise 22.1.

SUICIDE PREVENTION

Purposes

1. To enable trainees to learn some information about suicide.

2. To become aware of their own potential for suicide.

3. To learn signs of potential suicide in others.

4. To learn some intervention techniques for others considering suicide.

Approximate Time

Module 22—Introduction
Homework—10 to 15 minutes

Explaining the program—30 to 45 minutes

Exercise 22.1—30 to 60 minutes
Homework—30 to 60 minutes

Exercise 22.2—30 to 60 minutes
Homework—30 to 60 minutes

Exercise 22.3—30 to 60 minutes
Homework—20 minutes

Exercise 22.4—60 to 90 minutes
Homework—10 minutes

Exercise 22.5—60 minutes
Homework—30 to 60 minutes

Materials

Peer Power: Book 2, Applying Peer Helper Skills, one for each trainee

Optional: Slide show on suicide, "Preventing Teenage Suicide: You Can Help" or "Teenage Blues: Coping with Depression," Sunburst Communications.

Optional: Pamphlets from some of the suicide prevention organizations.

Speaker: From a hospice unit or a suicide prevention center.

Book: Rosenthal, Howard. *Not with My Life I Don't*, Accelerated Development, Inc., 3400 Kilgore Avenue, Muncie, Indiana 47304.

Introduction to Module

Suicide has been the epidemic of the 80s and is projected to continue in the 90s. It is very common these days for all individuals to know of someone who has committed suicide or who has attempted suicide. Apparently this approach to dealing with stress is becoming an alternative. Many persons have a difficult time coping with stress in a healthy manner. Peer helpers need to understand clearly that, should they run into this problem, rather than trying to handle it themselves, they must refer the individual to a professional. This module might be taught along with "Stress Management Moving Toward Wellness." Exercises from this module can be used in classroom presentations and/or small group discussions.

Audio-visual materials and speakers may be used with this module.

Training Procedures

1. Decide the number of training sessions and exercises to be included in this module.

2. Review the content to be covered as well as the suggested activities, as listed in *Peer Power: Book 2, Applying Peer Helper Skills.*

3. Be prepared to do a role playing or video tape of a suicidal person.

4. If a speaker is to be used, the trainer may want to schedule this early in the training.

5. Suggest that peer counselors order material from the resources listed.

6. Ask peer counselors to keep a reaction journal throughout this module.

Evaluation Process

As a trainer, you can evaluate the process used in teaching a skill through the feedback obtained from trainees and by observation of their written work as well as their behavior when practicing the skills during training sessions.

Measuring Outcomes

1. So that the trainees might find their own stress level, use Exercise 22.1.

2. Use Exercise 22.2 so that the trainees might judge their own vulnerability to suicide.

3. Watch and listen closely during the role playing in Exercise 22.5 to measure the ease with which trainees are using the techniques of intervention learned in Exercise 22.3.

EXERCISE 22.1
HOW STRESSFUL ARE YOU?

Purposes

1. To provide the trainees an opportunity to assess their own stress level.

2. To review introductory material.

Introduction to Exercise

In the introduction of Module 22, the trainees will learn some facts about suicide. This would be a good time to show a filmstrip.

In this exercise the trainees will learn their own level of stress.

Training Procedures

1. Review the material from the introduction as well as the reaction of the trainees to the filmstrip.

2. Discuss the material in terms of whether or not the trainees agree with it.

3. Have the trainees take "The Teen Scene: Stress Test."

4. Discuss their own results and what these results mean to the trainees.

5. As a group, use brainstorming techniques for reducing stress in the lives of the trainees.

6. Ask the trainees to set some goals to deal with stress.

Homework for Trainees
After Group Meeting

1. Ask the trainees to keep during this whole module a journal on their feelings and reactions to the discussion on suicide.

2. Ask the trainees specifically to focus on a plan to deal with their own stress level based on their score on "The Teen Scene: Stress Test."

3. Ask them to write some goal(s) to deal with stress in their lives.

EXERCISE 22.2
SUICIDE RISKS

Purpose

To provide an opportunity for trainees to examine their own risk for suicide and also to recognize suicide risk in others.

Introduction to Exercise

As individuals become aware of their own suicide risk many will begin to get professional help to reduce that risk. As peer counselors recognize these risk factors in others they will refer them to professional counselors. It has been found that once peer counselors are trained to recognize these risk factors, many of the referrals to professional counselors become more serious.

Training Procedures

1. Discuss their homework from previous exercise and review the goals set up by the trainees.

2. Have the trainees look over the list of possible suicide risk factors.

3. Ask the trainees to share their score with the group.

4. Have the trainees assist each other in suggesting intervention strategies to reduce risk factors.

5. Ask the trainees to think of someone they know and try to assess their potential for suicide.

Homework for Trainees
After Group Meeting

1. Continue with the trainees' journal.

2. Ask the trainees to write a plan to reduce their own potential for suicide.

3. Ask the trainees to think of someone they know who has several risk factors and plan an intervention to get professional help.

4. Prepare for Exercise 22.3.

EXERCISE 22.3
INTERVENTION TECHNIQUES

Purposes

1. To help trainees learn intervention techniques for coping with a potential suicide candidate.

2. To help trainees learn that they must refer to professionals.

Introduction to Exercise

The trainer must stress that this is a serious issue for peer helpers to deal with and that they must get additional help if the person with whom they are dealing is a suicide candidate.

Training Procedures

1. Review the homework journal from the previous exercise and discuss it.

2. Review intervention techniques, discuss them in the group, and help participants explore additional techniques.

3. Identify those techniques with which the trainees agree and disagree.

4. Brainstorm with the entire group a plan of action in dealing with a potentially suicidal person.

5. Have trainees to develop a resource list of professional people and materials for their use in working with suicidal persons and/or those affected by a suicide.

Homework for Trainees
After Group Meeting

1. Have the trainees continue writing in the journal.

2. Assign outside reading if available.

3. Prepare for Exercise 22.4.

EXERCISE 22.4
ASSISTING THOSE LEFT TO
LIVE ON AFTER A SUICIDE

Purposes

1. To assist trainees in understanding impact of suicide on others.

2. To assist trainees in setting up a plan to assist survivors.

Introduction to Exercise

This might be a good exercise for which to have a speaker, perhaps from a hospice or suicide prevention group. The issue of dealing with loss using Kubler-Ross material on grieving may be very appropriate for this exercise. Depending on the population served by the peer counselors (e.g., school, hospital, business), they may want to come up with a plan should a suicide happen.

Training Procedures

1. Review the journal from the previous exercise.

2. Review "Stages of Loss"; show a filmstrip if appropriate or have a speaker.

3. Discuss how the peer counselor would assist a survivor.

4. Discuss a plan for the local community if a suicide were to happen; how could the peer counselors assist the survivors?

Homework for Trainees
After Group Meeting

1. Have trainees to write how they might react to helping a survivor of suicide if this wasn't completed before class ended.

2. Write what they believe their thoughts and feelings would be if they were to lose someone close to them to suicide.

3. Prepare for Exercise 22.5.

EXERCISE 22.5
PRACTICE IN HELPING A SUICIDAL PERSON

Purposes

1. To help trainees practice helping a suicidal person.

2. To help trainees role play getting the potential helpee to a professional.

Introduction to Exercise

Peer helpers are often put in the position of being aware that someone is considering suicide, and they sometimes try to handle it themselves. This hopefully will help them learn the skills needed to get an individual to seek professional help. Each role play may last 20 to 30 minutes if they are using their basic skills (e.g., attending, empathy, questioning) and advanced intervention techniques. They may want to use for their own role that they have made up for practice.

Training Procedures

1. Demonstrate the following role play using information from the previous exercises, introduction material, and the skills from *Peer Power: Book 1.*

   Potential Suicide Victims: This is a white male, an excellent student, and a perfectionist. The boy slashed his wrist earlier this year when a good friend was killed in a car wreck. He has few friends and recently has been very depressed. To deal with depression, he has started drinking on the week-ends.

2. Divide the class into groups of three and role play a potential suicide victim, a helper, and an observer. Change roles until all have had a chance to play all three roles.

3. The observer should use the forms in the exercises containing guides for the observer.

4. Discuss the trainees' reactions to all roles.

Homework for Trainees
After Group Meeting

1. Ask the trainees to write in their journal their feeling about this activity.

2. Ask the trainees to request information from referral sources (list was developed in Exercise 22.3).

3. Ask the trainees to turn in their journals following this exercise.

4. Use the journal for evaluation.

5. Prepare for Module 23 and Exercise 23.1.

COPING WITH LOSS

Purposes

1. To learn about loss.

2. To help trainees understand how they deal with loss.

3. To understand grieving.

4. To practice helping others cope with loss.

Approximate Time

Module 23—Introduction, 10 minutes

Exercise 23.1—60 minutes
Homework—30 minutes

Exercise 23.2—60 minutes
Homework—30 minutes

Exercise 23.3—60 minutes
Homework—30 minutes

Exercise 23.4—60 to 90 minutes
Homework—30 minutes

Materials

Peer Power: Book 2, Applying Peer Helper Skills, one copy for each trainee.

Optional: Slide show or film on death and dying.

Speaker: Ask someone from a hospice unit.

Introduction to Module

This module can be very emotional for the group members. A high level of trust and skills is needed when you do this module. You may need to spend additional time with this module than that which is suggested.

Training Procedures

1. Decide the number of training sessions and exercises to be included in this module.

2. Review the content to be covered and the suggested activities as listed in *Peer Power: Book 2, Applying Peer Helper Skills.*

3. Be prepared to share your own loss and how you coped with it.

4. You might want a speaker to come into the group.

Evaluation Process

As a trainer, you can evaluate the process used in teaching a skill by the feedback obtained from the trainees and by observation of their written work and behavior when practicing a skill.

Measuring Outcomes

1. Use Exercise 23.4 to review skills.

2. Use written homework.

EXERCISE 23.1
MY OWN LOSSES

Purpose

To look at one's own loss and how one coped.

Introduction to Exercise

This exercise can be very powerful. It is important that you give enough time for the exercise as well as time to discuss it.

Training Procedures

1. Discuss with the trainees the loss line.

2. Show them an example.

3. Have them draw "My Age-Loss Line." If this is to be shared with the total group use newsprint or poster board.

4. Ask them to share their loss line within a small group or with the group.

5. Discuss how they coped.

6. Point out the impact if too many losses were to occur too close together.

Homework for Trainees
After Group Meeting

1. Have the trainees write down their reaction to the exercise.

2. Prepare for Exercise 23.2.

EXERCISE 23.2
TYPES OF LOSS

Purpose

To learn the types of loss encountered by the trainees and how they coped.

Introduction to Exercise

We all have dealt with loss at some time in our lives. How did we cope with it, and did formal rituals help?

Training Procedures

1. Discuss the exercise and have the trainees list their losses and identify ways of coping.

2. This would be a good exercise during which to show a film or have a speaker on rituals of loss—formal (Funerals) and informal (talking).

3. Explain rituals, formal and informal, and give examples.

4. Discuss the activity with the group.

Homework for Trainees
After Group Meeting

1. Write in your journal your reaction to this exercise with an emphasis on coping.

2. Prepare for Exercise 23.3.

EXERCISE 23.3
THE GRIEVING PROCESS

Purpose

To help the trainees understand the grieving process.

Introduction to Exercise

In this exercise the trainees will learn the grieving process and where they are in reference to their own grieving.

Training Procedures

1. Review the grieving process.

2. Lead a discussion on where each person is with the grieving process.

3. Explore with them the different feelings that they have at different stages.

4. Have a discussion on how can this knowledge be helpful in working with others.

Homework for Trainees
After Group Meeting

1. Write in your journal your reaction to the grieving process.

2. Prepare for Exercise 23.4.

EXERCISE 23.4
OFFERING SUPPORT TO OTHERS

Purpose

To provide practice in helping individuals with the loss process.

Introduction to Exercise

Often individuals are uncomfortable talking about loss. This exercise will help the trainees to be able to listen to others about their loss.

Training Procedures

1. Review "The Grieving Process" in Exercise 23.3.

2. Give referral sources here and have trainees to add to and possibly modify the list from Exercise 22.3.

3. Divide the training group into triads and appoint one a helper, one a helpee, and one an observer and ask them to discuss a personal example of a loss.

4. Have the observer give feedback and all play each role.

Homework for Trainees
After Group Meeting

1. Have the trainees to write their concepts about their role as support to someone experiencing grief.

2. Prepare for Module 24 and Exercise 24.1.

ETHICAL CONSIDERATIONS IN PEER COUNSELING/PEER HELPING

Purposes

1. To enable trainees to learn some information concerning ethics.

2. To assist trainees to develop a local code of ethics and conduct.

3. To assist trainees to learn how to refer.

4. To assist trainees in establishing a network.

Approximate Time

Module 24—Introduction
Homework—10 minutes

Exercise 24.1—30 to 60 minutes

Exercise 24.2—60 to 120 minutes

Exercise 24.3—120 to 160 minutes

Exercise 24.4—60 minutes

Exercise 24.5—60 minutes
Homework—30 minutes

Exercise 24.6—60 minutes

Materials

Peer Power: Book 2, Applying Peer Helper Skills, one copy for each trainee.

Code of Ethics, NPHA

Local referral sources

Introduction to Module

This module is probably one of the most important modules in the program. Therefore it might be good to do before you start training, at the start of the peer helping projects, and to review it regularly. The trainer should also write for the *Code of Ethics for the Facilitator and Program Standards* and *Peer Helper Code of Ethics from the NPHA.*

Training Procedures

1. Decide the number of training sessions and exercises to be included in this module.

2. Review the content to be covered in this module.

3. Be prepared with local resources, rules, laws, etc.

Evaluation Process

As a trainer, you can evaluate the process used in teaching this module by the finished Code of Ethics and Code of Conduct.

Measuring Outcomes

1. Use Exercise 24.5 to evaluate the learning

2. As the peer helpers go through their various projects, observe how they are operating ethically, etc.

EXERCISE 24.1
ETHICAL ISSUES IN TRAINING

Purpose

To address some of the issues involved in training.

Introduction to Exercise

For the training to be fully effective, local norms must be addressed.

Training Procedures

1. Review the "Issues Important During Training" as listed in *Book 2*. Add other points necessary to accommodate the local situation.

2. Discuss each one that fits your training program.

3. Ask the trainees to brainstorm the local norms and consequences for breaking them.

4. Write the finished product, duplicate it, and ask each trainee to sign it.

EXERCISE 24.2
CODE OF ETHICS FOR THE PEER COUNSELOR/HELPER

Purpose

To help the trainees learn about a national code of ethics and develop a local code of ethics.

Introduction to Exercise

In Exercise 24.2, the trainees will learn the national code of ethics and develop a local code of ethics.

Training Procedures

1. Review the national code of ethics.

2. Go over each major point listed in *Peer Power: Book 2.*

3. Develop a local code of ethics and ask some of the peer counselors to finalize it.

4. Have the counselors sign a local code of ethics.

EXERCISE 24.3
KNOWING YOUR OWN LIMITS

Purposes

1. To know how to refer.

2. To understand the limits of peer helping.

Introduction to Exercise

A list of possible local referrals is very important for each peer helper. To assure a quality program for helpers a wise procedure is to have peer helpers talk to you before giving a referral to determine the appropriateness.

Training Procedures

1. Discuss the referral sources. You might have peer helpers call the local referral sources to get information.

2. Have the peer helpers write to national organizations to obtain a list of local providers.

3. Discuss the guidelines for referral.

4. Develop local guidelines for referral.

5. Have trainees sign an agreement for referral techniques.

EXERCISE 24.4
CODE OF CONDUCT

Purpose

To develop a code of conduct based on local regulations and laws.

Introduction to Exercise

Each local program must follow state laws and local regulations, plus program guidelines. Each peer counselor must also serve as a role model.

Training Procedures

1. Discuss trust (e.g., role model).

2. Discuss state laws (e.g., child abuse).

3. Discuss local regulations (e.g., drug free).

4. Discuss program norms (e.g., referral).

5. Discuss your own personal code of conduct (e.g., being loyal to peer helpee).

6. Have the helpers develop and approve their own code of conduct.

EXERCISE 24.5
DEALING WITH ETHICAL ISSUES

Purpose

To discuss actual situations and relate them to the code of ethics and code of conduct.

Introduction to Exercise

One way to teach ethics is the case-by-case approach.

Training Procedures

1. Review both the national and local code of ethics. Review the code of conduct.

2. Review the examples and refer to the problems with the codes.

3. Discuss the consequences for violations.

4. Have the peer helpers brainstorm additional situations.

Homework for Trainees
After Group Meeting

Prepare for Exercise 24.6.

EXERCISE 24.6
NETWORKING

Purpose

To help the peer helpers set up a network.

Introduction to Exercise

Peer helpers need to understand networking and the need for networking. Then help them establish a local network as well as other ways to network.

Training Procedures

1. Discuss the concept of networking:

   a.   The benefits.

   b.   How it helps individuals.

2. Discuss local networking:

   a.   How it is now.

   b.   How to expand.

3. Discuss networking with others:

   a.   Help them plan to meet with other peer helpers.

   b.   Help them plan to write to other peer helpers.

   c.   Hold a local conference.

   d.   Other

4. Have the group develop a plan and assist them with their plan.

OPERATIONALIZING PEER COUNSELORS/HELPERS AND ADVANCED TRAINING

Operationalizing Peer Counselors/Peer Helpers is the next vital step in developing an effective peer counseling/helping program. The trainer needs to assist peer counselors/helpers in finding ways to put their newly developed skills to work. The terms peer helpers and peer counselors are frequently used interchangeably.

Several procedures can be followed to aid peer counselors in locating helpees. One procedure would be *for the trainer to recruit, organize, and establish groups* who could benefit from peer counseling. The trainer could have projects in mind to target such as a nursing home, handicapped students, tutoring elementary children, giving classroom presentations. A second procedure would be for the *trainer to offer a special training program* for peer helpers on how to recruit groups that the peer helpers could help. A *combination of the two procedures* could prove most beneficial for continued involvement of peer counselors over extended periods of time.

A third procedure is to utilize the peer counseling group to brainstorm possible projects. This provides the peer counselors to have ownership of these projects, which brings a certain amount of empowerment to the trainees. Much research is available to support the "ownership" concept. It is obvious that the peer counselor will be more motivated if they own the projects.

The involvement of peer counselors can provide an important component in the training of future peer counselors. Enabling others to observe what is and can be done by peer counselors is an excellent means of recruitment for future training programs. Peer counselors could be rap group leaders, tutors, outreach personnel, trainees of others, political leaders, discussion leaders, and public relations personnel in the peer counseling program. The list is offered not as an exhaustive list but rather as a stimulus for the creative development of peer counselors within different organizational settings.

One-on-One Helping

Research has supported the concept of one-on-one helping. This is done sometimes formally through identifying at risk youth or others, new students or newcomers to a group or community, handicapped students or persons, lonely students or other persons. Informal helping is done at any time with friends, co-workers, and families.

Conflict Resolution

In many institutions conflicts between individuals and groups can be distracting from the task at hand (learning, working); therefore many of the skills learned in basic training can be used to resolve conflicts. For example, two friends are having a disagreement over a misunderstanding. A peer counselor could help reduce the conflict through active listening and summarization and problem-solving skills. Members of a group representing two different cultures or minorities could be in conflict over an issue. The peer counselor could use small group skills, genuineness, and problem-solving skills to help resolve the conflict.

Cultural Differences

Often groups such as schools, community agencies, and religious institutions have students from minority groups or different cultures. There are often huge differences in the experiences of these two groups. Peer counselors can serve as friends, tutors, and rap leaders to help reduce these differences and help others of different minority groups feel good about themselves.

Rap Group Leaders

Groups can be recruited as helpers from people who have shown an interest in discussing problems with others. The trainer can either organize the group and assign one or two peer counselors to work with the group, or the trainer can suggest that each trainee develop his/her own group from among friends, acquaintances, or individuals with a common concern. If peer counselors choose their groups, the trainer needs to be aware of the composition of the group and meeting varied schedules. Without this trainer awareness and control, rap groups can lose their focus and become social groups. The trainer needs to interview the rap group members before starting the meetings. The interview should include discussing goals, rules of the group, and members' commitment to participate as fully as possible in the group meetings.

Tutors

Peer counselors can be used effectively as tutors, functioning primarily in training programs within schools or other settings. Adult learning centers are possible settings for peer tutors. Peer counselors and the trainer are involved in planning and developing the program. In this way, tutoring has a strong chance of being supported by teachers as well as by trainees who will function as tutors.

Students tutoring students is a valuable learning experience (Allen, 1976; Allen & Feldman, 1973; Cicirelli, 1972; Devin-Sheehan, Feldman, & Allen, 1976; Rogers, 1980). Students receive the help benefit and the tutors get an opportunity to practice concepts and skills. Tutoring others enables students to become more personally involved in the learning process, to accept more responsibility, and to find more meaningfulness in school.

Tutoring requires additional training of peer counselors to enable them to go into classes. This training will be explained later in the Chapter under "Advance Training Model."

Tutoring programs using peer helpers are used widely in Hillsborough County, Florida schools. According to Myrick and Bowman (1981), these programs are very successful because teachers believe that the trained peer helpers are more successful than are untrained students.

Discussion Leaders

Using peer counselors as discussion leaders is effective in schools, religious institutions, business and industry, and agencies such as Scouts, YMCA, and YWCA. Discussion leaders function as facilitators when working with a wide variety of discussion topics. The person in charge can use peer helpers in classrooms, problem-solving meetings, group training programs, camping programs, and other group settings. Peer helpers can relate to many topics. Individual procedures can be adapted to fit specific needs and facilities.

Persons of all ages, including children, can heighten student participation and involvement in the learning process when trained as small-group leaders. When a class is divided into small circle groups, each led by a trained peer helper, discussions become more stimulating and personalized.

Kern and Kirby (1971) trained fifth and sixth grade students to work as peer helpers. After completing training, the peer helpers assisted professional counselors with group counseling of poorly adjusted peers.

Gumaer (1976) described a nine-session program that prepared fifth grade students to facilitate small-group discussions with second graders. Training focused on developing communication skills after which the peer helpers led group discussions with small groups of second graders.

Hoffman's (1976) program also emphasized preparing students to work as small-group facilitators.

Gray & Tindall (1978) reported the work of trained rap leaders with ninth graders trained and working as small-group leaders of seventh and eighth graders.

Anderson (1978) described a program for high school students. Trained in small-group discussions, they lead groups each week in a high school with the help of a teacher.

Leading Class Discussions

Another method is having peer helpers trained with guidance materials so that a large class can be divided into small discussion groups with a student leader. Health educators are used to present prevention information such as drug and alcohol, eating disorder, smoking, and sexuality.

Peer Convention

Each year, all peer helpers in Hillsborough County participate in a special day of projects at a regional peer helper conference. Caning (1983) wrote that Project Promise in Baltimore, Maryland, holds an annual meeting with grade school through high school peer counselors.

Support Groups

Peer counselors have been extremely helpful in leading support groups such as AA, Alanon, Weight Watchers, and Narcotics Anonymous. Most of the leaders have not been formally trained, but this is slowly changing so that the support group experience can be more effective.

Career Center

Some schools are having students assist others in looking for information in the career center. Bowman and Rotter (1983) claim that some peer helpers have been trained to aid students with computer assisted instructions, career information, and cataloging information in the school's microcomputers.

Staff Trainers

Peer helpers have been used to train volunteers to augment the professional staff for a crisis telephone or drop-in center. With proper supervision by professional staff members, peers can effectively teach basic communication skills to volunteers. "Hotline" volunteers do not require a high degree of sophistication in communication skill development, and effective trainees often can be used with success as trainers in these situations. Supervision of peer helpers as trainers is imperative, however, and might be accomplished through the cooperation of the peer counselors' trainer and the crisis center personnel.

ADVANCE TRAINING OVERVIEW

As peer counselors assume their counseling responsibilities, they begin to undertake some real and practical problems in their relationships which develop as a result of their helping behaviors. For this reason, regular meetings need to be held with the peer counselors after their basic training has been completed. These meetings can serve several functions. They can be used as a sounding board for problems encountered by the peer counseling relationships. Advance training is often required as the problems develop and meetings form a natural time and setting to implement several advance training techniques, attitudes, and strategies. Another function the meetings serve is to enable the trainer to maintain surveillance over the peer counseling activities that are ongoing. Housekeeping and administrative concerns are another reason for holding regular meetings.

This time can be divided into two separate times. One time is for the peer counselors to share information about their activities and themselves, set personal and program goals, and deal with problems. The second part involves training in specific areas (Book 2) with which peer counselors may deal. Time needs to be spent in terms of self-understanding, sharing with peers, and problem solving personal issues.

Advance Training—Model

Using regular meetings as advanced training sessions form an effective segment in a developing peer counseling program. The major purpose is to provide a form for peer counselors who now are applying what they have learned in training.

The following model for advance training has been constructed to keep the program vital and ongoing—time for exchange, discussion, and specific additional training such as various techniques.

Exchange Time

An exchange time allows the trainer to be aware of what has been happening with the new peer counselors. To have the peer counselors fill out a "Peer Counselor Feedback Flow Sheet" in the *Peer Power: Book 2*, is desirable. The purpose of the flow sheet is to assist the peer counselor to focus on his/her behavior and skill development in the peer counseling sessions. The exchange time needs to be a free interchange between trainer and peer counselors as to the effectiveness of the skills and behaviors used in the peer counseling sessions.

Discussion Time

A discussion of special problems and/or successes experienced by the peer counselor is needed in the advance training meetings. The group discussion allows peer counselors the opportunity to air concerns and receive feedback from the trainer and other peer counselors. For example, a peer counselor may encounter difficulties in leading a group discussion or a rap session. The reasons could be varied, but with feedback from the trainer and others, additional resources become available for experimentation. Role playing the situation with various people taking different parts is a way of lending insight into alternative ways of dealing with the problem. In addition, the leader can get a periodic check on each trainee's skill development and competencies in working as a helper.

Specific Advance Training Skills

Time needs to be scheduled for specific advance training skills including topics such as the following (these topics are covered in Book 2).

1. Group discussion techniques

2. Value clarification skills

3. Self-awareness experiences

4. Psychological theories and philosophies

5. Tutoring techniques and skills

6. Referral skills

7. Awareness of other peer counseling programs

8. Drug and alcohol abuse intervention and prevention training

9. Wellness/stress management

10. Enhancing self-esteem

11. Leadership training

12. Goal setting

13. Facilitating small group discussion

14. Classroom presentations

15. Suicide prevention

16. Eating disorders

17. Coping with loss

18. Understanding self and others

19. Helping self and others through sharing

20. Ethical issues in peer counseling

Group Discussion Techniques. To function effectively as a group discussion leader, peer counselors will need to understand and experience group discussion techniques. Group discussion techniques include observation, awareness of nonverbal behavior and individual verbal behaviors, ability to keep the discussion moving through communication skills, group management, beginning a group, and handling conflicts. These group discussion techniques employ the peer training skills very heavily but require a different focus and direction. When teaching discussion skills to advanced peer counselors, trainers need to be flexible in their structure to model the kinds of flexible behaviors trainees will need to provide to others when they lead their own discussion groups.

Value Clarification Skills. Value clarification strategies may be used as group discussion topics in the advance training sessions. Each week peer counselors may prepare a different value clarification experience to use with the group in which they serve as helpers and to practice during the advance training session. Especially useful for teenagers and young adults, value clarification experience gives the group discussion leader an activity to use in a given week. Second, the experience provides an activity by which participants can look at themselves and their beliefs in relationship to others and their beliefs. Such activities can be developed by the trainer to fit needs of the group. Excellent resources are Values Clarification (Simon, Howe, & Kirschenbaum, 1972) and Values and Teaching (Raths, Harmon, & Simon, 1966).

Self-awareness Experiences. Peer counselors need to spend some time attempting to understand themselves either through self-awareness experiences, human potential seminars, or through discussions with others. In order to help others, peer counselors must understand themselves and work continuously toward being psychologically healthy persons. Many materials have been published related to this area of interest, including Jones and Pfeiffer (1972) and Sax and Hollander (1972).

Psychological Theories and Philosophies. Different kinds of training are needed to meet both the demands of various kinds of people and situations in which peer counselors find themselves. A trainer may need to spend time teaching different psychological frameworks to enable peer counselors to gain a better understanding of human behavior. For example, peer counselors helping children in a tutorial program would find the concepts of Adler or Transactional Analysis helpful in understanding the behavior of their students. If the peer counselors are working in a crisis center, an understanding of the theoretical helping process as developed by Carl Rogers (1980), Abraham Maslow (1968), and Arthur Combs (1974) will aid in understanding the role and function of a counselor.

Tutoring Techniques and Skills. Tutoring requires some additional information and strategies to be successful. At least four additional concepts need to be included in advanced training experiences when peer counselors are going to use their skills as tutors. They are as follows:

1. How to conduct one's self in a classroom as a tutor.

2. How to work with teachers (using newly learned skills).

3. What kinds of tutoring procedures can be developed and followed.

4. How interpersonal helping skills can be used in a tutoring situation.

Referral Skills. Referral skills are vital to the success of a peer counseling program. Different limits on the peer counselor need to be discussed at this time and appropriate referrals made. For example, in most peer helping programs, life-threatening issues (e.g., suicide) must be referred immediately to the supervisor. Each local program needs to develop guidelines for which kind of issues need to be referred. The list will be governed by life-threatening issues, local laws, and institutional rules.

Information relating to referral skills is not a training technique as such, the information needs to be included if an advance training program is to be complete. Advance training time must be spent in exposing peer counselors to the variety of psychological, vocational, and educational sources of help that are available to them.

The assurance of being able to refer difficult problems to professionals is an important aspect of any peer counseling program. The community has more confidence in a peer counseling program if a strong referral and professional support system is operating within the program. Therefore, the development of a directory of referral sources is crucial for any peer counseling program. The referral source list may range from a simple card with a listing of phone numbers to an extensive list of professional agencies and personnel for types of human problems. Crisis clients may need direct medical referral. The more contact peer helpers can have with referral agencies, the more smoothly the program will operate. The trainer is responsible for developing the referral sources appropriate for the type of peer helping program he/she supervises. For example, drug information, venereal disease, and pregnancy information may be helpful to teenagers. Hotline numbers may be helpful to individuals of all ages. A list of agencies with addresses and telephone numbers is provided in a book entitled *Not With My Life I Don't: Preventing Your Suicide and That of Others* (1988), by Howard Rosenthal.

Awareness of Other Peer Helping Programs. Peer helpers can learn about their function by visiting other peer helper programs. Personnel of one crisis center may want to visit and observe the operation of another crisis center to gather ideas for new techniques. Peer helpers in one school should visit with peer helpers in another school to observe new techniques in terms of implementing their program.

Drug and Alcohol Abuse, Intervention and Prevention Training. Chemical abuse is one of the leading problems in America. Most trainees are not aware of the problems with chemicals and what to do with them. This area will assist trainees to become aware of their own use and to begin to make lifestyle change. For specifics see Module 14.

Wellness/Stress Management. Wellness implies leading a healthy life, putting into balance the body, mind, and emotions. Stress management is a technique that demonstrates how to more effectively manage stressors that impact on the individual. For specifics see Module 15.

Enhancing Self-Esteem. Enhancing self-esteem focuses on assisting the peer counselors/helpers to focus on strengths and potential of themselves and to begin feeling better about themselves and gaining confidence (see Module 16).

Leadership Training. Leadership training assists the individual in becoming an effective leader with individuals and with tasks. For specifics see Module 17.

Goal Setting

Peer counselors participating in goal setting during advance training is needed. Each peer counselor may set goals for the following week that he/she wishes to accomplish. Refer to "Goal and Plan for Action, Exercise 13.2, Part I" in *Peer Power: Book 1, Introductory Program.*

Facilitating Small Group Discussion

Small group discussion can be helpful in helping any age group discuss topics and problem solving. Peer counselors/ helpers are often called upon to lead small discussion groups. Exercises in this can be found in Module 18.

Classroom Presentations

Classroom presentations can be made by peer helpers using a structured lesson plan and materials. These topics can range from health issues to wellness issues to prevention issues. Many of the exercises from *Book 2* can be adapted for classroom groups (for specifics see Module 19).

Suicide Prevention

Suicide prevention is needed in today's schools and work sites. Assisting others to learn about the problems of suicide can be very helpful. Assisting peer counselors to learn to recognize the signs of a potential suicidal person can often lead to needed referral and help. Peer counselors are often times called upon to help the survivors of suicide through listening and caring. An entire institution, school, church, and community can be immobilized as a result of a suicide (see Modules 22 and 23).

Eating Disorders

Eating disorders are prevalent in today's society. Equipping the peer counselors with the skills to recognize the symptoms of an eating disorder can help individuals get referred and obtain the help needed. Also, with the ability to lead small and large groups concerning eating problems, peer counselors can help prevent unhealthy eating problems (see Module 21).

Coping with Loss

Practically all individuals, helpers and helpees, face loss. This can often change their lives. Learning skills in coping with loss can be helpful throughout one's life (see Module 23).

Understanding Self and Others

As the peer counselors go through training, they need to understand themselves in terms of personality type, values, leadership styles, work style, and time management skills.

This can be done throughout the training through exercises found in both *Books 1* and *2*. You also may want to use formal assessment instruments such as the *Myers-Briggs Type Indicator*. One caution when using formal instruments, however: the trainer must possess the training and expertise to administer and interpret the testing. Therefore a trainer may want to use a psychologist or a professional counselor.

Helping Self and Others

Throughout all of the training (*Book 1* and *Book 2*) trainees should be encouraged to use their own personal experiences in the role playing. An extremely important aspect of the program is to provide sufficient time for peer counselors just to share their own concerns and receive help from others. This can be done at regularly scheduled times or done spontaneously in the training.

Ethical Considerations in Peer Counseling

Ethical issues will be faced by trainers and peer counselors during training as well as during their projects. An important aspect of a good peer helper program is the development of and utilization of a local "code of conduct" and "ethics" for peer counselors (see Module 24 for a lengthy presentation). Ethics should be discussed and dealt with throughout the training. The issue of confidentiality is important in the training sessions, as is the application of these skills with the helpees.

Feedback Flow Sheet

Peer helpers work to complete flow sheets and return them to the trainer at the next advance training session. The purpose of the flow sheet is to determine how the skill is used by the peer helper and plan the necessary training to overcome areas of weakness. (See "Peer Counselor Feedback Flowsheet," in *Peer Power, Book 1, Introductory Program.*)

CHAPTER

EVALUATION OF
THE PROGRAM

Evaluation needs to be done on the program, the peer counselor trainer and peer helper(s), and the community. Program evaluation is necessary for any peer counseling training if the venture is to be considered a competent one with continuing value. Evaluation is often a difficult task to complete effectively because certain built-in "booby traps" are difficult to avoid. If the evaluator does not avoid them, much distorted and incomplete results are accepted as valid outcomes.

Three traps exist that weaken or distort evaluation procedures. One is the **trainer's bias to demonstrate positive outcomes.** The amount of effort that a trainer invests in planning, training, and organizing the peer counselors creates pressure either to (a) distort the outcomes of effective evaluation procedures or (b) cause the trainer to omit evaluation of the program all together for fear of failure to meet goals. The need to have a successful program is a strong one in most of us and the fear of failure can cause unprofessional behaviors when evaluation procedures and outcomes are involved.

A second trap is the **lack of trainer skills in effective evaluation procedures.** Insufficient skills in evaluation procedures can create many minor or gross errors when attempting to evaluate a program. Evaluation procedures can become very technical and require expertise far beyond the average trainer. As a result, when those procedures are used by unskilled trainers, the evaluations frequently lack the quality needed to make valid judgments concerning the effectiveness of the program.

A third trap that negatively affects evaluation attempts is *timing.* Evaluation occurs after considerable effort has been invested in a focused direction. Outcomes that would suggest change of focus, reworking parts, or other major revision of the program can have deleterious effects on evaluation procedures or results if incentive is lacking on the part of the trainer to make the needed changes.

In spite of several possible pitfalls, evaluation needs to be an integral part of the peer counselor training program. Evaluation should take place on two levels: one, overall program evaluation and, two, constant evaluation of each trainee's progress in each learned step of the program.

PROGRAM EVALUATION

When considering overall program evaluation, many subjective evaluation procedures can be used. Objective evaluations are less available and not as easily used. Careful subjective evaluation procedures are valid for most programs, and "eyeball" (looking at it) evaluations can give much worthwhile information regarding effectiveness of a program.

In program evaluation, goals need to be identified clearly. These goals can be stated in general terms but should have a focus. For example, two goals would be "to complete an accurate needs assessment for the use of peer counselors in a system" and the second would be "to train a specific number of people to do peer counseling in the system." In this way, the outcomes reflect the goals.

Program objectives established in the program development stages can help in program evaluation by giving a guide which helps trainers identify outcomes. Program objectives should answer the questions *how, when,* and *how much change* is expected. When goals (broad concepts) and objectives (specific outcomes) are included in program planning, evaluation procedures can be established to meet both goals and objectives. When evaluation of the total program is included, the program itself feeds vital information to the trainer, which includes a review of all phases of program development and essentially resembles a single feedback system in itself as shown in Figure 10.1.

EVALUATION OF GOALS AND OBJECTIVES

The **goals** of a program, stated as general concepts, can be evaluated after the training procedure has completed one cycle. Since goals are general, broad non-evaluative constructs will identify how well the goals have been met. For example, one can easily identify how well the goal to train fifteen peer counselors by the end of the training sessions has been reached by counting the ones who have completed the program.

Reaching program **purposes** are evaluated best by having purposes initially stated by the trainer in as specific behavioral terms as is possible. Often humanistic concepts and objectives, such as this program teaches, can be stated in behavioral terms. For example, in teaching a person empathy skill, one can effectively state the objectives in terms of how frequently the trainee reflected accurately helpee feelings and meaning when in the role of helper. By stating behavioral objectives in frequency and quality of a particular behavior, a trainer can identify how well the objectives of that phase of training are being met.

Evaluating Purposes and Objectives

In this book are listed general purposes for each of the training modules from which one could form a basis for evaluation of each skill being taught. Those purposes listed are to be used as a basis for developing one's own specific objectives.

This book does not intend to teach people behavioral objective writing but simply to point out that, if the trainer would write the objectives of a program in trainee-outcome terms, the process of evaluation of the program would be simplified. When an objective is written in terms of outcomes relating to the behavior desired, an evaluation process is built into the written objective.

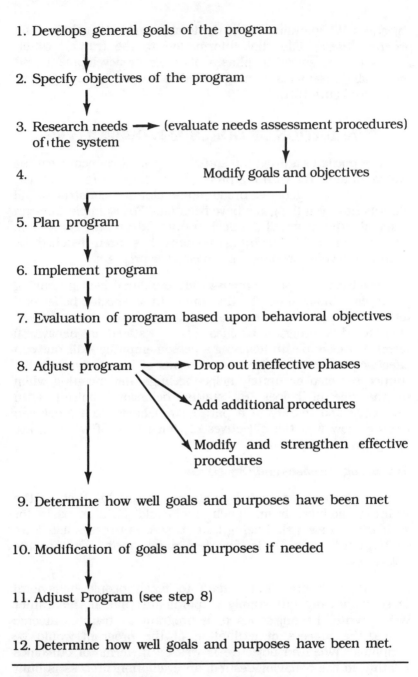

1. Develops general goals of the program

2. Specify objectives of the program

3. Research needs ⟶ (evaluate needs assessment procedures)
   of the system

4.   Modify goals and objectives

5. Plan program

6. Implement program

7. Evaluation of program based upon behavioral objectives

8. Adjust program ⟶ Drop out ineffective phases

   Add additional procedures

   Modify and strengthen effective
   procedures

9. Determine how well goals and purposes have been met

10. Modification of goals and purposes if needed

11. Adjust Program (see step 8)

12. Determine how well goals and purposes have been met.

Figure 10.1. Total review of program development.

Frequently when objectives are stated in specific behavioral terms these objectives describe the procedures needed to achieve them. However, behavioral objectives must be distinguished from the procedures, otherwise, one can easily superimpose process on results. Behavioral objectives need to state clearly what outcome is expected as the result of the training: how much change is expected and who or what is to change. Procedures will spell out how that change is to be accomplished and what experiences are going to be given trainees to reach the behavioral objective.

Evaluating Need Assessment Procedures

The concept of initiating a peer counseling program in all probability was born as the result of some recognized need within the system and with some goals, objectives, and possible procedures to meet the needs emerging concomitantly. As a result, the needs of the system probably will be assessed in close proximity to the development of goals and program purposes. Evaluating the effectiveness of the needs assessment procedures is best completed before the final program assessment and evaluation of the assessment procedure's effectiveness and accuracy can decidedly change the goals and purposes of a program. For example, when a needs assessment or feasibility study has been completed competently and evaluated effectively, the results are used to establish specific and attainable goals. By using accurate information gathering to establish specific goals and purposes, one is able to establish the format for a formal and final proposal. When a plan of action or procedure is added to the information gathered, the entire proposal reflects organization. By stating goals and objectives with specific action parameters and areas of responsibility clearly defined, including the names of people responsible, one has a complete and saleable program format.

EVALUATION OF TRAINING

In order to evaluate the training aspect of the program well, several aspects must be examined as to how well they meet the program goals and objectives. The following training components must be evaluated:

1. Selection of trainees

2. Effectiveness of training each module (Did the trainees learn the goals of the module?)

3. How well the trainees' skills are developing

   a. within each module
   b. within each of the eight skills

4. How the peer helpers are working with the helpee

   a. by trainer evaluation
   b. by other staff evaluations
   c. by helpee evaluations
   d. by research
   e. by advance training evaluations

Evaluation of the training aspect of the program is on two levels. The first level is concerned with the effectiveness of each segment of the training procedure in doing what is required of that segment. The second level of evaluation has to do with developing skills of the trainees. Evaluation procedures for the first level are accomplished by an assortment of procedures initiated by the trainer, other staff members, and research strategies. Evaluation procedures for the second level are identified almost wholly through the use of the feedback or rating process used by the trainer or trainees during practice sessions.

Selection of Trainees

Evaluation of the selection process can be done only upon completion of the basic training. However, selection procedures can be established in such a way that research can be done on the effectiveness of any one of several selection means. To establish these procedures requires that, prior to trainee selection, an evaluation (research) design be developed that will produce the kind of information at the end of the program which will identify the best selection procedures. For example, a design which selects three groups from three different populations can be developed. By giving a pre- and posttest and comparing the rates of changes on a pre-selected behavioral criteria, an assessment can be made. Another selection design is to pretest a population and then divide the training and control groups by skill level, academic achievement, or any one of a variety of criteria. A posttest will assess changes based upon selection procedures. A third design would be to have selected groups chosen based upon specific criteria and compare them with groups that were volunteer groups.

Evaluation of Training Module

Each module in the training program contains stated goals. Also contained in each module are evaluation procedures and outcomes that are to be measured. An evaluation process for each module is thus built into the training procedure. If module goals are changed, then the evaluation procedures and outcome measurements need to be altered to reflect new goals.

EVALUATION OF TRAINEES' SKILLS

In evaluating the skills learned by the trainees, the trainer is heavily dependent upon the feedback mechanism in which the trainer or trainee rated the quality of responses during practice sessions. The rating sheets in *Peer Power: Book 1* function as learning experiences as well as evaluation devices. The trainer can observe the skill of the trainees and use observation and review of the homework as a form of evaluation.

Each skill of the eight needs to be critiqued and evaluated during all practice sessions by both the trainer and trainees.

Evaluating Attending Skill

The trainer should establish minimum acceptance level for effective attending behaviors of the trainees when in the role of helper. When raters (trainees) give feedback during practice sessions, attending should always be one of the qualities critiqued. The most effective criteria for the helper are to have good eye contact, to be squared and open to the helpee, and to lean slightly toward the helpee. These behaviors can be evaluated consistently and easily.

Evaluating Empathy
and Discriminating Skill

Evaluation of discrimination is accomplished by identifying how accurately the rater was perceiving both the feelings of the helpee statements and the accuracy of the responses of the helper to those feelings. Discrimination is a quality that the rater must have both as a rater and as a helper. The ability to discriminate precedes the ability to provide helping communication and depends upon how accurately each person perceives feelings and meaning. Evaluation of empathy skill is subjective and variations among ratings are to be expected. Nuances of feeling cause discrepancy in how several trainees may perceive feelings or meaning. Discrimination abilities of the trainees become more consistent with practice.

In evaluating empathy, three conditions are rated:

1. helper's accuracy of identifying feelings communicated by the helpee,

2. helper's accuracy of identifying meaning communicated by the helpee, and

3. the degree of interchangeability between the helpees' statements and helpers' responses.

High levels of attending are included in evaluating (rater's feedback) empathic responses. When helper initiative or summary responses are included in the evaluation critique, the rater also will use criteria for summarizing and questioning skills to determine the helper's effectiveness in questioning and/or summarizing responses.

Evaluating Summarizing Skill

Evaluation of the summarizing skill is easily accomplished by rating a helper's ability to organize separate and discreet statements made by the helpee into a response that shows the integral relationship between those statements. Although the evaluation of the trainee's ability to summarize is subjective, it is valid enough to identify summarization skills effectively. See the preceding paragraphs on evaluating empathy in the previous section. The following question serves as an example.

Did the response tie together various aspects of the helpee's concern so as to help the helpee see how all parts relate to one another?

Evaluating Questioning Skill

Evaluating questioning responses takes some practice and experience but can be accomplished by following criteria listed earlier in this Chapter under "Evaluating Empathy Skill." Questioning responses widen a helpee's awareness, thereby creating greater understanding of the concern and identifying the goals to be gained. When these characteristics are present in a helper's responses, they can be rated high on initiative:

a. Did the initiative response expand the helpee's awareness of self or concern?

b. Did the initiative response identify where the helpee wanted to be?

c. Did the initiative response personalize the concern? Was it focused on the person rather than the problem?

Evaluating Genuineness Skill

Evaluating the quality of genuineness skill or non-phony behavior is more difficult than evaluating empathy. Genuine helper feelings cannot be identified until communicated either verbally or nonverbally. Therefore, a helper may be feeling a reaction to what a helpee is saying but may choose not to reveal these feelings for a variety of reasons. The most common reason for not revealing genuine feelings is self-protection or perceived threat by the helper if the helper's real feelings were revealed.

In evaluating helper genuineness the rater identifies verbal and nonverbal cues which show discrepant characteristics. For example, a helper may show nonverbal signs of retreating when a sensitive subject matter is explored by the helpee. This withdrawal can be a physical closing off by the use of nonverbal behaviors or actually moving away from the helpee. Verbal signs of retreat and nongenuine behavior can be identified when a helper withdraws from sensitive helpee concerns by not responding to feelings, asking irrelevant questions, or by other verbal behaviors which show a desire on the helper's part to move away from the subject being discussed. Evaluating the level of genuineness can be done only by raters when they are able to discriminate discrepant behaviors by the helper which may indicate that the helper's internal feelings and external behaviors are not the same. Genuine behaviors are identified rather easily when both nonverbal and verbal behaviors communicate the same message and when the helper reveals feelings that relate to the helpee that are risky for the helper to reveal but affect the helpee-helper relationship.

Evaluating Assertiveness Skill

Assertiveness is as difficult to evaluate as is genuineness. Assertive behavior cannot be identified until the trainee has practiced both verbally and nonverbally.

In evaluating helper assertiveness, the rater identifies verbal and nonverbal cues that show these specific characteristics. Use the material in *Peer Power: Book 1*, to assess the assertive skills of the trainees.

Evaluating Confrontation Skill

Evaluating confrontation effectively relies upon the rater's ability to identify whether or not the helper was able to point out discrepancies in the helpee's behavior. Therefore, the rater needs to be able to identify a helpee's discrepant behavior as well as the helper before the helper's confrontation skill can be evaluated. Three basic criteria of discrepant helpee behavior need to be confronted effectively by the helper:

1. Discrepancies between the helpee's real self and ideal self.

   Example: "I am very much interested in tennis, but I haven't played in over two years."

2. Discrepancies between self and others.

   Example: "You say you are a very gentle person, but your wife says she is terrified by your temper."

3. Discrepancies between self and helper.

   Example: "You tell me you want to be different, but you refuse to try any new behaviors we have decided would help you change."

When helpers identify and clarify discrepant behavior in a helpee, the helper can be rated high on confrontation skills. If helpers do not, they must be rated low on the same skill. Effective evaluation, however, depends upon the rater being able to identify discrepant helpee behaviors before he/she can rate the helper's ability to confront. In order to produce growth, confrontation should enhance the relationship and evaluation of its effectiveness should be made on that basis.

Evaluating Problem Solving Skill

Evaluating a helper's ability to problem solve with a helpee can be accomplished in either of two ways. One is based upon the adequacy of the devised solution. The other evaluation can be made regarding the helper's skill in following problem-solving procedures. Ultimately, the solution of the problem becomes the criterion for determining the quality of the helper's behaviors.

Evaluating Integration of Skills

The degree to which the eight skills are integrated into the normal behavior of the peer counselor can be measured in several ways. Measuring the total integration of skills requires general evaluation procedures and increased involvement of other people.

   —One method of evaluating the level of skill integration is to provide a composite rating sheet for raters to use during training sessions. The complete rating of all skills comes only near the end of the training program.

—Self-rating (from a rating sheet) is another way to measure the degree of helper/skill integration.

—Peer evaluation (from rating sheets) will add additional awareness as to how well the skills are being integrated by the peer counselor.

—Trainer evaluation is a final process to determine the degree of integration of the basic communication skills. Other advanced skills that may be taught later, need to be evaluated by the trainer also.

Assessment of the helper skills being taught is an ongoing process which takes place during basic training and advance training sessions by the trainer and other trainees.

EVALUATING BEHAVIORS
OF PEER HELPERS

Continued appraisal of the program is done most effectively by additional ongoing evaluation procedures carried out by a variety of people. Evaluating peer counselor effectiveness is essentially a process with great dependency on "eye ball" or subjective measures. Difficulty arises in making highly objective appraisals of subjective responses by others or in rating highly subjective material such as how I "feel" about something. Therefore, the evaluation procedures for the effectiveness of the peer counselors after training is more subjective than of the program but not necessarily less valuable material.

Trainer Evaluation

Advance training is needed to maintain contact with peer counselors and their follow through in using skills. By checking out skill levels of peer counselors through means previously identified, a trainer can identify weaknesses and strengths in both the program and the peer counselor skill levels.

In advance training a trainer can assess program effectiveness by working with the peer counselors in examining their counseling goals. How well the goals are met is a reflection on the effectiveness of the training. Reasons for peer counselors not meeting their counseling goals are varied. The peer counselor can reflect insufficient training, ineffective skills, lack of understanding on the part of the peer counselor, or unrealistic peer counselor goals. By examining the reasons for success or lack of success, the trainer can adapt either the program, peer counselor goals, the clientele, or future training so as to meet the emerging needs of each peer counselor.

Observing a peer counselor at work is an effective evaluative procedure. By using criteria for evaluating empathy, genuineness, attending, and other skills learned during training, a trainer can rate the peer counselor directly and the program indirectly. These observations can be made through audio or video tapes or through role playing with other peer counselors. Actual observation, if conditions permit, is an excellent way to evaluate the continued progress of peer counselors.

Other Staff Evaluations

Other members of the staff may have an opportunity to observe peer counselors in action. Staff observation could take place in the classroom, in a church school room with staff members participating in multiple counseling situations, or in any number of other situations where other trained or untrained staff personnel could be called upon to evaluate the performance of peer counselors. If staff members are in a position to evaluate, then they must be given some training, if only briefly, to identify the behaviors to be rated and how they are to be rated. If this brief training is not given, staff evaluations will be scattered and diverse and will be of little value in assessing the trainee's effectiveness. A worksheet that identifies the behaviors and attitudes that are to be evaluated, the qualities needed to be assessed, and in what manner they should be assessed could be an aid to the evaluation by the staff members. Using such a device, the staff observations will more consistently evaluate similar behaviors. Qualities that would be important to include on an evaluation form are the following: the quality of attending behavior, empathic responses, genuineness, and problem-solving skills. Evaluation of advance training peer counselors could also include group discussion behaviors, values clarification experiences, and leadership responsibilities by staff members.

Another easily followed procedure is to request a short prose evaluation of counselor behaviors observed by staff members. To do so may necessitate staff orientation as to peer counselors' behaviors that are to be evaluated. Also discuss how peer counselors are to be evaluated which will be necessary in order to gain consistency in the reporting.

Evaluating the Population Served

If one of the goals of your peer counseling program is to serve a specific population, you will need to obtain feedback from them. For example, if the program is in a school, a simple questionnaire can be given to a random tenth grade class to check whether or not they are aware of the program, if they used the peer counselor, and if so how effective was the help. Individual interviews can be performed by an unbiased outside agent.

Overall changes can be looked at in terms of reducing areas that are targeted. Examples might be increased scores on standardized testing (tutoring), reduced drug use (prevention), reduced smoking (prevention), reduced drop out rate (helping the lost and lonely person), increased attendance, and productivity (special friend, big sister/brother project, focus group, quality check groups), and increase in wellness (through information relative to diet, smoking, exercise, etc.) This type of evaluation may be difficult, but it is important to do to change training or refocus.

Evaluation of Personal Growth

The peer counselor goes through a growing period. Feedback to each trainer as well as important information for the trainer might be from formal and informal feedback from the peer counselors themselves. Such formal instruments ought to be the *Communication Test (Book 1)*, pre- and post. Formal instruments such as the *Tennessee Self-concept and Self-evaluation*, as found at the back of *Book 2*, may be important not only for the peer counselor but also the trainer to give pretraining and postraining. Observation of outside behavior may be helpful, for example, increased GPA, attendance, reduced conflict with friends and family, happier person, and so forth.

Evaluation Through Research

Formal and informal research designs are excellent evaluation procedures. Researching a program provides the most useful feedback on the quality and effectiveness of a program. The methods previously mentioned are worthwhile and can give general information regarding the progress of the training, but serious research will give the best kind of information to answer questions about the program's ultimate value to the people involved in the program.

When researching the program, two areas will prove to be most fruitful for program development and public relations. They are **program design** and **effects of training on trainees.** Although the basic training design is well supported by research, much work remains to be completed in improving on teaching techniques and procedures. The effects of the training on the trainees or on those people whom they attempt to help has considerable research data, but, as is usually the case, has opened up many questions that need to be answered.

Taking pre- and post-measurements on one or more characteristics of behavior provides data which allows the drawing of conclusions regarding the merits of a program. Using schools as an example, pre- and post-measurements can be taken on grades of trainees, grades of the people with whom they work, school attendance, a variety of student attitudes, discipline referrals, or parental attitudes toward the children who participated in the program before and after training.

More complex research can be done. Experience frequently shows, however, that time and working conditions do not allow for highly sophisticated research designs. Some trainers who develop programs will be close enough to colleges and universities so that, with assistance, more complex studies can be attempted. Help from the National Peer Helper Association (NPHA) also can be requested for suggestions in needed research design. In studying peer helping programs, the researcher may want to look at the impact of the program on classroom behavior, attendance, changes in academic grades, self-concept, discipline, referrals, and property damage. They may want to simply chart types of problems and number of contacts (Hensley & Mickelson, 1978). Peer counseling training is still in its initial stages of development and the continual input of many people is needed to improve this process.

Public Relations as an Evaluation Process

Programs such as peer counselor training need consistent and effective public relations work. Emphatically, the results of program evaluation give much valuable material that can be used to sell the program and to insure that the program remains acceptable to those who have supported the program.

Staff members can sabotage programs unless they are involved in the feedback. Specifically, counselors, teachers, and parents need to be asked for their feedback. Teachers and administrators also can be important friends for you and your program. Therefore, if the projects that your peer counselors are doing meet the addressed needs of the school, you will gain a lot of support.

Other staff members, administrators, and the public need to know the results of any evaluation that is undertaken. The importance of continued evaluation and reporting of that evaluation to many people should be stressed to those interested in developing programs. Informing the public once at the onset of the program is not adequate if continued support is expected from people not directly involved. Conditions and people change and as a result, they need to be reminded periodically of the work that the program is accomplishing. Without such follow up, one may lose support for the program. The reporting of program results can be accomplished by speaking to any number of groups or reporting results through news media. Public relations can be in the form of posters, flyers announcing the program, letters to other staff members, articles from publications given to targeted audiences (e.g., parents, teens, administrators, CBOs).

Also, a unique program of this nature involves sharing program results with other professionals in the field. The helping profession grows through the sharing of resources and experiences. Exchange can be effected through seminars in which people involved with peer counselors meet to discuss common concerns and problems. Giving programs at professional meetings or writing in journals or newsletters are two additional means of speaking to other professionals. Another option is to inform other professionals about a peer counseling program and invite them to attend the training sessions. Much can be learned by observing such a program in action.

Feedback from the public is one of the best criteria of intent of acceptance of the peer counseling program. Consider the public relations aspect as a two way flow: (1) sharing with the public what is being done and what the evaluation supports as accomplishments, and (2) asking for and listening to what the public has as perceptions. From the feedback, a determination can be made as to a match with goals and objectives and whether or not changes are necessitated in training, goals, objectives, criteria for trainees selected, and/or places where trainees practice/apply their skills.

PEER COUNSELING/HELPING IN ACTION

The final step in the book is to provide specific and general examples of peer counseling/helping programs selected from junior high through young adult levels. The purpose of describing these programs is to demonstrate the outcomes and effects of successful programs which have used the concepts set forth in the book. Hopefully, these examples will further support individual creativity in developing a peer counseling program to fit specific needs.

The several examples given have used basically the format and procedures described in the book. This format has produced a significant degree of success for participants, helpers, and various systems needed to support the program.

The one junior high program that will be examined in detail in this Chapter is the school system which supported the original research and much of the program development procedures and concepts. Other reports of other programs are not as detailed because of the lack of intimacy with them. Other programs included in this Chapter have been identified by various means. Some have been visited, or trainers have corresponded by phone and mail. Written reports and evaluations have been received and included as additional sources to show program effectiveness.

JUNIOR HIGH SCHOOL PEER COUNSELING/HELPING PROGRAM

A peer helping program in a junior high school needs to be structured for students of that age. Such a program took place at Pattonville Heights* from 1970 to 1975. Training for the program involved basic skills in training and advanced skill training. A description of the program and a specific evaluation of it follows.

Program Description

The first step was to inform teachers and administrators who would be affected by giving them a description of the program. Then the other steps outlined in this book were followed. The program and its outcomes are presented to illustrate a peer counseling program in action.

Summary Report to the Faculty

The Communication-Leadership training program at Pattonville Heights Junior High is a productive program organized to assure complete skill training, utilization of skills learned, and comprehensive evaluation of effectiveness. In the fall of 1974, thirty-nine ninth grade students completed twenty sessions of training as part of the "Youth and Understanding" English course; a course designed to enhance communication and insight into young adolescents. The students were given the choice of Communication-Leadership training or regular English curriculum.

The Communication-Leadership training program, the term used at Pattonville Heights Junior High instead of Peer Counseling Training Program, used the guidance office as the physical facility for the training session. A "rap room" adjacent to the guidance area provided a relaxed atmosphere in which to conduct the training sessions. The sessions' format included an introduction and explanation of each skill, followed by modeling the behavior involved in performing the skill, and then followed by practice sessions with feedback from fellow trainees. Time was allotted so that each student could practice the skill and receive feedback on his/her performance of the skill. By designing practice sessions as part of the training, each student had the opportunity to become competent in the skill and to

---

*Pattonville Heights Junior High School, Maryland Heights, Missouri, Mrs. Judy Tindall, Counselor; Mr. George Cavanaugh, Principal

receive helpful feedback in a non-risk situation. Conceptual and practical implementation of certain skills comprised the course in communication skills. Each session, or at least every other session, introduced a particular skill and allowed time for practice. Rating by students of their own performance provided feedback to them as well as measuring group progress. The skills stressed included:

1. attending,
2. empathy,
3. summarizing,
4. questioning,
5. genuineness,
6. confrontation, and
7. problem solving.

(**Note:** The assertiveness skill as a separate skill has been added since the study reported here was conducted.)

Practice in leading discussion groups and learning the "Vocational Exploration Group Process" were included toward the end of the program. Audio and video taping were utilized in the training.

Following the basic training, the leaders (peer counselors) served as "rap" leaders in seventh grade English classes and ninth grade Career Awareness classes.

Evaluation of communication skills leadership training included five ratings:

1. Change in the value continuum of seventh grade students.

2. Leaders (peer counselors) evaluated themselves after each seventh grade discussion session and indicated skills which they used.

3. English teachers evaluated the leaders (peer counselors) in terms of similar criteria at the conclusion of the seventh grade "rap" sessions.

4. Students (helpees) in the seventh grade made a subjective evaluation of their group leaders' skills after the completion of "rap" sessions.

5. Students (helpees) in the ninth grade Career Awareness unit made a subjective evaluation of their group leaders' (peer counselors') skills after the completion of the Vocational Exploration Group experience.

Seventh Grade "Rap" Groups

Following the training, the peer counselors led small "rap" groups of seventh graders in the students' English classes. Eight teachers organized class schedules to allow thirty minutes once a week during which seventh graders could participate voluntarily in discussions. Each peer counselor was provided with a series of activities, primarily values games, which could be used as the basis of discussion. The leader had the prerogative of initiating the values games or spending the thirty minutes in other discussion. About 250 students in the seventh grade participated in the program which involved the thirty-nine peer counselors.

Change of Value Continuum
of Seventh Grade Participants

A measure of effectiveness of the discussion materials and peer counselor-led groups included a values continuum as a pre- and posttest for group activities. A random sample was selected of twenty students to determine changes, if any, on the Value Continuum. See Appendix A for *Positive Values Continuum.*

Discussion. Peer counselors leading value clarification discussion groups at the seventh grade level were able to bring about changes in three areas. One was to affect the values of the students with whom they worked as evidenced by changes the students made in responding to pre-and posttest questionnaires designed to identify values. These changes as reported occurred in the frequency students listed "important" as opposed to "sometimes important" when responding to the values continuum exercise. A second change occurred in the way students perceived their own behavior more accurately as a result of the peer helper lead discussion groups. A third change was that students' responses moved from both extremes to the middle in terms of how students thought that others viewed his/her behavior or ability. When viewing the data on the three changes, the trainer concluded that the changed responses indicated a movement toward a more realistic self evaluation, a clearer conception of one's behavior, and how that behavior was viewed by others.

Leaders Self Evaluation of
Seventh Grade "Rap Group"

The rap leaders who were required to fill out the self evaluation form reported that they used the skills taught to varying degrees. In particular, attending, empathy, summarizing, questioning, genuineness, confrontation, and problem solving were all used frequently and relied upon by these leaders. Confrontation and problem-solving skills, both of which required more active commitment on the part of the leader, were used often but not predominantly. The summarizing skills were used infrequently.

In general, skills which required initiation on the part of the leader were used less frequently, and skills involving listening were used more frequently. This condition was congruent with the goal of the "rap" groups, that is, to have ninth grade leaders serve as a sounding board. In future training, initiating skill may need more stress and practice.

Seventh Grade Teacher's
Evaluation of Communication Skills

Teachers rated leaders individually upon completion of the seventh grade "rap" sessions. The leaders' (peer counselors') use of skills as viewed by the teacher can be used in comparison to the students' own evaluations. Comparisons made in attending, empathy, genuineness, and problem-solving skills revealed two distinct notions: (1) teachers, overall, responded favorably to the "rap" leaders as did the "rap" leaders to themselves; and (2) teachers' evaluations and students' self evaluations compared almost identically in rating and in the number of skills used. The students on self evaluation who used these skills and rated high the number of times the skills were used were given higher ratings by the teachers. (See Appendix B for samples of evaluation forms used by students and teachers.)

Teachers' evaluations were similar to the evaluations of the peer counselors in skills used. Skills observed most often by the teachers and students were empathy, attending, and genuineness. Problem-solving skill although not rated low by the teachers was, nevertheless, observed less frequently. This report was consistent with the self report of the peer counselors. As a result of the two evaluations, the following conclusions were made regarding future training procedures:

1. More stress on skills of problem solving, questioning, and confrontation is needed.

2. Teachers need to reinforce students more frequently when they use these skills effectively.

3. Teachers indicated more assertion skills such as punctuality, regularity of attendance, and keeping the group on task needed additional attention in training.

Discipline Referrals for Seventh Grade Students at Pattonville Heights

A study of discipline referrals was made of seventh grade referrals to the principal. Two comparisons were made. The first comparison was from the seventh grade classes participating in the "rap" groups as compared to other classes. The second comparison was between student discipline referrals first and third quarters (first nine weeks of school year and third nine-week period) when the "rap" groups were not being held and referrals second and fourth quarters (second nine-week period and fourth nine-week period) when the "rap" groups were being held. Two conclusions were drawn from the data. One, as the year progressed, more total discipline referrals were made but those classes in the "rap" program reduced discipline referrals to a minimum. Two, during the second quarter the discipline referrals increased in the participating classes; whereas, the discipline referrals, fourth quarter, decreased rather markedly. One factor contributing to the results as expressed by trainers and cooperating teachers was that fourth quarter leaders were better trained. The second and fourth quarters represent times when the ninth grade "rap" leaders led groups in the seventh grade classrooms.

Implications. Possibly, teachers of seventh grade classes that participated in the program did try to handle their own discipline problems, or possibly the small group experience enabled seventh graders to experience group cooperation and discussion skills. As a result, class members were able to express themselves openly with their peers, thus reducing behavior that caused discipline referrals.

Ninth Grade Student Participant Evaluation

Peer counselors also worked with the ninth graders on a career awareness group. About 250 ninth grade students were taken through two days of the Vocational Exploration Group Experience. The class was divided into groups of five students each with a "rap" leader. The ninth grade students answered questions more directly pertaining to the leaders. (See Appendix D for sample of complete questionnaire.) In almost all cases, the rap leaders were rated high by the ninth graders. Negative responses came only for rap leaders who were not present at all of the meetings or in groups where lack of communication with the rap leader was felt. Those rap leaders who rated themselves favorably in the seventh grade "rap" groups on skills used also were rated favorably by the ninth graders. Considerable agreement existed between those rap leaders who saw themselves using fewer skills and leaders whose ninth grade groups responded with less favorable evaluations. The ratings by ninth graders were significant for two apparent reasons.

1. The manner in which the Vocational Exploration Group was organized required extensive use of the peer counselors for each activity and, therefore, to complete the activity without the peer counselor was impossible.

2. The ninth graders (helpees) were peers of the peer counselor and, therefore, made valuable "peer assessment" of the peer counselor.

Comments from Youth and Understanding Teachers (Sue Heggarty and Diane Wolf)*

A peer communication ("rap" group) program has made a marked difference in the functioning of our ninth grade English classes. Two of our classes were designed to include a peer communication leadership training program as a part of the curriculum. A distinct difference in atmosphere existed in these two leadership training classes as compared to our other nonparticipating three classes. Students in the leadership training classes seemed to have a much greater tolerance for each other, which was important because of the heterogeneous mixture of abilities. The second quarter of this semester course was designed for independent study. During independent study the peer communication really improved the activity of these classes. Students worked together willingly helping each other.

In contrast, the other three nonparticipating classes we had this year were traditional classrooms. When asked to work in groups on projects that were to be presented, students had decidedly more trouble in reaching a consensus including every member in the group and in making allowances for the individual differences. Antagonism existed between members of a group and the students did not know how to resolve this problem.

A student who has experienced peer communication or leadership training usually understands the workings of a group and, generally, is more sensitive to the needs of others. Students who have had these peer communication experiences function very well in a normal classroom.

---

*Ms. Sue Haggarty and Ms. Diane Wolf were 9th grade English teachers at Pattonville Heights Junior High, Maryland Heights, Missouri.

Comments from Social Awareness Teachers
(Clara Clark and Barry Hapner)*

In doing the career simulation, we used "rap" leaders previously trained in communication skills. These leaders were effective in several areas.

The simulation and its method of division into small groups was designed to allow participants to risk expression of their goals and to motivate them to that end. The leaders helped in providing a secure atmosphere in which to take this risk because they had personally experienced the risk. Also, the fact that the groups were peer groups and peer led enabled new ideas to be expressed and, perhaps, heard and adopted more readily. Peer pressure to try something new was much more effective than teacher pressure. Also, encouragement from the leaders was effective in helping some students open up and become expressive.

Being in six places at once is an impossibility; so six leaders, who had already experienced the simulation and were trained in communications, were probably a much better training agent than a hurried teacher. The leaders also enabled us to get a better perspective of all the group dynamics in the room. We honestly can say that we learned several things from watching these leaders in action.

Grade Point Comparison

The grade point averages of "rap" leaders trained during the second semester of 1974 were compared with students not included in the program. The following is a comparison of the grade point average of "rap" leaders with 25 students selected at random. As is noted, the grades of the "rap" leaders improved; whereas, the other 25 randomly selected students showed little change over the same period.

---

*Ms. Clara Clark and Mr. Barry Hapner were Social Studies teachers at Pattonville Heights Junior High, Maryland Heights, Missouri.

25 Rap Leaders		25 Students Selected at Random
60%	Grades Improved	28%
24%	Grades Stayed the Same	20%
16%	Grades Dropped	52%

Overall reaction to the peer leaders was favorable. The use of skills and the evaluation of those skills were positive. The peer evaluation was moderately improving on the seventh grade level and positively improving on the ninth grade level.

For future training, communications skills which require more assertive techniques need to be stressed. A more accurate scale of evaluation also needs to be designed. The peer counselors' evaluations were made in terms of the number of skills he/she used each session, an additional qualitative assessment similar to the teachers' seventh graders, and ninth graders assessments need to be made. Because the leader's assessment was based on his/her own count, however, this assessment may be seen as a qualitative judgment.

Volunteer Rap Group

The same "rap" leaders also formed informal rap groups made up of volunteer students from the eighth and ninth grades. They met weekly, alternating hours. The leaders were trained in group discussion skills, open-ended discussion, and specific activities (value clarification and problem solving). These groups affected approximately 250 students weekly for one semester. The results reported by the group members were positive, but the time involved in administration hall passes, scheduling, and supervising was extensive. These peer groups served as a vehicle to reduce tension in an extremely overcrowded school.

Elementary School Helpers

Students in the ninth grade served as cadet teachers to students located at a nearby elementary school. These peer counselors were trained in the easier helping skills, tutoring, and small group discussion. The first project was to work with two sixth grade classrooms that were trying an "open" concept. They served as ongoing helpees and tutors. The other projects involved working with small groups in other classrooms of younger students to lead small discussion groups. Both teachers and students (elementary and junior high) felt good about the program.

HIGH SCHOOL
PEER COUNSELING/HELPING PROGRAMS

One high school* has developed a peer counseling program by training students who signed up for a course entitled "The Art of Helping." After training, students were assigned peer counseling tasks. Lindbergh High School in St. Louis County, Missouri, trained peer counselors during the months of July and August. These peer counselors were used as one-to-one counselors, "rap" leaders, and discussion leaders.

Peer counselors supervised "rap" groups and met with individual students during study halls in the "commons" and cafeterias. Peer counselors were supervised by outreach workers, interested teachers, and counselors. These peer counselors were involved in leading "rap" groups during class time that was volunteered by interested teachers. The peer counselors went into a classroom once a week, divided the class into small groups and led "rap" sessions. The "commons" area of the high school was the focal point for these peer counselors. Peer counselors also were available before and after school for discussions with other students.

Supervision of peer helpers and their related activities was the ultimate responsibility of the outreach worker, a professional counselor in the school with the responsibility of setting up student help programs that reached out to where students were. The superintendent was informed of the progress of the

---

*Note: Nancy Sefaf and Chris Keathy were involved in implementation of the program.

program. However, the aid and cooperation of teachers, counselors, and principals were necessary for the smooth functioning of the program. Peer helpers were not seen as part of the counseling staff of the school but as student "helpers" or listeners who used counselors as a resource. They referred students with serious problems to the counselors.

Supervision consisted mainly of each group of peer counselors meeting together once a week during the school year to discuss problems, receive extra training, and evaluate themselves. These meetings were open to teachers, counselors, and administrators who had concerns or wished to observe the group. The school staff was encouraged to bring their comments, negative or positive, directly to outreach workers (professional counselors).

Peer counselors kept records of contacts made with students, and these records were reviewed by the outreach worker. The evaluation process was ongoing during the supervision groups through objective observation and testing of skills of peer counselors.

School personnel involved with peer counselors or those who had contact with them were surveyed periodically concerning the peer counselors' attitudes, performance in class, and observation skills. Comments also were elicited from school staff relevant to their feelings about effectiveness of the peer counselors.

COLLEGE PROGRAMS

One junior college (Meramec Junior College, 1133 Big Bend Boulevard, St. Louis, MO) reimburses peer counselors financially. College personnel have hired students to work as peer counselors with other students on an ongoing basis. Peer counselors often have been located in the counseling center, the student center, and throughout the college. Training often has taken place in groups but sometimes is conducted on an individual basis.

COMMUNITY CENTER PROGRAMS

The community center may spend much time advertising for peer counselors and setting up its program. The center may have the training time contained in a concentrated time period. The emphasis at a community center aside from basic communication skills may be in the areas of crisis counseling, giving over-the-phone information related to drugs, venereal disease, or pregnancy or aiding runaways. Community service centers which provide the services described are Youth Emergency Service (6808 Washington, St. Louis, MO 63130) and Youth In Need (St. Charles, MO.). Involvement with local juvenile authorities, police, and the community is important to assure the success and continuance of the program. The population to be served is extremely broad. The only controlling factor is the creative ability of the trainer. The trainer can design a program to meet needs of most communities.

CREATIVE RESOURCES OF TRAINER

Everyone has some creative ability in which to approach a given situation in a different way. Using this training book as a base, the next step is to supplement parts of the training with plans to meet one's own particular area of need with individual talents. This *Peer Counseling* book was designed only for a structured base so that *the trainer may add his/her own creative supplementary material. However, the program model and training session model should be followed exactly.* Procedures to implement the models need to be suitable to trainees.

The implementation of the program may involve one individual helping the other person on a one-to-one basis. On the other hand, implementation of the program may require peer counselors to lead "rap groups" in which the groups talk about everyday, common concerns. The groups are designed to allow people to air some of their concerns with someone who is interested in listening and to help them through use of other helping skills learned in the peer counseling program.

Value clarification group activities have been led successfully by peer counselors with training in discussion skills and value clarification activities. An example of this type of program was explained earlier in this Chapter under the heading "Change of Value Continuum of Seventh Grade Participants."

Many groups have initiated activities-centered groups which are led by peer helpers. The activities have involved physical games, such as baseball and basketball, and activities centered in areas such as art and sewing.

"YOUR BALL GAME, GO GET THEM!"

The hope is that this book has planted ideas and methods that will bring about the initiation and development of a peer counseling program. This last Chapter can serve as a springboard for additional ideas of how to use a peer counseling program in different settings.

Hopefully, this written communication will encourage others to try new risk-taking behavior with their own approaches for helping others. Actually, this book calls on individuals to train lay populations in helping skills. The concept is to develop mentally healthy people who can listen, communicate, and problem solve. Individuals have the potential to train people in schools, churches, and community organizations, and the authors of this book are extremely interested in learning about successes and/or failures you may have with your peer counseling program. Please write or call us. Written communication can be sent through the publisher. Only by sharing successes and failures will the process be feasible of developing a more workable peer counseling model. As the authors, we are throwing the ball to you, so go with it, and see what programs evolve.

GUIDELINES FOR THE PARAPROFESSIONAL IN HUMAN SERVICES

A POLICY STATEMENT

The contents of this Chapter were developed by California Personnel and Guidance Association, 654 East Commonwealth Avenue, Fullerton, California, 92631, and copyrighted in January 1977. The material is reprinted with permission.

The scope of the Guidelines includes paid and non-paid paraprofessionals in various Human Services capacities. We have included the entire set of guidelines in order that you may have some understanding of the scope of ethics as they apply to the paraprofessional in a variety of settings.

A STATEMENT OF GUIDELINES FOR THE PARAPROFESSIONAL IN HUMAN RIGHTS

A PROPOSED POLICY STATEMENT

It is the position of the California Personnel and Guidance Association that appropriately prepared paraprofessionals performing clearly defined functions in a carefully coordinated program under the supervision of the professional can contribute to meeting client's needs and thereby enhance the work of the professional. The appropriate use of such personnel will facilitate the work of the professional, increase the impact of the program, and make the total endeavor more meaningful and effective for the client.

Rationale for Paraprofessionals in Human Services

The California Personnel and Guidance Association Task Force Committee in accepting the challenge of the California Paraprofessional Counselors' Association has developed this policy statement of guidelines for the Paraprofessional in Human Services.

The utilization of paraprofessional support personnel in the human services in neither new nor innovative. The human services professional has felt the need for such support personnel for several years and has indeed trained them and worked with them in a wide variety of settings. Paraprofessionals have been supported both in their training and in the delivery of their services by federal, state, and local funding. Their effectiveness is well attested to by the generally enthusiastic acceptance of them by the community they serve.

However, as the utilization of paraprofessional support personnel continues to increase, the need to develop specific guidelines becomes urgent; both professionals and paraprofessionals express this need. The many concerns relating to the role of the paraprofessional, his/her function, responsibilities, competencies, and training, as well as the line and staff relationships, need to be addressed directly. This paper is an attempt to do just that—to offer definitions and clarifications for the paraprofessionals and professionals working together in the human services.

Guiding Principles

It is the purpose of this document to identify the principles and concepts that underline the roles and preparation of human services paraprofessionals. It provides guidelines for the development of specific functions within specific settings. There is no intention of providing detailed job descriptions for such personnel. This document offers general guidelines for the development of such job descriptions. It is hoped that each CPGA Division and Affiliate will apply these guidelines to its work setting and thus will develop appropriate job descriptions.

The concept of the human services paraprofessional does not refer to the lateral relationships between the human services professionals and collaborating occupations, such as social workers, psychologists, physicians. The services performed by the paraprofessional must be recognized as a supplement to and not a substitute for the services provided by the professional.

This statement deals only with a discussion of relationships between the professional and the paraprofessional. This approach is not based upon a lack of interest and/or understanding of the importance of "reciprocal lateral relationships between the counselor and collaborating occupations." It is based upon a recognition of the importance and scope of such relationships, which means that each of these occupations may establish policies relative to paraprofessionals, and finally that the concept of reciprocal relationships is by itself quite worthy of separate research and study.

Career patterns must also be considered in delineating between the professional and the paraprofessional. It may be appropriate for paraprofessional jobs to provide the steps in the career lattice to professional status. Moves on the career lattice must come with evidence of appropriate competency.

Even though agency policy and hiring practices will ultimately determine the actual role of the paraprofessional, the professional must have an active voice in determining what specific duties can most appropriately be performed by such support personnel. There are certain services for which the professional must maintain responsibility. There are certain other services which may be more appropriately provided by specially oriented and appropriately prepared paraprofessionals. It is essential that a coordinated pattern of professional and paraprofessional services be provided.

Direct counseling services provided by the paraprofessional must always be with the approval of the institution, agency, and the professional and must be under the supervision of the professional.

The activities of paraprofessionals differ from the work of the professionals in several basic respects:

1. The human services professional performs the functions described in the professional policy statements of the profession. The paraprofessional performs important and necessary activities which supplement the overall service.

2. The work of the human services professional involves the development, organization, and coordination of the total program. The work of the paraprofessional deals with specific parts of the program and becomes an integral part of the larger whole under the direction of the professional.

3. The human services professionals base their performance on the use of relevant theory, authoritative knowledge of effective procedures, application of technical skills, and evaluation of the total endeavor. Functions of paraprofessionals are characterized by similar but more limited theoretical background and specialization in support functions.

4. The introduction of paraprofessionals in the human services team brings about changes in the roles of the other team members. The professionals are expected to function at levels of competency appropriate to their specialized training and to accept responsibilities inherent in the supervision of the paraprofessional staff members. It is incumbent upon the professionals to develop good supervisory skills.

Typical Activities of Paraprofessionals

The role of the professional is subtly but constantly changing, a fact that is characteristic of any dynamic profession. Since the definition of roles for the paraprofessionals is dependent on the professionals' roles and their relationship to the total program, it is inevitable that support personnel roles will also change. It is advisable to consider an analysis of the total complex of roles, responsibilities, and functions involved in order to identify activities that may be performed satisfactorily by paraprofessionals rather than by the professionals. Such activities are related to the total complex of the program.

The performance of identified activities by paraprofessionals will contribute to the work of the professional and enhance the quality and quantity of services delivered to the client. Sometimes the tasks supportive of professional functions are assigned to persons who are not working in paraprofessional positions. It should be noted that nothing in this paper should be construed as meaning the paraprofessionals should take the place or the responsibility of the professional.

Direct Helping Relationships

Paraprofessional activities may involve direct person-to-person helping relationships under the supervision of the professional. They are not identical or equivalent to counseling as conducted by the counselor. In specific instances, certain paraprofessionals may have received sufficient appropriate training and education to perform individual counseling functions under the direct supervision of and in frequent consultation with the professional counselor. It should be clearly understood that this section does not suggest that all or most paraprofessionals are capable of performing individual or group counseling. The professional needs to make a careful judgment in consultation with the paraprofessional regarding the level of competence of the paraprofessional. Among direct helping functions and activities performed by the paraprofessional would be the following:

1. Functions with Individuals

    a. Secure information from an interviewee by means of a semistructured or structured interview schedule.

b. Provide information prepared in advance and approved by the counselor for its appropriateness for the interviewee.

c. Explain in terms understandable to the community the purpose and procedures involved in the services to the client.

d. Serve as an active liaison between the clients and the sources of services.

e. Serve as an initial contact person to explore with the counselee the nature of his/her problem.

f. Decide in consultation with the professional appropriate referral sources.

g. Assist in orientation and articulation of the client to the institution or agency.

h. Provide on-going follow-up support to clients.

i. Serve as an "input" source in team case study consultation.

j. Perform outreach function for the counseling agency.

k. Under the supervision of and in consultation with the professional, appropriately prepared paraprofessionals may engage in personal counseling.

2. Functions with Groups

a. Guide discussions as a discussion leader in a structured group with established program objectives.

b. Describe staff and material available to a group, as an information resource person, or tell a group how and where to acquire needed resources.

c. Act as recorder in a variety of small group discussions or counseling situations under the supervision of the professional.

d. Observe verbal and nonverbal interaction in groups following predetermined cues and procedures for making observations.

e. Participate in informal conversation in a small group of clients to help put them at ease and to establish the beginning of helping relationships that may be provided by forthcoming counseling.

f. Provide information and support to former clients.

g. Perform outreach activities.

h. Explain services and programs to community groups.

i. Participate in counseling groups as leader, co-leader, or active member, when appropriate level of competency is present and with the approval of the supervising professional.

Indirect Helping Relationships

Many of the activities of paraprofessionals provide help indirectly rather than directly to clients, even though some of these activities do involve face-to-face relationships with clients. Among the functions and activities under the direction of the professional may be these:

1. Information Gathering and Processing Function

    a. Administer, score, and "profile" routine standardized tests and other appraisal instruments (non-clinical type).

    b. Contact sources for needed records and related information relevant to counseling.

c. Search for new sources of information about clients and/or the environment.

d. Obtain, maintain, and prepare for dissemination of educational, occupational, and personal-social information.

e. Search for new sources to which the clients may be referred.

f. Secure specific special information about former clients upon request of the professional.

g. Operate technical communications media.

h. Disseminate information regarding the institution or agency, its purpose, functions, and programs.

i. Consult on cases with other members of the human services staff.

2. Referral Function

a. Initiate liaison contacts with specific referral agencies.

b. Initiate contact for specific individuals with given referral agencies.

c. Aid individuals in making proper contact with referral agencies.

d. Report on cases to professional supervisor.

e. Refer cases to appropriate resources within the institution/agency.

3. Placement and Follow-Up Function

a. Through appropriate channels, establish and maintain working relationships with placement agencies in the community.

b.   Search for and develop placement opportunities.

c.   Maintain continuous surveys of placement conditions and trends as requested by the professional.

d.   Secure follow-up information of a routine nature according to a general follow-up plan.

4. Program Planning and Management Function

a.   Perform routine collection of information and analytical statistical operations as a research assistant.

b.   Procure and prepare supplies of materials of various sorts for the professional.

c.   Prepare standardized reports of contacts with clients and potential clients, and referral, placement, and follow-up agencies.

d.   Maintain appropriate personnel and information records for the professional.

e.   Supervise and coordinate the activities of clerical or other skilled personnel or paraprofessionals under the general supervision of the professional.

f.   Perform activities related to organizing, scheduling, promoting, hosting, evaluating, and following-up special activities and programs.

The Preparation of
Human Services Paraprofessionals

The preparation of human services paraprofessionals will vary according to a number of factors. Among those that must be considered are the following:

1. People who wish to become paraprofessionals in human services must be selected for their potential ability to perform specific duties, and for their suitability for working with human services workers and clients in

particular settings. Selection must not be restricted to those who may be capable of earning academic degrees. People may come from a wide variety of educational and experimental background required of its paraprofessionals. It may be possible to find people who already possess the necessary competencies, depending upon the local setting and the accumulation and organization of specific duties and/or tasks into payroll jobs. Planning by supervising professionals and agency or institutional administration personnel relative to the development of each job will be imperative.

2. The pre-service preparation for the paraprofessionals will be fairly brief compared to that of the professional. In-service preparation of paraprofessionals on the job is essential to the ultimate success of the program. Such preparation should be initiated on a carefully planned basis.

3. A preparation program must involve opportunities to work in the field under the supervision of professionals. There should be supervised preparation as members of a human services team.

4. The staff for human services paraprofessionals' preparation programs would include experienced, highly successful paraprofessionals as well as professionals, and other personnel.

5. In order to provide opportunity and encouragement for the paraprofessional to grow, it would be advantageous for paraprofessional training programs to be coordinated with professional education programs in order to develop a continuous preparation ladder.

PARAPROFESSIONALS IN THE HUMAN SERVICES

Definition

A paraprofessional is a person who performs duties related to those of the professional and under the professional's direct supervision.

Furthermore, the paraprofessional in human services may be defined as a person who performs duties in support of the functions of the professional in human services, under the direct supervision of the professional, and as an integral part of a totally planned human services program.

Rationale

To meet the demands of society for quality and extensive human services, personnel must be employed from varying backgrounds and possess skills appropriate to the tasks to be performed. Paraprofessionals, by supplementing the work of professionals in human services, make it possible to provide more intensive as well as more extensive assistance. The primary purpose of employing paraprofessionals is to serve the client more effectively.

Role

Clarification of the roles of the paraprofessional and of the professionals under whom he/she works is essential. Indefiniteness in defining these roles or a lack of understanding of them may lead to confusion and disruption of the program.

Recommendations:

1. That the tasks the paraprofessional can perform, as well as those that the professional can perform, should be carefully delineated.

2. That paraprofessionals' duties should include both those that are "task oriented" and those that are "client oriented."

Career Lattice

The career lattice would permit an employee either upward or horizontal mobility when the requisite experience and the needed personal qualities and competencies are acquired and developed.

Recommendation:

That the concept of a career lattice for paraprofessionals in human services be accepted.

Recruitment & Selection

One purpose of adding paraprofessionals to a human services team is to broaden the base of contact people, e.g., as to age, ethnicity, cultural background, sex.

Recommendations:

1. That the recruitment of paraprofessionals be based on the tasks to be performed and the competencies required.

2. That jobs should be opened to as large a pool of qualified applicants as possible.

3. That the selection of a paraprofessional be based on the skills and competencies which a person possesses. The attempt should be made to "screen in" rather then to "screen out" capable applicants. A focus on specific competencies performed in human relationships and the possession of certain personal qualities should be emphasized. The person selected should demonstrate the capability of performing the defined tasks as well as a willingness to continue in training and employment.

4. CPGA recommends that no employing organization, institution, or agency recruit and hire those with professional skills to do paraprofessional tasks. That those employees using professional skills and assuming professional responsibilities as an integral part of their work be renumerated accordingly. Those using paraprofessional skills and assuming paraprofessional responsibilities should be hired to perform paraprofessional tasks, and professionals should be hired to perform professional tasks.

Licensing

Licensing of trained paraprofessionals protects the public from incompetence and ensures that the paraprofessional assumes his/her share of responsibility in providing services to clients in the human services area.

Recommendation:

> That licensing of paraprofessionals in human services be established.

Training

Training is likely to have a greater effect on the program than any other factor. It should be well planned, continuous, and cooperatively organized, involving both the paraprofessionals and the professionals who will be supervising their work.

Recommendation:

1. That pre-service, in-service, and on-the-job training be under the supervision of human services professionals.

2. That the tasks to be performed will dictate the type and kind of training needed.

3. That the relevant skills and knowledge which the paraprofessionals bring to the job should be considered when planning their training programs.

4. That part of the paraprofessionals' training programs should involve team training with the professionals with whom they work.

5. That the agency employing the paraprofessionals has the continuing responsibility to provide in-service training.

6. That universities or community colleges continue to develop training programs for human services parapro-fessionals.

Supervision

Supervision of the paraprofessionals is the direct responsibility of the professionals to whom they are assigned. This supervision must relate to the overall goals and objectives of the program.

Recommendations:

1. That direct supervision of a paraprofessional be the responsibility of a professional in the area to which the paraprofessional is assigned.

2. That the supervising professional has responsibility for seeing that the paraprofessional perform assigned tasks efficiently, and at the same time is responsible for creating a climate in which the paraprofessional's competencies can be effectively utilized.

3. That the supervising professional and the paraprofessional being supervised develop a staff relationship involving mutual respect for one another's person, roles, skills, and competencies.

4. That universities can make a real contribution by training professional human services workers to plan cooperatively with paraprofessionals and to supervise their work.

Selection of Supervisors

Selection of the paraprofessional and of the professional with whom the paraprofessional will work are equally important.

Recommendation :

That the selection of the professionals with whom the paraprofessionals are to work is based on their ability to accept the responsibilities of working with the paraprofessionals, their willingness to supervise their work, and their participating in the training programs.

It is incumbent on the professionals to develop the necessary supervisory skills for working with the paraprofessionals.

ASCA POSITION STATEMENT ON PEER HELPING

(The following position statement was approved by the Governing Board of the American School Counselor Association in December of 1978 and later revised.)

It is the position of the American School Counselor Association that Peer Counseling Programs enhance the effectiveness of the helper program by increasing outreach programs and expanding guidance services. Through proper selection, training, and supervision, peer helper can be a positive force within the school and the community, one that will meet the needs of a sizable segment of the student body.

Teenagers often communicate their problems to their peers rather than to parents, administrators, or counselors. There exists in every school community a segment of the student population that rejects adult relationships. In our society, peer influence may be the strongest single motivational force in a teenager's life. Peers can be selected and trained by professional counselors in communication and counseling skills through a carefully planned peer counseling program and can produce additional guidance services that otherwise might never have been realized.

Peer Helping Defined

Peer helping is defined as a variety of interpersonal helping behaviors assumed by nonprofessionals who undertake a helping role with others. Peer helping includes one-to-one helping relationships, group leadership, discussion leadership, advisement, tutoring, and all activities of an interpersonal helping or assisting nature. A peer helper refers to a person who assumes the role of a helping person with contemporaries. Peers are individuals who share related values, experiences, and life-styles and who are approximately the same age.

Peer Helping Roles

Peer helpers can provide a variety of useful and helpful services for schools, depending on the individual school's needs. It should be emphasized that peer helpers should not be used as mere clerical assistants since they have been trained to function in an interpersonal capacity.

The most obvious role of peer helpers is that of one-to-one counseling. Talking with students about their personal problems, referring peers to other sources of help in the community, giving information about drugs, sex, and venereal disease, and helping students with their school problems are some of the types of assistance given by peer helpers on a one-to-one basis.

Peer helpers can be effective in group settings. Their training enables them to be used as group leaders, assistants in counseling groups, or as communications skills trainers in the classroom. They can also help to train new groups of peer counselors/peer helpers.

There are several educational functions that peer helpers can perform effectively such as tutoring students in academic areas, serving as readers for nonreaders, and assisting Special Education consultants in working with learning and behaviorally disabled students.

Peer helpers can be helpful in many guidance capacities. They are very effective in greeting new students and their parents and in making them feel welcome. They can be used to help with the registration process by aiding students in the selection of their classes and serving as assistants and runners on registration nights. Other guidance functions that peer helpers can perform are serving as career center helpers, being open house guides, writing the guidance newsletter, helping with organizational details of testing, and engaging career program speakers.

Professional Counselors' Responsibilities in Peer Counseling

The professional counselor must accept the responsibility for adequately meeting the needs of the school population and for writing a peer counseling program designed to meet those needs. The counselor must then accept the additional responsibilities of:

1. Devising a plan for selection of peer helpers that is compatible with the population to be served.

2. Coordinating the leadership of an adequate training program for the peer helpers selected.

3. Planning the professional helper's time budget so that adequate time is scheduled for work with the peer helpers.

4. Constructing a support system through positive, factual, and honest public relations.

5. Providing time for meeting with the peer counseling group on a weekly basis for continued training, supervision, sharing, and personal growth.

6. Continually monitoring and evaluating the training and the impact of the program, and instituting any necessary changes to help the program meet the assessed needs of the population it serves.

The professional counselor must serve as a support and a resource person to peer helpers. The counselor must have a broad, reliable awareness of competent resources, and support professionals in the community who can and will accept referrals when needed.

The professional counselor should accept responsibility for the design and completion of research on the program. Follow-up studies and program effectiveness must be conducted and studied in an objective manner. Results should be reported to the population served and to interested professionals; it is the responsibility of the counselor to share information, research, and expertise with other interested counselors.

How Peer Helpers Help
the Professional Counselor

After training and with ongoing supervision, peer helpers can work as important members of the guidance team. Peer helpers often are able to help accomplish things that the professional cannot do alone or cannot do as quickly alone. Therefore, peer helpers help increase the services of the counseling center. They are able to serve in an outreach function and be of help to any population that may feel uncomfortable talking with a professional counselor.

The peer helpers may assist peers with a variety of problems by serving as listeners. As listeners, they are able to help others to stay healthy mentally and to reduce crisis situations by alerting professional counselors to serious problems.

As peer helpers are trained with helping skills, they grow as individuals and become more functional at a higher level. The experience of counseling peers also may help them decide if they want a future occupation in the helping profession. Peer helpers are trained to become more effective adults.

It is imperative that all guidance and counseling departments in the schools plan, initiate, and implement a peer counseling program. Well-trained peer helpers can have a positive effect on students such as no one else can provide. Students sometimes relate and accept alternative patterns of behavior from peers who are struggling with similar feelings and problems. Peer helpers can create a tremendous positive impact on the student population.

NATIONAL PEER HELPERS ASSOCIATION

--Standards

—Ethics for Facilitators/Supervisors

—Ethics for Peer Helpers

These are in the process of being developed. If you are interested, you can contact the NPHA to obtain the final document. These can be used as you develop and operate your program.

APPENDICES

A. PRETEST AND POSTTEST POSITIVE VALUES CONTINUUM

B. TEACHER EVALUATION FORM FOR DISCUSSION GROUPS

C. RAP GROUP EVALUATION

D. VOCATIONAL EXPLORATION GROUP

E. SOCIOGRAM

F. NOMINATIONS OF PEER HELPERS

G. PEER HELPING APPLICATION

H. ADDITIONAL QUESTIONS TO USE WHEN INTERVIEWING PROSPECTIVE PEER HELPERS

I. TEACHER RECOMMENDATION FORM

J. PEER FACILITATOR TRAINEE SELF-RATING SHEET

K. INTERVIEWER RATING SHEET OF PROSPECTIVE PEER HELPER

APPENDIX A

PRETEST AND POSTTEST
POSITIVE VALUES CONTINUUM

Part One

The words listed below are examples of values that one may or may not have. Some words represent ways one behaves, some one's abilities. For the exercise rate the importance of each of the following behaviors and abilities. Put an X on the continuum at the appropriate place for each behavior or ability. Use own personal opinion *about each one.*

Behavior or Ability	Important	Sometimes Important	Never Important	Don't Know
Physical Ability	.	.	.	.
Intellectual Ability	.	.	.	.
Learning	.	.	.	.
Attractiveness	.	.	.	.
Honesty	.	.	.	.
Considerate of Others	.	.	.	.
Able to Take Criticism from Others	.	.	.	.
Independence	.	.	.	.
Being a Friend	.	.	.	.
Close to Family	.	.	.	.
Having Money	.	.	.	.

Part Two

Now that these values have been rated according to how important they are, let us see how it is felt about these values as they pertain to daily living. Think carefully about the way one believes in what he/she does and how he/she does it.

Read the following carefully. The statement may describe how you behave all of the time, some of the time, or never, or the statement may describe how you feel about your abilities. Mark an X on the continuum at the spot which best describes your behavior or ability on each item.

Behavior or Ability	Always	Sometimes	Never
I am physically fit.			
I learn easily.			
I am a person who is getting a lot from my education.			
I am a person who plans for the future.			
I work hard at my appearance.			
I am honest.			
I am considerate of others' feelings.			
I am able to listen to criticism from others without anger or fear.			
I am independent.			
I am a friendly person.			
I am a good family member.			
I can make (will make) a lot of money.			

Part Three

In Part Two, you described your own behaviors and abilities as you see them. In Part Three, we would like you to look at yourself the way that others look at you. Read the following statements carefully. These statements may describe you as others think of you all the time, some of the time, or never. Mark an X on the continuum at the spot which best describes **how you feel others feel about you** regarding each item.

I Feel	Always	Sometimes	Never
People believe that I am in good physical condition.	·	·	·
People believe that I am intelligent.	·	·	·
People believe that I am getting a lot from my education.	·	·	·
People believe that I am good-looking.	·	·	·
People believe that I am honest.	·	·	·
People believe that I am considerate of others' feelings.	·	·	·
People believe that I am a person who can accept criticism without anger or fear.	·	·	·
People believe that I am an independent person.	·	·	·
Many people want to be my friend.	·	·	·
People believe that my family is important to me.	·	·	·
People believe that money is important to me.	·	·	·

APPENDIX B

TEACHER EVALUATION FORM FOR DISCUSSION GROUPS

TEACHER _____

DATE _____ HOUR _____

    In order to develop a group discussion procedure, an evaluation of this program seems important to improve future discussions. The rating may be used to give feedback to the Peer Counselor. Please rate each peer counselor on his/her communication and discussion skills. Rate on a five (5) point scale with one (1) being not effective and five (5) being very effective.

Peer Counselor's name _____

Item Rated	Not Effective				Very Effective
	1	2	3	4	5
Attending Behavior					
Empathic Behavior					
Genuine Behavior					
Problem-Solving Behavior					
Group Management					
Leadership (Promptness)					
Overall Rating					

APPENDIX C

"RAP" GROUP EVALUATION
(To be completed by participants)

1. How often has your group met? _____

2. Leader's name _____

3. Do you think the same leader each week is important?

   Yes _____
   Depends on the discussion _____
   No _____

4. Your feeling toward the discussion group in general, is that it is

   a waste of time. _____
   just to get out of class work. _____
   sometimes worthwhile. _____

5. Your "rap" leader

   doesn't understand what you say. _____
   most of the time understands what you say. _____
   really understands what you say. _____

6. Benefits from the "rap" group:

   Doesn't help _____
   Some help _____
   Very helpful _____

7 Did the group get you to think about yourself?

   All the time _____
   Sometimes _____
   Very helpful _____

8. Would you like to continue with the same group?

   Yes _____
   No _____

9. Do you feel the program should be continued and expanded to include other peers

   Yes _____
   No _____

APPENDIX D

VOCATIONAL EXPLORATION GROUP
(To be Completed by Participants)

Leader Survey

	Yes	Don't Know	No
1. Did your leader seem interested?	_____	_____	_____
2. Did your leader explain the material well?	_____	_____	_____
3. Did your leader keep the group busy with the activity?	_____	_____	_____
4. Did the game get you to consider occupations you had not considered?	_____	_____	_____
5. Did the leader listen to you?	_____	_____	_____

APPENDIX E

ST. CHARLES HIGH SCHOOL
PEER FACILITATOR PROGRAM
SOCIOGRAM*

The purpose of this sociogram is to determine the three or four most trusted students at each grade level, ninth through twelfth, for the Peer Facilitator Program, which will begin at the high school next fall. The students with the most votes will not necessarily be the peer facilitator: first, they may not be interested, and second, they may not be selected in the final interview. The survey is confidential and anonymous, so please do not sign your name. Your **serious** considerations are greatly appreciated.

1. If you had a problem and wanted to talk with one of your fellow students about it, someone whom you know you could

    a. Trust
    b. Would care about and try to help you
    c. Would keep your problem between the two of you

    Who would you go to? (SELECT THREE)

    First choice: _____

    Second choice: _____

    Third choice: _____

---

*Used with permission from Gale Horn and Charles Meeker, St. Charles High School, St. Charles, Missouri.

APPENDIX F

TO: Faculty

FROM: Peer Helper Advisors

DATE: February 22, 1988

RE: NOMINATIONS OF PEER HELPERS FOR 1988-1989

We are beginning the process of selecting Peer Helpers for the new Peer Facilitators class for next year. Please give me the names of any of your sophomore or junior students who would be good Peer Helpers.

A good nominee is one who shows caring and concern for others, has leadership qualities, is willing to take responsibility, is respected by other students, and shows a high level of maturity.

Thank you for your help.

Gayle Horn, Charlie Meeker
Peer Helping Advisors

STUDENTS RECOMMENDED:

_____

_____

_____

_____

_____

This list will be kept confidential. If you would be willing to have us contact you for further information, please sign your name below.

_____

Please return this memo to the Guidance Office by Monday, February 25, 1988.

APPENDIX G

ST. CHARLES HIGH SCHOOL
PEER HELPING APPLICATION

Name: _____ Phone: _____

Address: _____

1. List the various groups to which you belong both in school and out of school.

2. Of the groups listed above, which one is the most satisfying and why?

3. List two experiences that you have had that would be useful to you as a peer group leader (e.g., camp counselor, Sunday School teacher).

4. List two things that you have done that make you feel proud.

5. List two values or principles that are important to the way you conduct your life.

6. What three qualities do you look for in a friend?

7. What contributions do you feel that you can personally add to the Peer Helping Program?

8. If you could change one thing about St. Charles High School, what would it be?

9. My description of me as a person (what kind of person):

10. A stranger's first impression of me would include:

11. I would like others to see me as:

12. I spend too much time:

13. What I have done lately that really turned people off:

14. What I have done lately that really turned people on:

15. Do my friends confide in me? Why or why not?

16. My reputation includes:

17. Things I value:

18. The best advice I ever got:

19. The worst advice I ever got:

20. When I have a problem I handle it by:

21. When someone criticizes me, I:

22. When someone becomes angry with me, I:

23. When I become angry, I:

24. I like me because:

25. Describe what your idea of a Peer Helper is and what a Peer Helper does.

APPENDIX H

ADDITIONAL QUESTIONS TO USE
WHEN INTERVIEWING PROSPECTIVE PEER HELPERS

1. What do you do when individuals tell you that they have a problem?

2. What does confidentiality mean to you? Are there any exceptions?

3. Do you have any duties or chores at home? Do you have to be reminded to do them?

4. Have you ever been in charge of a project? If so, how did you feel? If not, how do you think you would feel?

5. How do you feel in front of other people (younger, same age, older)?

6. Examples of dependability, honesty:

7. Any unusual experiences, trips, and so forth:

8. Name a significant person in your life and explain why that person is significant.

APPENDIX I

TEACHER RECOMMENDATION FORM
PEER HELPING CLASS

Name of Student: _____

In your recommendation, please include the student's attitude, sense of responsibility, dependability, leadership potential, commitment, honesty, and genuine willingness to help others. Because the peer helper will be trained to help students with problems, the student whom you are recommending should possess the ability to listen and to understand others.

Signed: _____

Dated: _____

Recommendation must be complete and returned by March 7, 1988. Please return to Mrs. Horn's mailbox or the Guidance Office.

APPENDIX J

PEER FACILITATOR TRAINEE
SELF-RATING SHEET

_____

Name of Student

Codes (CIRCLE ONE):

SA = Strongly Agree
A = Agree
U = Uncertain
D = Disagree
SD = Strongly Disagree

1.	Concern for the welfare of others	SA	A	U	D	SD
2.	Ability to listen to and understand others	SA	A	U	D	SD
3.	Flexibility: ability to adjust to new situations	SA	A	U	D	SD
4.	Self-confidence	SA	A	U	D	SD
5.	Dependability: responsible and able to follow through with assigned tasks	SA	A	U	D	SD
6.	Honesty	SA	A	U	D	SD
7.	Potential for leadership	SA	A	U	D	SD
8.	Ability to keep confidential information	SA	A	U	D	SD
9.	Ability to work without constant supervision	SA	A	U	D	SD

APPENDIX K

INTERVIEWER RATING SHEET
OF PROSPECTIVE PEER HELPER

Name of Interviewer: _____

Name of Nominee: _____

Code:

5 = the statement is completely and consistently descriptive of the nominee and your rating is **outstanding** (top 5%).

4 = it is almost always descriptive and your rating is **excellent** (top 15%).

3 = it is almost always descriptive and your rating is **good** (top third).

2 = it is occasionally descriptive and your rating is **average** (middle third).

1 = it is not descriptive at all and your rating is **poor** (bottom third).

DK = you do not feel that you can evaluate the candidate on the item.

Concern for welfare of others	1 2 3 4 5 DK
Ability to listen and to understand others	1 2 3 4 5 DK
Ability to keep confidential information	1 2 3 4 5 DK
Ability to work without constant supervision	1 2 3 4 5 DK
Potential for leadership	1 2 3 4 5 DK
Self-confidence	1 2 3 4 5 DK
Dependability	1 2 3 4 5 DK
Honesty	1 2 3 4 5 DK
Sense of humor	1 2 3 4 5 DK
Energetic	1 2 3 4 5 DK
Self-initiative and motivation	1 2 3 4 5 DK
Diversity of experience and background	1 2 3 4 5 DK
Good rapport with other students	1 2 3 4 5 DK
Good rapport with teachers	1 2 3 4 5 DK

My overall recommendation:

_____ Recommend without reservation
_____ Recommend
_____ Recommend as an alternate
_____ Do not recommend

COMMENTS: (Use back side if necessary)

REFERENCES

Allbee, R. (1976). *A comparison of the effects of two variations of micro-counseling paradigm on the development of human relations skills of students in community college setting.* Unpublished doctoral dissertation, Saint Louis University, St. Louis, MO.

Allen, D.A. (1973). Peer Counseling and professional responsibility. *American College Health Association Journal, 21,* pp. 35-40.

Allen, V.L. (1976). *Children as Teachers: Theory and research on tutoring.* New York: Academic Press.

Allen, V.L., & Feldman, R.S. (1973). Learning through tutoring: Low-achieving children as tutors. *Journal of Experimental Education, 42,* pp. 1-5.

Anderson, R.A. (1978). *Stress power! How to turn tension into energy.* New York: Human Sciences Press.

Aspy, D.N. (1972). *Toward a technology for humanizing education.* Champaign, IL: Research Press Company.

Bell, C.M. (1977). *Changes in self-concept and academic achievement of peer counselors in an urban school district.* Unpublished doctoral dissertation, University of Maryland, College Park, MD.

Bowman, R.P. (1982). *A student facilitator program: Fifth graders helping primary-grade problem-behavior students.* Unpublished doctoral dissertation, University of Florida, Gainesville, FL.

Bowman, R.P., & Myrick, R.D. (1980). I'm a junior counselor having lots of fun. *School Counselor, 28,* 31-38.

Bowman, R.P., & Rotter, J.C. (1983). Computer games: Friend or foe? *Elementary School Guidance and Counseling, 18,* 25-34.

Briskin, A.S., & Anderson, E.M. (1973). Students as contingency managers. *Elementary School Guidance and Counseling, 7,* 262-268.

Brown, W.F. (1974). Effectiveness of paraprofessionals: The evidence. *Personnel and Guidance Journal, 53*(4), 257-264.

Caning, J. (1983). Peer facilitator projects for elementary and middle schools. *Elementary School Guidance and Counseling, 18*(2), 124-129.

Carkhuff, R.R. (1969). *Helping and human relations (Vol.1).* New York: Holt, Rinehart, and Winston.

Carkhuff, R.R. (1971). *The development of human resources.* New York: Holt, Rinehart, and Winston.

Carkhuff, R.R. (1972). New directions in training the helping professions: Toward a technology for human and community resource development. *Counseling Psychologist, 3*(3), 12-30.

Carkhuff, R.R., & Truax, C.B. (1969). Lay mental health counseling. *Journal of Consulting Psychology, 29*(5), 5-10.

Carroll, M. (1973). The regeneration of guidance. *The School Counselor, 20*(5), 355-360.

Cicirelli, V.G. (1972). The effect of sibling relationship on concept learning of young children taught by child-teachers. *Child Development, 43*, 282-287.

Combs, A.W. (1974). *Professional education of teachers.* Boston: Allyn and Bacon.

Cooker, P., & Cherchia, P. (1976). Effects of communications skill training on high school students' ability to function as peer group facilitators. *Journal of Counseling Psychology, 23*(5), 117-126.

Creange, N. (1982). *The effects of individual and peer group counseling on a sample of disruptive high school students.* Unpublished doctoral dissertation, University of the Pacific, Stockton, CA.

Dellworth, U., Moore, M., Mullich, J., & Leone, P. (1974). Training student volunteers. *Personnel and Guidance Journal, 53*(1), 57-60.

Devin-Sheehan, I., Feldman, R.S., & Allen, V.L. (1976). Research on Children Tutoring Children: A Critical Review. *Review of Educational Research, 46*, 355-385.

Egan, G. (1975). *The skilled helper.* Monterey, California: Brooks/Cole.

Eisdorfer, C., & Golann, S.E. (1969). Principles for training of new professionals in mental health. *Community Mental Health Journal, 5*, 349-357.

Emmert, B.A. (1977). *An analysis of the effectiveness of large group peer-helper training with pre- and early adolescents in the middle school.* Unpublished doctoral dissertation, University of Northern Colorado, Greely, CO.

Engle, K.B., & Szyperski, T.A. (1965). *A demonstration study of significant others in producing changes in self-concept and achievement in Kalamazoo secondary school underachievers.* Kalamazoo, Michigan: Kalamazoo Board of Education.

Feldman, R.A., & Caplinger, T.E. (1983). *The St. Louis conundrum: The effective treatment of anti-social youth.* Englewood Cliffs, NJ: Prentice-Hall.

Foster, E.S. (1982). *Tutoring: Learning by helping.* Minneapolis: Educational Media Corporation.

Froman, F.R. (1972). Effect of peer tutoring, brief individual and group counseling, and reinforcement on the academic achievement of risk college students. (Unpublished doctoral dissertation, University of Tennessee). *Dissertation Abstracts International, 32*, 4346A.

Gartner, A., & Riessman, F. (1974). The paraprofessional movement in perspective. *Personnel and Guidance Journal, 53*(4), 253-256.

Gazda, G.M. (1973). *Human relations development: A manual for educators.* Boston: Allyn and Bacon, Inc.

Golin, N., & Safferstone, M. (1971). *Peer group counseling: A manual for trainers,* Miami, Florida: Dade County Public Schools.

Gordon, T. (1970). *Parent effectiveness training.* New York: Peter H. Wyden.

Gray, H.D., & Tindall, J. (1974). Communications training study: A model for training junior high school peer counselors. *The School Counselor, 22*(2), 107-112.

Gray, H.D., & Tindall, J. (1978). *Peer counseling.* Muncie, Indiana: Accelerated Development.

Gumaer, J. (1976). Training peer facilitators. *Elementary School Guidance & Counseling, 11,* 26-36.

Hamburg, B.A., & Varenhorst, B.B. (1972). Peer counseling in the secondary schools: A community mental health project for youth. *American Journal of Orthopsychiatry, 42*(4), 566-581.

Hensley, B., & Mickelson, E. (1978). You give a little for great return with peer counseling. *The Guidance Clinic.* New York: Parker Publishing Co.

Hoffman, L.R. (1976). Peers as group counseling models. *Elementary School Guidance and Counseling, 11,* 37-44.

Ivey, A. (1971). *Microcounseling: Innovations in interviewing training.* Springfield, Illinois: Charles C. Thomas.

Ivey, A. E. (1973). Microcounseling: The counselor as a trainer. *Personnel and Guidance Journal, 51,* 311-316.

Ivey, A.E., & Alschuler, A.S. (1973). Editors psychological education: A prime function of the counselor. *Personnel and Guidance Journal, 51*(9), 586-682.

Jakubowski-Spector, P. (1973a). Facilitating the growth of women through assertive training. *The Counseling Psychologist, 4*(1), 75-96.

Jakubowski-Spector, P. (1973b). *An introduction to assertive training procedures for women.* Washington, D.C.: American Personnel Guidance Association Press.

Jones, J., & Pfeiffer, J.W. (1972). *A handbook of experiences for human relations training*. Iowa City, Iowa: University Association Press.

Jourard, S.M. (1971). *The transparent self* (revised ed.). New York: Van Nostrand Reinhold.

Kelley, E.R. (1980). *Peer group facilitation with secondary students in an alternative high school*. North Texas State University, Denton, TX.

Kern, R., & Kirby, J. (1971). Utilizing peer helper influence in group counseling. *Elementary School Guidance and Counseling Journal, 6*, 70-75.

Koch, J.J. (1973). Counselor power. *School Counselor, 20*(4), 288-292.

Kohlberg, L. (1971). The concept of developmental psychology as the central guide to education: Examples from cognitive, moral, and psychological education. In M.C. Reynolds (Ed.), *Proceedings of the conference on psychology in the next decade: Alternative concepts*. Minneapolis: University of Minnesota Press.

Kum, W., & Gal, E. (1976). Programs in practice. *Elementary School Guidance and Counseling, 11*, 74.

Lobitz, W.C. (1970). Maximizing the high school counselor's effectiveness: The use of senior tutors. *School Counselor, 18*(2), 127-129.

Luepker, R.V., Johnson, C.A., & Murray, P.M. (1983). Prevention of cigarette smoking: Three-year follow-up of an educational program for youth. *Journal of Behavioral Medicine, 6*, 53-62.

Luther, R.K. (1972). The effect of peer counseling upon the self-esteem and acand adult-led group counseling of behavioral problem girls in middle school. (Unpublished doctoral dissertation, Fordham University.) *Dissertation Abstracts International, 34*, 137A.

Mager, R. (1962). *Preparing behavioral objectives*. Belmont, CA: Fearon Publishers/Lear Siegler.

Margro, A.L. (1973). *The effectiveness of peer-led and adult-led group counseling of behavioral problem girls in a middle school*. Unpublished doctoral dissertation, Fordham University.

Maslow, A.H. (1968). *Toward a psychology of being* (2nd ed.). New York: Van Nostrand Reinhold.

Mastroiani, M., & Dinkmeyer, D. (1980). Developing an interest in others through peer facilitation. *Elementary School Guidance and Counseling, 14*, 214-221.

McCann, G.B. (1975). Peer counseling: An approach to psychological education. *Elementary School Guidance and Counseling, 9*(3), 180-187.

Mizell, M.H. (1978). Designing and implementing effective in-school alternatives to suspension. *Urban Review, 10,* 213-226.

Murphy, F.L. (1975). *A study of the effects of peer group counseling on attendance at the senior high level.* Unpublished doctoral dissertation. George Washington University.

Murry, J.P. (1972). The comparative effectiveness of student-to-student and faculty advising programs, *Journal of College-Student Personnel, 13*(6), 562-566.

Myrick, R.D., & Bowman, R.P. (1981). *Children helping children: Teaching students to become friendly helpers.* Minneapolis: Educational Media Corporation.

Myrick, R.D., & Bowman, R.P. (1983). Peer helpers and the learning process. *Elementary School Guidance and Counseling, 18,* 111-117.

Nicoletti, J., & Flater-Benz, L. (1974). Volunteers in a community mental health agency. *Personnel and Guidance Journal, 53*(4), 281-284.

Olsen, C. (1974). *The base church.* Atlanta, Georgia: Forum House.

Otto, H. (1970). *Group methods to actualize human potential: A handbook.* Beverly Hills, CA: Holistic Press.

Rapp, H.M., Dworkin, A.L., & Moss, J.L. (1978). Student-to-student helping program. *Humanistic Educator, 18,* 88-98.

Raths, L., Harmon, M., & Simon, S. (1966). *Values and teaching: Working with values in the classroom.* Columbus, Ohio: Merrill.

Rogers, C.H. (1980). *A way of being.* Boston: Houghton Mifflin.

Samuels, D., & Samuels, M. (1975). *The complete handbook of peer counseling.* Miami, Florida: Fiesta Publishing.

Sax, S., & Hollander, S. (1972). *Reality games.* New York: Macmillan.

Sciacca, J.P. (1987). Student peer health education: A powerful yet inexpensive helping strategy. *Peer Facilitator Quarterly, 5*(2), 4.

Scott, S.H., & Warner, R.W., Jr. (1974). Peer counseling. *Personnel and Guidance Journal, 53*(3), 228-231.

Shorey, A.E. (1981). *Peer counseling and achievement motivation: A comparison of two counseling approaches to an urban middle school.* Chicago: Northwestern University.

Simon, S., Howe, L., & Kirschenbaum, H. (1972). *Values clarification: A handbook of practical strategies for teachers and students.* Hart Publishing.

Sobey, G. (1970). *The nonprofessional revolution in mental health.* New York: Columbia University Press.

Telch, M.J., Kellen, J.D., & McAlister, A.L. (1982). Long term follow up of pilot project on smoking prevention with adolescents. *Journal of Behavioral Medicine, 5,* 1-8.

Terrell, D.C., McWilliams, S.A., & Cowen, E.L. (1972). Description and evaluation of group work training for non-professional aides in a school mental health program. *Psychology in the Schools, 9,* 70-75.

Thomas, L., & Yates, R., (1974). Paraprofessionals in minority programs. *Personnel and Guidance Journal, 53*(4), 285-288.

Tindall, J. (1978). *A partial replication of effects of communication skill training on high school students' ability to function as peer group facilitators.* Unpublished study, Saint Louis University, St. Louis, MO.

Tindall, J. (1979). *Youth Listener Evaluation Survey.* St. Louis: Lafayette High School.

Tobler, N. (1986). Meta-analysis of 1433 adolescent drug prevention programs: Quantitative outcome results of program participants compared to a control or comparison group. *Journal of Drug Issues, 16*(14), 537-567.

Truax, C.B., & Carkhuff, R.R. (1967). *Toward effective counseling and psychotherapy: Training and practice.* Chicago: Aldine Co.

Upcraft, M.L. (1971). Undergraduate students as academic advisors. *Personnel and Guidance Journal, 49,* 827-831.

Varenhorst, B. (1973). Middle junior high school counselors' corner. *Elementary School Guidance and Counseling, 8*(1), 54-57.

Varenhorst, B. (1987, May). Research and publications. *Peer Facilitator Quarterly, 4,* 3.

Vriend, T.J. (1969). High performing inner-city adolescents assist lower performing peers in counseling groups. *Personnel and Guidance Journal, 47*(9), 897-904.

Ware, C., & Gold, B. (1971). *The Los Angeles City College peer counseling program.* O.E.O/A.A.J.C. Report -2. Washington, D.C.: American Association of Junior Colleges.

Zwibelman, F. (1977). Effects of training. *Journal of Counseling Psychology, 24*(4), 359-364.

ADDITIONAL READING

Ackerman, R.J. (1983). *Children of Alcoholics* (2nd ed.). Holmes Beach, FL: Learning Publications, Inc.

Baker, V. (1973). Big friend: A tutorial program. *Educational Leadership, 30,* 733-735.

Bandura, A. (1969). *Principles of behavior modification.* New York: Holt, Rinehart, and Winston.

Belloc, N.B., & Breslow, H. (1972). Relationship of physical health states and health practice. *Preventive Medicine, 1,* 409-421.

Benson, H. (1975). *The relaxation response.* New York: Avon Publishers.

Berenson, B.G., & Carkhuff, R.R. (1967). *Beyond counseling and psychotherapy.* New York: Holt, Rinehart, and Winston.

Black, C. (1982). *It will never happen to me!* Denver, CO: MAC Publications.

Blakeman, J. (1971, May). *Correspondence.* University of Georgia, Athens, GA.

Botvin, G.J., Baker, E., Renick, N.L., Filazzola, A.D., & Botvin, E.M. (1984). A cognitive-behavioral approach to substance abuse prevention. *Addictive Behavior, 9* 137-147.

Caplan, G., & Killilea, M. (1976). *Support systems and mutual help: Multidisciplinary explorations.* New York: Grune and Stratton.

Carkhuff, R.R. (1972). *The art of helping.* Amherst, ME: Human Resource Development Press.

Carroll, M. (1973). The regeneration of guidance. *The School Counselor, 20*(5), 355-360.

Carroll, M.(Ed.). (1973). Special feature: Psychological education. *The School Counselor, 20*(5), 332-361.

Combs, A.W. (1974). *Professional education of teachers.* Boston: Allyn and Bacon.

Cooper, J. (1977). *Aerobics.* New York: Bantam Books.

Corey, G., & Corey, M. (1982). *Groups: Process and practice.* Monterey, CA: Brooks/Cole.

Corey, G., Corey, M., & Callanan, P. (1982). *A casebook of ethical guidelines for group leaders.* Monterey, CA: Brooks/Cole.

Corey, G., Corey, M., Callanan, P., & Russell, J.M. (1982). *Group techniques.* Monterey, CA: Brooks/Cole.

Cravitz, H.L. (1974). *Peer counselor program.* Unpublished paper, University of California, Santa Barbara, CA.

Crosson-Johnson, B. (1976, October). Peer counseling programs. *Focus on Guidance, 9*(2), Denver, CO: Love Publishing.

Davis, M., & Eshelman, E. (1980). *The relaxation and stress reduction workbook.* Richmond, CA: New Harbinger Publications.

DeLuca, W.R. (Editor) (1981). *Fourth special report to the U.S. Congress on alcohol and health from the Secretary of Health and Human Service.* Rockville, MD: National Institute on Alcohol Abuse and Alcoholism.

Doran, E.P.A. (1975). *Model Peer counseling program: Presentation of peer counseling of Archbishop Mallory High School.* Jamaica, NY. Paper at APGAP Convention, New York.

Durphy, D.C. (1969). The social structure of adolescent groups. In R.E. Grinder (ed.) *Groups in studies in adolescence.* Toronto: MacMillan.

Edelwich, J., & Brodsky, A. (1980). *Burn-out stages of disillusionment in the helping profession.* New York: Human Sciences Press.

Ehlert, R. (1975). Kid counselors. *School Counselor, 22*(4), 260-262.

Engle, M. (1959). The stability of self concepts in adolescence. *Journal of Abnormal Social Psychology, 58,* 211-215.

Forsyth, L. (1978). *American School Counselors Association Leadership Manual.* Washington, DC: ASCA.

Frank, M., Ferdinand, B., & Bailey, W. (1975). Peer group counseling: A challenge to grow. *School Counselor, 22,* 267-272.

Gartner, A., Kohler, M., & Riessman, F. (1971). *Children teach children.* New York: Harper and Row.

Gazda, G.M. (1969). *Theories and methods of group counseling in the schools.* Springfield, IL: Charles C. Thomas.

Gazda, G.M.(Ed.). (1975). *Basic approaches to group psychotherapy and group counseling.* Springfield, IL: Charles C. Thomas.

Gherman, E.M. (1981).*Stress and the bottom line.* New York: AMACOM.

Girdano, D., & Everly, G. (1979). *Controlling stress and tension: A holistic approach.* Englewood Cliffs, NJ: Prentice—Hall.

Gossberg, J.M. (1964). Behavior therapy: A review. *Psychological Bulletin, 62,* 73-88.

Gravitz, H., & Bowden, J. (1985). *Guide to recovery: A book for adult children of alcoholics.* Holmes Beach, FL: Learning Publications.

Greenberg, H. (1980). *Coping with job stress: A guide for all employers and employees.* Englewood Cliffs, NJ: Prentice-Hall.

Greenwood, J.W., III, & Greenwood, J.W., Jr. (1979). *Managing executive stress: A systems approach.* New York: John Wiley.

Gumaer, J. (Ed). (1976). Special issue: Peer facilitators. *Elementary School Guidance and Counseling Journal, 11*(1).

Hansen, J.C., Zimpfer, C.D., & Easaterling, R.E. (1969). A study of the relationship in multiple counseling. *Journal of Educational Research, 6,* 461-463.

Harris, T. (1967). *I'm O.K., you're O.K.* New York: Avon Books.

Heinemann, M.E., & Estes, N.J. (1977). *Alcoholism development: Consequences and intervention.* St. Louis: The C.V. Mosby.

Hendricks, G., & Roberts, T. (1977). *The second centering book.* Englewood Cliffs, NJ: Prentice-Hall.

Hoper, C., Kutzleb, U., Stobbe, A., & Weber, B. (1975). *Awareness games.* New York: St. Martin's Press.

Hoppenbrowers, T. (1972, September). *Peer counseling.* Paper presented at the American Psychiatric Association, Honolulu, HI.

Jacobson, E. (1938). *Progressive relaxation.* Chicago, IL: University of Chicago Press.

James, M., & Jongeward, D. (1971). *Born to win: Transactional analysis with Gestalt experiments.* Reading, MA: Addison-Wesley.

Johnson, D. (1972). *Reaching out.* Englewood Cliffs, NJ: Prentice-Hall.

Jones, J., & Pfieffer, J.W. (1972). *A handbook of experiences for human relations training.* Iowa City, IA: University Association Press.

Kagan, N., & Kratkwohl, D. (1967). *Studies in human interaction: Interpersonal process recall by videotape.* East Lansing, MI: Michigan State University Education Publication Services.

Kern, R., & Kirby, J. (1971). Utilizing peer helper influence in group counseling. *Elementary School Guidance and Counseling Journal, 6,* 70-75.

King, J. (1983). *Alcohol/drugs and kids: A handbook for parents.* St. Louis: St. Louis Area National Council on Alcoholism.

Kuntz, A. (1967). Experimental evaluation of short-term group counseling with non-conforming adolescents. Unpublished doctoral dissertation. *Dissertation Abstracts, 27,* 3290.

Leibowitz, A., & Rhoads, D.J. (1974). Adolescent peer counseling. *School Counselor, 21*(4), 280-283.

Lodato, E.J. (1964). Group counseling as a method of modifying attitudes in slow learners. *School Counselor, 12,* 27-29.

McBride, J.R. (1967). *A study of relationships between the self concepts of 7th grade disadvantaged children and certain counseling motivation techniques.* Unpublished doctoral dissertation, Arizona State University, Tempe, AZ

McCarthy, B.W. (1975). Growth and development of a university companion program. *Journal of Counseling Psychology, 22*(1), 66-69.

McLaurin, R., & Harrington, J. (1977). A high school instructional peer counseling program. *Personnel and Guidance Journal, 55*(5), 262-265.

McWilliams, S.A., & Finkel, N.J. (1974). High school students as mental health aides in the elementa N. (1971). Psychological education: A means to promote personal development during adolescence. *The Counseling Psychologist, 2*(4), 3-85.

Murphy, F.L. (1983). *A study of the effects of peer group counseling on attendance at the senior high level.* Unpublished doctoral dissertation, George Washington University, Washington, DC.

Nye, S.L. (1973). Obtaining results through modeling. *Personnel and Guidance Journal, 51,* 380-384.

Ohlsen, M. (1970). *Group Counseling.* New York: Holt, Rinehart, and Winston.

Pease, V.P. (1981). *Anxiety into energy stress management.* New York: Hawthorn/Dutton.

Pelletier, K. (1977). *Mind as healer, mind as slayer; A holistic approach to preventing stress disorders.* New York: Delta Books.

Pelletier, K. (1979). *Holistic medicine from stress to optimum health.* New York: Dell Publishing Co.

Pfeiffer, J., & Jones, J. (1972). *Structural experiences for human relations training.* Iowa City, IA: University Associates Press.

Pyle, K.R. (1977). Developing a teen-peer facilitator program. *School Counselor, 24*(4), 278-282.

Reichert, R. (1970). *Self-awareness through group dynamics.* Fairfield, N.J.: Pflaum/Standard.

Reissman, F. (1987). *National Peer Helper conference.* St. Charles, MO: Paper presented.

Robert, M. (1974). *Loneliness in the schools.* Niles, IL: Argus Communications.

Rogers, C.H. (1980). *A way of being.* Boston: Houghton Mifflin.

Rosenman, R.H. (1966). Coronary heart disease in the western collaborative group study: A follow up experience of 2 years. *Journal of the American Medical Association, 195,* 86-92.

Rosenthal, H. (1988). *Not with my life you don't: Preventing your suicide and that of others.* Muncie, IN: Accelerated Development.

Sachnoff, I.S. (1984). *High school peer resource programs: A directors perspective.* San Francisco, CA: Peer Resource Programs.

Satir, V. (1972). *Peoplemaking.* Palo Alto, CA: Science and Behavior Books.

Satir, V. (1976). *Making contact.* Berkeley, CA: Celestial Arts.

Sax, S., & Hollander, S. (1973). *Reality games.* New York: Popular Library.

Schmitt, L.C., & Furniss, L.E (1975). An elementary adjunct: High school helpers. *Personnel and Guidance Journal, 53*(10), 778-781.

Schnert, K.W. (1981). *Stress/unstress.* Minneapolis: Augsburg Publishing House.

Sears, P.C., & Sherman, V.S. (1964). *In pursuit of self esteem.* Belmont, CA: Wadsworth.

Schnert, K.W. (1981). *Stress/unstress.* Minneapolis: Augsburg Publishing House.

Selye, H. (1974). *Stress without distress.* New York: J.B. Lippincott.

Selye, H. (1978). *The stress of life* (rev. ed.). New York: McGraw-Hill.

Sergiovanni, T.J., Metzcus, R., & Burden, L. (1969). Toward a particularistic approach to leadership style: Some findings. *American Educational Research Journal, 6,* 62-79.

Simon, S. (1973). *I am lovable and capable (IALAC).* Allen, TX: Argus communications. (Also available as a filmstrip.)

Simon, S., Howe, L., & Kirschenbaum, H. (1972). *Values clarification: A handbook of practical strategies for teachers and students.* Denver, CO: Hart Publishing.

Sprinthall, N.A. (1972, March). Paper presented to National Association of Independent Schools conference in New York.

Sprinthall, N.A. (1973). A curriculum for secondary schools: Counselors as teachers for psychological growth. *School Counselor, 20*(5), 361-369.

Tindall, J. (1982). *The effectiveness of a wellness program: Coping with stress in schools.* Unpublished doctoral dissertation, Saint Louis University, St. Louis, MO.

Truch, S. (1980). *Teacher burnout and what to do about it.* Navato, CA: Academic Therapy Publications.

Wegscheider, S. (1981). *Another chance.* Palo Alto, CA: Science & Behavior Books.

Wegscheider, S. (1985). *Choicemaking.* Pompano Beach, FL: Health Communications.

Weinstein, G., & Fontain, M. (1970). *Toward humanistic education.* New York: Praeger.

Woititz, J. (1983). *Adult children of alcoholics.* Hollywood, FL: Health Communications.

Woititz, J. (1985). *Struggle for intimacy.* Pompano Beach, FL: Health Communications.

Wyrick, T.J., & Mitchell, K.A.A. (1971). Relationship between residents assistants: Empathy and warmth in their effectiveness. *Journal of College Student Personnel, 12*(1), 35-40.

INDEX

A

Abt, L.E. 62
Abuse
    alcohol 12
    drugs 12
    intervention 12
    prevention 12
Ackerman, R.J. 401
Ainsworth, T. 68
Alberti, R.E. 60, 61, 63
Alcohol 69
Allbee, R. 30, 32, 33, 395
Allen, D.A. 45, 46, 395
Allen, V.L. 317, 395, 396
Alschuler, A.S. 17, 63, 397
American School Counselor Association (ASCA) 32, 47
    position statement 375-8
Anderson, E.M. 32, 39, 395
Anderson, R.A. 68, 319, 395
Application
    peer helping 389-90
Ardell, D. 68
Asbury, F. 63
Aspy, D.N. 19, 57, 63, 395
Assertiveness
    communication skills 11
Assertiveness skill
    evaluation 338
    module 184-94
Association for Specialists in Group Work (ASGW) 66
Attending
    communication skills 10
Attending skill
    evaluation 335
    module 127-33
Attributes
    trainer 1-2
Austin, N. 61
Awareness
    other peer counseling programs 325

B

Bailey, W. 402
Baker, E. 40, 401
Baker, V. 401
Balzer, F. 63
Bandura, A. 62, 401
Barry, H. 355
Bates, M. 65
Behavior modification 61-2
Bell, C.M. 28, 395
Belloc, N.B. 401
Benson, H. 68, 401
Berenson, B.G. 401
Black, C. 401
Blakeman, J. 401
Book
    goal 1
Botvin, E.M. 40, 401
Botvin, G.J. 40, 401
Bowden, J. 403
Bowman, R.P. 27, 28, 32, 39, 318, 319, 395, 399
Bratter, T. 69
Breslow, H. 401
Briskin, A.S. 32, 39, 395
Brodsky, A. 402
Brown, W.F. 15, 24, 46, 395
Budget 78-9, *Figures* 78 & 80-1
Burden, L. 405

C

California Personnel and Guidance Association (CPGA) 32
Callanan, P. 67, 401
Caning, J. 319, 395
Caplan, G. 401
Caplinger, T.E. 41, 396
Career center 319
Carkhuff, R.R. 2, 10, 28, 33, 47, 51, 52, 56, 57, 61, 86, 90, 93, 95, 395 400, 401

ABOUT
the
AUTHOR

Judith A. Tindall

Psychologist
Counselor
Consultant
Author

Dr. Tindall has worked for 18 years in public schools as a counselor and guidance director; for several years she has also been in private practice as a psychologist and consultant. She is presently associated with Rohen and Associates Psychological Center in St. Charles, Missouri. She has been a consultant to, and has conducted workshops with, businesses, schools, church groups, and hospitals concerning a wide range of topics. She has consulted with such companies as Ralston Purina, Monsanto, McDonnell Douglas, TWA, Webster University, and numerous schools and churches. She has also been on the staff of Webster University and the University of Missouri at St. Louis teaching group process.

Dr. Tindall has been active in professional associations, holding offices and committee chairs at the local level (St. Louis Association of Counseling and Development), state level (Missouri Guidance Association and Missouri Association of Counseling and Development), and national level (American School Counselor Association and American Association of Counseling and Development) and the National Peer Helper Association. She serves on the Board and was co-conference coordinator for the first Peer Helper Conference in St. Charles. She is the co-author of two books, *Peer Counseling: In-depth Look at Training Peer Helpers* and *Peer Power: Book 1, Introductory Program,* and author of *Peer Power: Book 2, Applying Peer Helper Skills,* and one audio tape on *Problem Solving.*

Dr. Tindall received a B.S.Ed. degree in Speech and Political Science from Southwest Missouri State University, an M.S. from the University of Missiouri at Columbia in Counseling, a Specialist degree in Counseling and Psychology from Southern Illinois University at Edwardsville, and a Ph.D. in Psychology from Saint Louis University. She has also recieved extensive training in hypnosis, communication skills, drug and alcohol counseling, Adlerian counseling, career education, wellness, stress management, imagery, biofeedback, pain management, and group work. Research topics include communication skills, stress management, self-esteem, problem solving, wellness, and group work.

Dr. Tindall is a proficient practitioner in training peer counselors. She conducts workshops and classes and serves as consultant in peer counselor training programs.